Get Updates and More on Nolo.com

Go to this book's companion page at:

www.nolo.com/back-of-book/USFTL.html

When there's an important change to the law affecting this book, we'll post updates. You'll also find articles and other related materials.

More Resources from Nolo.com

Legal Forms, Books, & Software
Hundreds of do-it-yourself products—all written in plain English, approved, and updated by our in-house legal editors.

Legal Articles
Get informed with thousands of free articles on everyday legal topics. Our articles are accurate, up to date, and reader friendly.

Find a Lawyer
Want to talk to a lawyer? Use Nolo to find a lawyer who can help you with your case.

NOLO
LAW for ALL

5th Edition

First-Time Landlord
Your Guide to Renting Out a Single-Family Home

Attorney Janet Portman
Ilona Bray, J.D. &
Marcia Stewart

Fifth Edition	SEPTEMBER 2020
Book Design	SUSAN PUTNEY
Editors	ILONA BRAY AND ANN O'CONNELL
Proofreading	IRENE BARNARD
Index	ACCESS POINTS INDEXING
Printing	BANG PRINTING

Names: Portman, Janet, author. | Bray, Ilona M., 1962- author. | Stewart,
Marcia, author.
Title: First-time landlord : your guide to renting out a single-family home
/ Attorney Janet Portman, Ilona Bray, J.D., & Marcia Stewart.
Description: Fifth edition. | [Berkeley] : Nolo, [2020] | Includes
bibliographical references and index.
Identifiers: LCCN 2020012785 (print) | LCCN 2020012786 (ebook) | ISBN
9781413327939 (paperback) | ISBN 9781413327946 (ebook)
Subjects: LCSH: Real estate management--United States. | Rental
housing--United States--Management. | Landlord and tenant--United
States.
Classification: LCC HD1394.5.U6 P67 2020 (print) | LCC HD1394.5.U6
(ebook) | DDC 333.33/8--dc23
LC record available at https://lccn.loc.gov/2020012785
LC ebook record available at https://lccn.loc.gov/2020012786

This book covers only United States law, unless it specifically states otherwise.

For information on bulk purchases or corporate premium sales, please contact the Sales
Department. Nolo, 2550 Ninth Street, Suite 113-A, Berkeley, California 94710.

Please note

We know that accurate, plain-English legal information can help you solve many of
your own legal problems. But this text is not a substitute for personalized advice from
a knowledgeable lawyer. If you want the help of a trained professional—and we'll
always point out situations in which we think that's a good idea—consult an attorney
licensed to practice in your state.

Acknowledgments

We couldn't have written this book without the help of many people. Former Nolo legal editor Alayna Schroeder was particularly invaluable.

Also integral were the many first-time or accidental landlords who provided stories from around the country, including Amy Benton, Catherine Berryessa, Danielle DeBray, Phil Cunliffe, Dennis Deen, Kathy Eldridge, Lisa Guerin, Stuart Jacobson, Darren Johnston, John Lindenmeyer, Laura Macht, Michael Molinski, Dan Nguyen, Sergio Raddavero, Amy Shelf, Kyung Yu, Sharon Vallejo, Gordon and Connie Finwall, and others who wished not to be named. Current Nolo editor Ann O'Connell helped bring the latest edition up to date, and offered insights based on her considerable experience as a real estate broker, attorney, and landlord.

Thanks also go to Nolo authors and editors Steve Fishman and Diana Fitzpatrick for their help regarding the tax deductions associated with owning rental property, Richard Stim for contributions regarding the small business aspects of being a landlord, Mary Randolph and Emily Doskow for their advice on taking title and co-owning rental property, Matt Larson for information on investment considerations when buying rental property, Amy Loftsgordon for legal insights on buying properties undergoing foreclosure, and Stan Jacobsen for research help.

Thanks to the ever-helpful Mike Mansel, a Certified Insurance Counselor (mmansel@rlmilsnerc.com), for providing information and tips on converting homeowners' insurance when a home is converted to rental use ... and much more.

None of this information would help anyone if it weren't designed attractively by Jaleh Doane, Susan Putney, and Rebecca Bond. Hats off to Nolo's production team for their fine efforts and patience.

About the Authors

Janet Portman is an attorney and a nationally recognized expert on residential and commercial landlord-tenant law, including legal issues related to courts, landlords and tenants, and neighbor disputes. Portman is the author or coauthor of *Every Landlord's Legal Guide, Every Landlord's Guide to Finding Great Tenants, Every Tenant's Legal Guide, Renters' Rights, Negotiate the Best Lease for Your Business, Leases & Rental Agreements, The California Landlord's Law Book: Rights & Responsibilities,* and *California Tenants' Rights*, all published by Nolo.

Ilona Bray is a former attorney turned Nolo author and editor. Among her many popular titles (authored or coauthored) are *Nolo's Essential Guide to Buying Your First Home* and *Selling Your House: Nolo's Essential Guide.* Check out her real-estate related blogs on blog.nolo.com.

Marcia Stewart has written and edited books on landlord-tenant law, real estate, and other consumer issues. She is the coauthor of *Nolo's Essential Guide to Buying Your First Home, Every Landlord's Legal Guide, Every Tenant's Legal Guide, Leases & Rental Agreements,* and *Renters' Rights*.

Table of Contents

Your First-Time Landlord's Companion

This book is for the millions of people who rent out (or want to rent out) a single-family house or condo, and who might want to do much of the work themselves. You might not consider yourself a "real" landlord—you might not even like the term. Yet you no doubt want to make money and avoid legal hassles.

If you're balancing a day job and a family, taking on the tasks of being a landlord can actually seem overwhelming, especially if it's not a role you actively chose. An increasing number of landlords are the "accidental" sort, having come into their rental property in one of the following ways:

- **Inheritance.** Many people become accidental landlords by inheriting a property (usually a single-family home) from a family member or friend. You might be deciding whether to sell or keep the place.

- **Divorce.** When couples separate, they often agree—or a court decides—that one or the other gets to keep a property, whether a family home or investment or vacation property. And if two divorcing parties decide to share a property, renting it out can actually help them recover from the financial difficulties of the split, or at least put off selling until the market improves.

- **Trading up or moving out of the area.** Perhaps you need more space or are moving to a new location, but aren't prepared to sell your current home, maybe because the housing market is soft or you're thinking you might move back someday.

- **Trading down or fighting foreclosure.** You might be having trouble paying the mortgage on your current home—but reluctant to sell if prices are down. Renting out your home, while you live somewhere less expensive, can provide the cushion you need until you're ready to move back or sell.

- **Having extra space.** Perhaps your kids have graduated from college or you've divorced and the extra living space within your home could be rented out. Or you might own a duplex or a house with an in-law unit. If there's room for a tenant, you might be looking at a handy way to raise extra cash without much change to your fixed expenses.

- **Caring for a loved one's property.** A close relative or friend might need help renting out a property, for example, because he or she has moved to a nursing home.

- **Temporary move.** If you're taking an overseas sabbatical, serving in the military, or making some other temporary move, you probably don't want your house sitting empty. You can prevent this, and make money, by renting it out.

In any of these situations, you might be wondering whether to sell the property immediately, rent it out temporarily before selling, or turn it into a long-term investment property. This book will start by helping you make that decision, then orient you to all the financial, legal, and practical rules every landlord needs to know. It will also help you if you're thinking of going out to buy real estate for use as a rental (not to "flip" and sell quickly).

We provide nuts-and-bolts information on how to:

- find and choose good tenants (the number one key to your success)—from low-cost ideas for sprucing up a property to writing ads to checking prospective tenants' credit and references

- prepare a solid lease or rental agreement, which will help ensure that tenants pay rent on time, respect your property, and cause you little hassle

- make the most of landlord tax deductions, and manage financial record keeping

- handle repairs and maintenance legally and efficiently—without driving yourself crazy or going broke

- use careful landlord practices and a good insurance policy to stay out of legal trouble (and limit your liability) when it comes to tenant health and safety, discrimination, and crime on the property

- maintain a good relationship with your tenant, or deal with a tenant who's skipping out on the rent, damaging your property, or otherwise causing you sleepless nights
- manage rental property from a distance
- hire a property manager and other professionals as needed
- share the work (and ownership and tax benefits of landlording) with a spouse, relative, or friend—while maintaining your personal relationship
- take over a rental house with tenants in place, and
- get out of the landlording business while maximizing profit and minimizing taxes.

We've tried to concentrate on the things that every first-timer needs to know as well as some tips for people who are in unique situations (for example, if your rental property was recently in foreclosure).

We also include lots of hands-on practical anecdotes and advice from real landlords who've come before you—people like Catherine, who rents out a cottage behind her own house, or Laura, who lives in Washington but rents out properties in three states.

We hope this book provides a valuable companion on your path to being a successful and satisfied rental property owner.

Get Updates and More at This Book's Companion Page on Nolo.com

When there are important changes to the information in this book, we'll post updates on a dedicated webpage:

www.nolo.com/back-of-book/USFTL.html

We call this the book's "companion page." You'll find other useful information on this page, too, such as legal blogs.

Helpful Nolo Resources for Landlords

For many readers, this book will provide all the information needed to become a first-time landlord. But if you want specific legal forms or detailed legal information for your state, you'll want to check out other Nolo resources.

Let's start with what's available from Nolo for free: Nolo.com offers lots of relevant information, on topics such as property management, fair housing rules, occupancy standards, evictions, landlord liability for crimes and tenant injuries, and real estate investment. Check out Landlords under the Legal Articles tab. Here, you'll also find charts with your state laws, including state security deposit limits, required landlord disclosures, tenant privacy, small claims rules, repair responsibilities, termination and eviction rules, and much more. Throughout this book, we'll refer to the state-specific information available on Nolo.com.

Nolo also publishes a comprehensive library of books (hard copy and electronic versions) for landlords and rental property owners. Three of Nolo's most popular titles are *Every Landlord's Legal Guide*, *Every Landlord's Tax Deduction Guide*, and *Every Landlord's Guide to Managing Property*. Nolo's many other books for landlords include California-specific titles, such as *The California Landlord's Law Book: Rights & Responsibilities*. Look to these books for state-by-state legal information, legal forms, checklists, and letters, including a lease and rental agreement, rental application, tenant repair request form, property manager agreement, security deposit itemization, and more.

Nolo also has many single-copy interactive online forms, such as state-specific leases and rental agreements.

For Nolo's full library, see the Landlord-Tenant and Leases & Rental Agreements sections of the Nolo store on Nolo.com, or call Nolo at 800-728-3555.

Finally, be sure to see the legal updates on this book's companion page (described above).

Will Landlording Bring You Money and Happiness?

Being a landlord might sound appealing in theory—you find a decent tenant, collect a monthly rent check, and celebrate your good fortune. If only it were that simple. Before you start fantasizing about a multiunit building on Park Place, let's look at what it takes to own and manage rental property, and how to decide whether a particular property is actually going to make you money. Along the way, we'll share some helpful advice from other first-time landlords.

Great Things About Being a Landlord

Owning rental property offers both financial and lifestyle benefits. As Laura, a landlord with properties in Washington, Nevada, and Florida, says, "I like people and the feeling that I'm doing a good job. In fact, I have to be careful not to get too friendly—I have tenants in Florida with adorable kids, and I'm often tempted to volunteer to babysit, but have to remind myself to keep it all business. Of course, it's also nice to earn money through my efforts, and to be able to take tax-deductible trips. I remember the first time I sold one of my rental properties, and made a nice profit on the sale; it made me very happy."

> *Of all U.S. households, 36.1% are occupied by renters.*
> (*Source:* 2018 American Community Survey, U.S. Census Bureau)

Below is an overview of the various benefits that Laura and other landlords enjoy. Try to remember these later, when you're cursing the latest plumbing problem or fretting over how to fill a vacancy.

Appreciation and wealth building

If you hold onto your property long enough, it will almost certainly go up ("appreciate") in value—eventually. Since World War II, real estate prices in America have risen an average of around 5% a year (with some nerve-wracking ups and downs in between). And even if the house's value isn't rising, renting it might allow you to build equity until you own it outright. Owning investment property is a great way to increase your net worth.

Income

A well-managed investment property, with tenants who pay the rent on time and monthly expenses that are less than the rent, can bring you a steady stream of income. Most landlords who chose to buy single-family homes did so with this purpose in mind.

Diversification of income

You never know what life is going to throw at you. If you're laid off from your job, or your health takes a turn for the worse, your primary source of income—presumably your salary—could be jeopardized. Owning an investment property diversifies your income stream and can give you somewhat of a cushion.

Low-risk investment

Unlike more volatile investments, the returns on real estate are fairly steady. While stock values can fall or even disintegrate entirely, land and property won't disappear on you. And history shows us that they almost always hold their value—or at least bounce back after a tumble.

Also, even when property values are down, people need places to live —a fact that keeps rents relatively high even during recessionary periods.

Investment diversification

Owning property also diversifies your investment portfolio, which is a cardinal rule of investing. The reasoning for the rule is pretty easy to understand, if you get the idea of not putting all your eggs in one basket: Should something unforeseeable happen to your riskier investments, such as stocks, you'll have the backup of a tangible, relatively low-risk asset. As you approach retirement, it's good to start shifting into lower-risk investments, to ensure the cash you need doesn't disappear when you're relying on it.

Leverage

Unlike other investments, a little bit of cash will buy a lot of real estate: A down payment of 20%—or in some cases, as low as 10% of the value of the property—is usually enough to get you started. You could, for example, buy a $400,000 property with a $40,000 down payment, while that same amount will buy you only $40,000 worth of stock. And if the value of that stock were to increase by 10%, you'd have a $4,000 profit, whereas if the value of the property increased 10%, you'd have a $40,000 profit. (These are, of course, rough figures, in that they do not account for sales commissions, depreciation, capital gains taxes, and so forth.)

This is called being highly "leveraged"—in one sense, deeply in debt, but in another sense, poised to gain high returns based on a relatively small up-front investment. Leveraging your investment allows you to trade up to more profitable properties.

Short-term tax advantages

While the rental income from your property is taxable, you can deduct most of the expenses related to owning and maintaining the property. Among these are mortgage interest, insurance, repairs, and upkeep. They also include your business expenses, such as your phone line, office supplies, professional fees (for example, to the accountant who helps you figure out your business taxes), and more.

Another major tax advantage is the ability to "depreciate" your property—to take an annual deduction that reflects the decreased value of the property caused by wear and tear. (In the most literal sense, depreciation could turn out to be a fiction if the value of the property goes up a lot—but it can be a wonderful fiction for tax purposes.) Chapter 6 of this book discusses tax issues in detail.

Long-term tax advantages

Even if your property skyrockets in value on paper, the IRS won't expect you to pay taxes on that increased value until you sell. (Your state and local property taxes will probably be another matter, however, rising steadily to catch up with the property's value.) Unfortunately, when you do sell, you might lose the advantage of the capital gains tax exclusion ($250,000 per owner), if you haven't lived in the place for two out of the previous five years. However, there are several strategies you can use to decrease your tax liability. We'll discuss those in Chapter 11.

Part-time commitment

If you own just one property, and it's not too far from where you live, you can probably handle its management in your spare time, while still working a full-time job. A little job flexibility will help, of course. Although weeks might go by when the property needs little or no attention, there will be times when it will need hours from you, for example, when you're getting the place painted while dealing with the departure of the old tenant and interviewing prospective new tenants.

Your time commitment will be even less if you hire a property management company—though your profits will decrease as well. We discuss the pros and cons of hiring property managers in Chapter 10.

Professional development

Being a landlord and owning property can give you a sense of accomplishment (and some stories to tell at parties). It shows that you've broken out of the mold of the average working stiff, and are willing to take risks and accept major responsibilities. You're learning new skills involving finances, dealing with people, and maybe even home repair, which may help you in other areas of life.

Personal satisfaction

Being a competent and conscientious landlord will pay dividends in other respects, too—you're going to feel pleased about the way you're doing business. As Amy, who lives in Berkeley, California, and rents out her former home in Austin, Texas, puts it: "I've rented from a few crummy landlords myself, so it's very satisfying to be able to give my tenants a positive experience, for example, quickly taking care of repairs if something goes wrong."

Tough Parts of Being a Landlord

Landlording is not for everybody, and not every property is worth keeping or buying as an investment. The main reasons that people tend to give up on landlording are the time required to manage a property effectively, the risks involved (such as problem tenants, long vacancies, and legal risks), and the cost. Here's a quick overview of these issues. Later chapters in this book provide detailed advice on minimizing and dealing with problems.

Time

Even though landlording isn't a full-time job, it will take more than an hour or two of your time every few weeks. For one thing, you'll need to be reachable and available nearly around the clock, to respond to calls from tenants when the plumbing backs up or the neighbor's dog is barking all night. Occasionally, you'll need to put in large chunks of time, for tasks like listing and showing the property during a vacancy, screening and approving tenants, and handling rent checks and deposits, to name a few.

> ### Landlord Stress Levels
>
> *According to a 2019 survey from Porch.com, 83% of landlords say they experience stress in renting out their properties, in most cases (41%) at a rating of three out of five. At the same time, 80% said that the money they earn from this activity makes the stress worthwhile!*

In this book, we'll help you strategize ways to cut down on the time you spend landlording. For example, Chapters 3 and 4 will give you tips on how to market your property, attract and choose the right tenants (who will hopefully stick around for awhile), and list the property so as to fill vacancies quickly and efficiently.

Problem tenants

One of the pitfalls of owning rental property is the possibility that you're going to get that rare "tenant from hell"—someone who doesn't pay the rent on time, trashes the property, or constantly bugs you about every little thing that goes wrong—all of which can be expensive to remedy. Catherine, who rents out a cottage behind her house in Berkeley, describes often feeling "vulnerable" because someone else has day-to-day control of property she owns and cares about.

It's more likely that your tenants will be perfectly decent, responsible people. Good screening procedures (as described in Chapter 4) will help assure this. Nevertheless, people can change. Catherine's low point as a landlord came, she says, when "one of my tenants, who six months before had a nice job and drove a BMW, developed a crack addiction. The neighbors formed a watch group around my house, and I'd see drug deals going on and find vials in the backyard."

> **Lucky for landlords, people tend to stay in one place for a long time.**
>
> The percentage of people moving over a one-year period in the United States is low: down to just under 10% for 2018–2019. (Source: U.S. Census Bureau)

A properly structured lease or rental agreement (as covered in Chapter 5) will help deal with difficult situations like this and reduce many of the risks associated with problem tenants. And knowing how to deal with bad tenants (Chapter 9) will also help you do damage control when needed.

Difficulty renting

There might be times when the market is soft and it will be difficult to rent your place out. Vacancies are a reality of life for most landlords, but can be made worse by local economic conditions, the need for major repairs in your property, or just sheer bad luck. That's why we'll make sure you factor vacancies into your analysis of potential profits on the property.

Legal risks

If you really want to talk worst-case scenarios, you could worry about the legal risks that come with owning rental property—that is, the possibility that a tenant, prospective tenant, or someone else on your property will sue you over a health, safety, environmental, discrimination, or other legal matter. You could even face legal trouble from third parties, stemming from misbehavior of your tenant. For example, if a tenant's drug dealing results in injury to a neighbor, you might be liable if the neighbor can prove that you knew what was going on but failed to take action.

Landlording Duties

☐ Research and set rental price.

☐ Establish a bookkeeping system for tracking income and expenses.

☐ Participate in a local landlords' association (optional).

☐ Learn the key laws and ordinances that cover renting residential property in your state and city.

☐ Advertise property for rent.

☐ Respond to people interested in renting the property.

☐ Clean property and make any necessary repairs in preparation for tenants.

☐ Show property to prospective tenants.

☐ Review tenant applications, obtain credit reports, and conduct reference checks.

☐ Draft and negotiate lease or rental agreement.

☐ Supervise tenant move-in.

☐ Collect and manage security deposit.

☐ Respond to tenant problems or inquiries.

☐ Collect rent.

☐ Respond to late rent and other violations of the rental agreement.

☐ Pay mortgage, utilities, insurance, etc.

☐ Prepare regular tax paperwork.

☐ Evaluate and fix problems and contact maintenance repair people.

☐ Supervise tenant move-out.

☐ Evaluate the condition of the vacated rental and return tenant security deposit.

☐ Handle disputes among tenants (multifamily rentals) or disputes or complaints from neighbors.

Knowing your own responsibilities and potential liabilities (which we'll describe in Chapter 8) and acting to reduce the risk of problems occurring will limit the chances that you'll face serious legal situations.

Costs

The costs of owning an investment property go well beyond the mortgage. They include property taxes, insurance, utilities, upkeep, repairs, property management costs (if you choose), wages for a handyperson, legal costs when needed, and much more. All in all, operating a property as a rental is probably more expensive than using it as your primary residence.

As Dennis, a landlord since 1982, describes it, "We haven't had much of a negative cash flow on our properties, but we have sometimes. From a financial point of view, if people are really tight, they shouldn't get into the landlord business. There's always the unexpected plumbing problem, or an appliance that wears out."

Reducing costs is one of the keys to being a successful landlord. We'll advise you on how to assess the cost side of your property in Chapter 6.

The Unexpected

Situations you never anticipated can throw a wrench into your well-laid landlord plans. At the time this book went to print, for example, the world was gearing up to deal with the COVID-19 pandemic. Landlords in some parts of the United States were facing new rules prohibiting the eviction of nonpaying tenants as well as challenges in showing property in person. By the time you read this, some of these issues will have been settled, but new ones might have arisen.

Location, Price, and More: Features of the Ideal Rental Property

Whether you're planning to buy a rental property or deciding whether to keep a property you already own, one of your first considerations should be whether the place is actually suited for renting. Look especially hard at features of the property that can't be changed, like its location and whether it has a yard. Let's consider its suitability from both the tenant's vantage point and yours.

What gives a property "tenant appeal"?

Here are the most important, primarily physical characteristics of a house that will appeal to a wide range of tenants:

- **Size.** This depends on the local population. For example, a house with several bedrooms will be attractive to large families.

- **Location.** Nearby transportation access—particularly public transport, when gas prices are running high—is a big plus. So is proximity to shopping and commercial areas.

- **Security.** Safe neighborhoods appeal to all tenants. No one likes to live in a high-crime area—and making sure the property is secure enough for your tenants can add to your to-do list as a landlord, too.

- **Good nearby public schools.** A family that wants to make sure their children go to the best schools and finds a good home nearby to rent might settle there for years. But even short-term renters appreciate a good school and the corresponding community spirit.

- **Affordability.** With rare exceptions, it's difficult to find tenants for large, luxury houses. Any prospective tenant who has the money to afford the monthly rent can probably also afford to buy a house.

- **In good repair.** Even if it's otherwise in good shape, a house with ongoing maintenance issues—perhaps having a nearby creek that often floods, or being so old that everything is falling apart—might put off tenants who don't want to be dealing with inconveniences or calling you with numerous repair requests.

> ### What type structure most renters live in:
> - *single-family home, 33.5%*
> - *two-to-four–unit structure, 17%*
> - *five-plus–unit structure, 44.6%*
> - *mobile home, 4%*
>
> (*Source:* 2018 American Community Survey *by the U.S. Census Bureau*)

- **Layout.** Like everyone, rental tenants want a place that's well designed. Don't assume, for example, that a renter will be content with a tiny kitchen. And if the house is likely to be shared among roommates, each bedroom should be reasonably private and have bathroom access that doesn't involve invading someone else's room.

- **Charm and aesthetics.** Like home buyers, renters will be drawn to a place that looks nice. But you can't know every prospective tenant's taste. That's why a house with broad appeal rather than quirky features is your best bet.

Of course, tenants will also be concerned with certain nonphysical parts of the property, like how much rent you charge and whether you allow dogs. However, such policies are largely within your control, and don't affect whether you'll buy or keep the house in the first place, so we'll discuss them in Chapter 3.

What makes a good rental from the landlord's point of view?

After thinking about whether your property has sufficient tenant appeal, turn your attention to whether the house you're considering is appropriate for you, given your available time, skills, and interest. In most cases, this is a house that:

- **Requires little fixing up and maintenance.** For example, a house that's relatively new isn't likely to need new plumbing or wiring anytime soon. But this doesn't mean a newly built house is necessarily the best. A place that's well constructed but isn't on the verge of becoming "historic" is your best bet.

- **Is close to your own home or work.** Who wants to drive for an hour—or get onto an airplane—to interview new tenants or see to a maintenance problem? And even if you hire a property management company, it's good to be able to check on the property yourself from time to time.

! **CAUTION**
Dealing with maintenance gets a lot harder at a distance.
As Kyung, who formerly rented out her triplex home in New Haven, Connecticut, explains, "For the ten years we lived in the unit above the rental, we had practically no maintenance problems. But wouldn't you know it, as soon as we moved to Pennsylvania, things started to fail. The tenants were calling in the middle of the night, and I'd have to call some 24-hour service and pay a premium to get the repairs made."

- **Isn't in a heavily regulated city or area.** If your property is in an area with rent control or other restrictions on landlords, take a careful look before you leap. Read the regulations and talk to other local landlords about their experiences. If you'll be buying a property with existing, long-term tenants who show signs of planning to stay there forever, you'll have to make do with below-market rent well into the future. In situations like this, your investment might be a losing proposition.

- **Will attract long-term renters.** For example, a house near a vacation resort or a college might not be optimal if you're hoping for year-round tenants. (Students tend to leave at the summer break and switch housing every year, which means regular turnover and repairs.) If there's high turnover, you'll at least want correspondingly low vacancy rates and high rents.

- **Doesn't require evicting long-term tenants.** See "Evaluating resident tenants" in the discussion of buying foreclosed property, below.

- **Is convenient to commercial supply sources and repair people.** Avoid houses in remote locations where you'll have to struggle to get to a hardware store or find high-quality help for maintaining or improving the property.

> *Rental occupancy rates are on the rise nationwide*
>
> *The average occupancy rate hit 96% in May 2019, the highest since 2001.*
>
> *(Source: RealPage Analytics Blog)*

- **Is in a strong rental market.** Ideally, you're looking for a property that's cheaper to buy than to rent, so you can bring in income. But you're also looking for a market with lots of would-be renters: Otherwise, you'll find profits eaten up by vacancy periods.

Special concerns when renting out a condo or co-op

Whether you already own a condominium or another home in a common-interest development (CID) or are thinking of buying one, you need to be aware of how the property's unique features impact its suitability as a rental property. (In some regions of the U.S., CIDs are referred to as "common interest communities" or "CICs.")

Condos and townhomes are the most common types of homes in CIDs. Renting them offers special advantages, including:

- **Less maintenance responsibility.** The homeowners' association (HOA) will take care of common areas, freeing you from hands-on responsibilities like tending the garden or (in most cases) repairing the roof. (Of course, you pay to get these things done via your monthly HOA dues.)

- **Affordability.** A condo or townhouse is usually cheaper to buy than a single family home, because you own less—you own your particular unit, and own common areas jointly. And the maintenance can be less expensive too, because costs that might otherwise be individually paid—like landscaping and insurance —are instead shared.

- **Amenities to attract tenants.** Without having to buy a whole apartment building, you might be able to offer your tenants access to a pool or other recreational or meeting spaces.

But let's not forget the disadvantages:

- **Community rules and regulations.** In a CID, residents typically must agree to live by a set of rules. These might govern everything from the size of residents' dogs to whether they can hang clothes on the line, smoke in the unit, change the color of the curtains, or change the color of the outside paint. Getting your tenants to read and abide by these rules, when they don't have a long-term stake in the community, can be challenging.

- **Restrictions on renting.** Possibly the most significant rule in a CID is a restriction on renting. Some CIDs place numerical limits on how many units can be rented or how long a unit can be rented, or ban renting altogether. Although the association is unlikely to weigh in on your choice of tenants (which would expose it to liability for discrimination and the like), it might insist that you put certain clauses in your lease (for example, committing the tenant to abide by community rules), or exert other oversight.

- **Community fees and costs.** Every CID charges regular (usually monthly) dues for maintenance and shared costs, and the rules typically also allow special assessments for major expenses like a new roof on the property or dealing with a flood or another emergency. These fees can run into the hundreds, even thousands of dollars per month, which you'll need to figure into your budget. (The landlord is normally responsible for making these payments, not the tenant.)

- **Slow property appreciation.** Historically, condos and townhomes have appreciated in value at a slower rate than single-family homes.

We've given a broad description of CIDs, which can vary immensely in physical features and character. Your job, before deciding to buy or rent out one of these properties, will be to fully research its costs, rules (often in a document called covenants, conditions, and restrictions, or CC&Rs), and current community concerns. Read the CC&Rs and recent meeting minutes thoroughly, talk to neighbors, and investigate the reputation and financial strength of the property's builder or owner.

Is Airbnb or VRBO for you?

Many people who own rental property in popular tourist destinations, such as San Francisco, or in college towns, such as Ithaca, New York, choose to rent their homes through Airbnb or another short-term hosting or rental service.

This book focuses on more traditional rental situations, where you sign a fixed-term lease or month-to-month rental agreement with one or more tenants. You will have screened these longer-term tenants by running a credit report and checking references.

Renting through Airbnb or a similar service involves a separate set of legal and practical issues concerning taxes, insurance coverage, local registration, liability for guest injuries, and so forth. Having different people come in and out of your rental house can cause major headaches for neighbors and might even violate the law.

Many municipalities, including large cities such as New York City, San Francisco, and New Orleans, have legal restrictions (often quite severe) on short-term home rentals. Local registration or licensing requirements, tax rules, and other policies, vary greatly from place to place, so check yours if you're even thinking about renting your home through Airbnb or a similar service. The Responsible Hosting section of Airbnb.com has a summary of the legal requirements of more than 50 cities, with links for details. If your city isn't listed on the Airbnb site, call your city's zoning board or local housing authority for information, or do your own research on local law at www.statelocalgov.net or Municode.com. Another useful resource is the Short Term Rental Advocacy Center (www.stradvocacy.org), created by Airbnb, HomeAway, TripAdvisor, and FlipKey.

> **Renting out your castle?**
>
> Airbnb has grown dramatically since its founding in 2008, with more than half a billion guests and over seven million property listings (over 4,900 of which are actual castles) worldwide.
>
> (Source: Airbnb.com)

If you own a condo, co-op, or other property in a planned development, ask your homeowners' association or co-op board about its short-term rental policies.

While you might end up bringing in more money each month by renting your house through VRBO or a similar service, carefully consider all the relevant issues, including how much time you'll need to spend screening guests or arranging for cleaning in between visitors. To get further informed, see the Short-Term Rentals of Your Home area in the Real Estate & Rental Property section of Nolo.com. You'll find articles on insurance, taxes, screening renters, legal restrictions, and neighbor concerns. Also, to prevent your tenants from renting a room or space within their rental via a short-term rental service, make sure your lease or rental agreement prohibits sublets, as recommended in Chapter 5.

Is sharing your home with a lodger for you?

Some homeowners decide (either for financial or social reasons) to stay in their homes and rent out a room in their house to a lodger. Because this is different than the typical landlord-tenant relationship, we've devoted a special chapter to the subject. See Chapter 12 for details.

Thinking About Buying an Investment Property?

Not all landlords are accidental landlords. You might be thinking about buying a property so that you can rent it out. (If not, and you already own a property, skip down to the section below, "What Will Your Monthly Profit Be?")

Before you make that decision, you'll want to do a careful analysis of the costs and potential returns of your investment. Keep in mind that real estate is not a get-rich-quick business. You'll have to invest some significant cash up front. And while your rental income might be a source of ongoing profit (we'll help you calculate how much below), a large portion of the financial gain will come about as time passes and the value of the property increases. And you won't actually realize that benefit until you sell (though you could use your increased equity as collateral for a loan).

While some people have gotten rich in real estate, you've probably seen the headlines about the many who've been disappointed—the would-be house "flippers" who, during a real estate downturn, found they couldn't buy and sell property for quick profits as they'd planned, and ended up in foreclosure or bankruptcy. For many of them, turning their houses into rental property wasn't an option—their carrying costs were too high compared to the rents they could charge, and they faced a long road of losses ahead.

We're going to assume you don't have aspirations toward house flipping, but are looking to invest in rental property over the long term, and ride out the inevitable ups and downs of the market. Or perhaps your ultimate goal isn't to sell, but to live in the home yourself, after you've retired. Let's evaluate your budget and how buying a rental property will fit in, both as a short- and long-term investment.

RESOURCE
This book doesn't attempt to present a complete guide to choosing a house to buy or financing investment property. Some good resources for that include:

- *Nolo's Essential Guide to Buying Your First Home,* by Ilona Bray, Ann O'Connell, and Marcia Stewart, and
- The Real Estate & Rental Property section of Nolo.com, which includes hundreds of useful articles on buying, owning, and selling real estate, including investment property.

How much cash you can put down

To determine whether buying an investment property is even a financial possibility for you, let's start with a simple calculation: How much cash can you free up for a down payment, and how much house will that buy? Most lenders require 20% down, especially on an investment property. (The days of zero down payments are gone, victims of the bursting real estate bubble and subsequent foreclosure crisis.) A quick visit to the real estate section of your local paper, or to an online site like www.realtor.org, will show you typical prices in the location where you're interested in buying.

You'll also need to budget around 2%–3% of the house's price for closing costs, depending on what state you live in, what kind of mortgage you get, and what you can expect to pay in escrow fees, title fees, real estate agent commissions, and taxes and insurance at closing.

So if you can put down $80,000 plus pay $12,000 in closing costs, you're well on your way to buying a $400,000 property. If your cash on hand will likely buy a worthwhile rental in your area, keep reading.

> ⓘ **CAUTION**
> **Looking at a fixer-upper?** In that case, you'll need even more cash on hand. Major home improvements always seem to take more time and money than originally expected, so think twice about this strategy if you're not experienced with home repairs or construction.

How large a loan you'll qualify for

You'll probably be taking out a loan with which to buy your property (unless you're among the approximately 36% of real estate investors who pay all cash). That means you'll need to show a lender that you can afford the monthly payments. One of the tests that lenders use is your credit history and score, or your record of paying debts on time. We're not going to discuss credit scores in detail here—for more information, see the free articles in the Debt Management section of Nolo.com.

The other test that lenders use is the comparison between your income and your debt load, called your "debt-to-income" ratio. The more debt obligations you already have hanging over you, the less likely the lender is to let you take on more. In fact, the lender might be stricter than when you bought your first home, because lending practices have tightened and mortgages on investment properties are considered riskier.

> ⓘ **CAUTION**
> **Evaluate your monthly expenses even more strictly than your lender does.** What we're discussing here is how much mortgage you'll qualify for. But if you tend to spend everything you earn each month—and perhaps aren't even sure where the money is going—you need to get your first house in order before taking on a second one.

The concept of "debt-to-income ratio" isn't as complicated as it sounds. The lender looks first at your household's gross monthly income (the amount you earn before taxes and other monthly withdrawals, plus income from all other sources, like rents, royalties, alimony, or investments). Then it makes sure that your combined minimum debt payments on the property—going toward your PITI (principal, interest, taxes, and insurance), plus any community association fees, credit card payments, car debt, student loans, and more—don't eat up more than a certain percentage of that gross income. See the "Sample Debt-to-Income Front-End Ratio Worksheet," below.

How high can your debt-to-income ratio go? Traditionally, lenders require that your PITI payment not exceed 28% of your gross monthly income (sometimes called the "front-end ratio"), and your overall debt shouldn't exceed 36% (the "back-end ratio"). Federal guidelines also say that a home borrower's total debt-to-income ratio for a "qualified mortgage" should not exceed 43%.

With such ratios in hand, the lenders set your maximum monthly mortgage payment. Using the calculators listed below, you can arrive at a roughly equivalent figure—and then decide whether that amount is enough to buy a rental property in your chosen area.

Sample Debt-to-Income Front-End Ratio Worksheet		
Gross monthly income:	$4,000	
Gross monthly income x .28	$1,120	= Maximum monthly PITI payment
Gross monthly income x .36	$1,440	= Maximum monthly debt overall

RESOURCE
Ready to run some real numbers? Find online affordability, as well as household budget, calculators at Nolo.com/legal-calculators, HSH.com, and Interest.com. Make sure any calculator you use factors in the amount of your down payment, income and debts, and estimated taxes and insurance.

Keep in mind that interest rates are higher on investment properties, so your calculations shouldn't assume that you'll qualify for the rock-bottom rate offered to buyers with stellar credit who are buying primary residences. You won't be offered these rates, because lenders know they're in a riskier position when their borrower is paying two mortgages: If you hit hard financial times, you'll pay the mortgage on your primary residence first.

Some investors with lots of equity in their primary residences get around these higher rates by doing a cash-out refinance (drawing out cash from their main home to pay for a second) or taking out a home equity loan. This strategy is beyond the scope of this book; in general, while you can use it to get a lower interest rate, the lender will subject you to the same financial evaluation discussed above.

Fortunately, lenders will allow you to include your expected income from the rental property in your calculations. This will help you qualify for a bigger loan. However, lenders will probably be conservative in estimating your likely income, for example, by figuring a higher-than-expected vacancy rate.

You'll need to know how much loan you qualify for so you can estimate what kind of property you can buy, how much it will cost you each month, and how much you can expect it to bring in. Later in this chapter, we'll cover whether it's profitable to buy based on these factors.

Buying a Foreclosed Property

Although fewer foreclosure properties are available now than in past years, many buyers continue to brave the uncertainties and frustrations associated with such transactions to buy homes for use as investments.

Foreclosure properties tend to be in rough shape (there's a reason they're known as "distressed"), and some come with resident tenants and even recalcitrant former owners. You'll need to be prepared for the special challenges that come with them.

The main advantage to buying a foreclosure is price—you're likely to get a good bargain, whether you buy from the owner (preforeclosure), at a foreclosure sale, or directly from the bank (known as "real estate owned," or REO). The main disadvantages to buying foreclosure properties are:

> **Where are most foreclosures happening?**
>
> In early 2020, according to RealtyTrac, the five states with the highest foreclosures rates were New Jersey, Delaware, Illinois, Maryland, and Ohio.

- **Going without the usual buyer protections.** As we'll explain further, below, at most stages in the foreclosure process you'll forgo at least some of the normal protections available in a typical transaction. For example, you might not get to see the property before you buy, have to accept it "as is," and have to go without title insurance.

- **Waiting to make sure the owner's rights are protected.** All states have laws to make sure banks can't rip properties out from under late-paying owners on a moment's notice. For buyers, that means deadlines, delays, court rules, and uncertainty—particularly in the many states that allow the former owner to "redeem" or buy back the property within a certain period of time after it was sold in foreclosure (usually from ten days to one year). Of course, if the owners redeem the property, you'll get your money refunded. But do you really want to be held in limbo, unsure of whether you'll ever be able to occupy the house?

RESOURCE
To find out your state's redemption period and get other summaries of your state's law regarding foreclosures, see Nolo.com (choose Foreclosure).

- **Competition from experienced real estate investors.** If there are good deals to be had, you can bet real estate investors will be lined up in front of you, with cash at the ready.
- **Risks of undisclosed repair needs, tax liens, or other issues with the property.** Remember, these homeowners were probably financially stressed for a while. They might have held back on maintenance, gotten behind on their taxes, or used the house as collateral for other debts.

Still interested in pursuing foreclosed properties? Find an agent who specializes in them—most don't handle them at all, while some go so far as to arrange bus tours of local foreclosures. A good source is REONetwork.com. If you still have a regular real estate agent, explain to both agents what you're doing, so that you can agree on each agent's limited role. You'd also be wise to hire a real estate attorney to help navigate this somewhat touchy area.

> **RESOURCE**
> **For information on foreclosures, see the following sites:**
> - Zillow.com (under "Buy" you can filter for foreclosure properties)
> - PropertyShark.com (you'll need to register for some information)
> - RealtyTrac.com (includes state-by-state statistics)
> - HomeSales.gov (includes listings of houses foreclosed upon by the federal Department of Housing and Urban Development after owners failed to pay their FHA loans), and
> - Foreclosure.com.

Investigating the home's maintenance history

If you are buying during preforeclosure, the current owners should (depending on the laws in your state) give you a filled-out disclosure form and answer any questions you might have. (And of course, before closing the deal, you'll want to have the house inspected.) There's a good chance that you're dealing with a home that has already been a rental.

If you don't have access to the prior owner, ask the neighbors about the house's maintenance history. Did the owners take pride in their home and leave it in good shape? Or was the home occupied by malicious tenants who were unsupervised by an owner already demoralized by the property's imminent loss? Or was the home occupied by resident owners who spitefully trashed the home before moving out?

No matter whom you talk to, be prepared for disappointing news. As neighbors, brokers, banks, and eventual new owners of distressed properties have learned all too well, the prospect of losing one's property —whether owned or rented—spurs some to acts of vengeful destruction. Refurbishing these properties will involve considerable expense.

Even if the property was a rental that escaped the wrath of its last occupants, think about the extent of wear and tear it has undergone. Often, rental properties suffer more deterioration than owner-occupied homes. (In fact, 37.5% of renters admit that if they owned the home, they would treat it better, according to a 2019 Porch.com survey.) Take this into consideration when setting your purchase bid.

Dealing with former owners

Occasionally, you'll find former owners still in residence right through the foreclosure proceedings—and beyond. Some of these folks simply have nowhere to go, and figure that they'll stay on as long as possible. The sight of a new owner may be the last straw that will trigger their departure, but maybe not.

If you inherit former owners, you'll need to evict them. (Do not resort to self-help measures, which can turn nasty.) But you might not be able to evict using the same methods as you would to evict ordinary tenants. (Under normal circumstances, tenant evictions are very quick compared to other types of civil cases; many states provide simple fill-in-the-blank forms, making it possible to handle the matter on your own.) Instead, evicting a former owner might involve a more complex lawsuit, for which you will probably need a lawyer.

Dealing with current tenants

It's possible that the house you're considering will come with resident tenants who were renting from the prior owners. For years, most tenants lost their leases when a rental property was foreclosed on, which gave the new owners the option to keep the tenants (under a new lease) or evict them. But that changed in 2009, when President Obama signed the "Helping Families Save Their Homes Act." This legislation specifies that all leases will survive a foreclosure, except when new owners intend to personally occupy the premises (in which case, the current tenant's lease may be terminated with 90 days' notice). Month-to-month tenants may be terminated with 90 days' notice (which is longer or as long as any notice period required by the states).

The federal law came to an end in 2014; however, many states and municipalities continue to provide the same protection. As a result, if you are buying a home that you intend to use as a rental, if was foreclosed on or after May 19, 2009, and it comes with a lease-holding tenant, it's likely that you'll have to honor the lease. You can terminate month-to-month tenants with 90 days' notice, but keep in mind that if the home is subject to state and local rent control requiring landlords to have a "just cause," or good reason, to terminate a tenant (or is in New Jersey or Washington, DC, which impose statewide "just cause" eviction protection), you cannot give the tenant a notice to vacate the property. You'll be stuck with these tenants for as long as you use the property for rental purposes, or until you fit within one of the rent control ordinance's allowable reasons for termination.

Evaluating resident tenants

If you're inheriting month-to-month tenants in a non-rent-controlled property, should you allow them to stay? Evaluate these tenants as you would any others. If they've been paying rent on time (which, admittedly, might be hard to find out unless you can talk to the prior owner), and have been taking reasonable care of the property, you could decide to keep them and negotiate your own new rental agreement or lease (after giving the tenants 90 days' notice).

But if you sense trouble, particularly if the property comes with tenants who have lots of time left on a lease, think twice about purchasing this property. You don't want to be saddled with tenants whom you'd never have rented to in the first place. If you go ahead and purchase the property, while counting on evicting the residents, understand that if these tenants refuse to leave, you'll need to begin an expensive and drawn-out eviction. This is hardly the way to begin your new rental business.

What Will Your Monthly Profit Be?

Earning steady profits from the rent stream off your investment property should be at the top of your goals list. So don't just guesstimate or hope for the best. Do the research and run through the analysis below to determine whether you'll make money each month.

Calculate rental income

Wouldn't it be nice if you could just add up your expenses for the property, tack on a little extra for profit, and call the result your monthly rental amount? Unfortunately, it doesn't work that way (except by coincidence). The local rental market largely sets the prices, based on how many properties are available and what amount tenants are willing and able to pay. That's why many landlords must settle for rental amounts that don't actually cover their costs, hoping that long-term appreciation in property value will make their investment worthwhile.

As a first-time landlord, your safest bet is to rent out your property only if the rent you can charge will cover your expenses (unless you have no other realistic choice). To figure out whether that's feasible, look at local ads for comparable properties of the same size and condition, in the same neighborhood and school district. Or check Rentometer.com, which provides median rent amounts by area.

If the house is already being rented, the existing landlord will of course tell you what the monthly rent has been—and will continue to be, if the tenant has a lease that lasts beyond the property transfer. (You can't raise the rent until you renew the lease.) But if the tenant will be leaving, your outside research will come in handy, because the landlord might have kept the rent below market rates, perhaps in order to keep a good tenant. And even a tenant who wants to stay might have only a month-to-month rental agreement, which you are free to either terminate or renegotiate (unless your state or local laws add restrictions).

For more on rentability, see "What gives a property 'tenant appeal'?" above. And see Chapter 3 for ideas on how to spiff up your house for added appeal. When setting your rental policies (which we'll detail in Chapters 3 and 5), consider whether you might be willing to, say, allow pets or charge a lower security deposit in trade for a higher rent. Depending on who your likely tenants are, a furnished property might also allow you to raise the rent—for example, if you'll be renting out a downtown condo to busy young professionals. This will be particularly handy if you inherited a fully furnished property.

Also visit other rentals (say, during open houses) to see how yours stacks up. There's no need to be undercover about it—identify yourself as a new landlord researching the market, and you might find a fellow landlord who's eager to share tips and stories.

After figuring out a likely market rent, your next task is to check into the local vacancy rate, usually expressed as a percentage. A real estate or property management company should be able to tell you how many rental houses like yours are sitting empty. You can also get a sense of likely demand for your house by considering factors such as whether your area is growing economically (so that new employees need housing), whether there's a steady stream of likely renters (such as students), and whether home prices are out of reach for the average local resident, who will turn to renting instead. Nationwide, the average annual rental vacancy rate is up to 6.7%, according to U.S. Census Bureau figures. Of course, this is just a ballpark, and varies depending on where your property is located; but you might be able to lower the vacancy rate by using some of the methods in this book to find and keep long-term tenants.

Putting it all together, you should be able to come up with a monthly and annual dollar figure that your rental is likely to command—the monthly rent figure times twelve, minus expected vacancies. Assume that your vacancy rate will be the same as the average where you live, even if you expect to have a long-term renter.

When Will You Be Able to Raise the Rent?

After you're in full swing as landlord, keep an eye on changes in your local rental rates, by watching the ads and talking to local real estate management experts. If rents go up, then you might be able to renegotiate a raise at the next lease renewal, or, if you have a month-to-month rental agreement, within the next month or two (depending on your state's requirements for giving the tenant advance notice). State and local rent control laws, if any, will also affect when and by how much you can raise the rent.

The next question is whether you'll want to raise your rent. Dennis (the longtime landlord mentioned earlier) says, "I usually don't raise the rent on anyone in the property. I raise it when I rent to someone new. Maybe I can save 50 bucks a month by raising the rent, but I can save thousands by not having it vacant. I have one set of tenants whose rent I haven't raised in 12 years. They're the nicest, neatest people. They put in their own blinds; they garden and mow."

TIP
Consider setting your rent slightly below market rates. In the experience of Gordon, a landlord with a single-family property in San Jose, California, "It's important to not charge as much as you can get away with. If you charge top dollar, you're more likely to have a tenant not take care of it. But if you give them a fair rent and they feel you're treating them fairly, they'll return the favor by taking care of the place."

Subtract expenses

If you're already a homeowner—as most people are before becoming landlords—you know that keeping up a home isn't cheap. Your regular annual expenses will include the mortgage (both principal and interest, assuming it hasn't already been paid off), homeowners' insurance, property and other taxes, and property management services if you decide to use them. You'll also face less predictable expenses, such as maintenance and improvements, accounting fees now that you're in business, and more.

Now's the time to draw up a budget, estimating what it will cost to keep your property. The worksheet below will help with this task. We've broken it down so that you enter monthly figures—of course, you'll need to fiddle with some of the numbers, for example dividing your annual property tax payment by 12.

CAUTION
Double the amount you think you'll spend on maintenance. If you base your likely maintenance figures on what you usually spend on your own home, you'll probably come out low. Tenants tend to be harder on houses than owners and blind to minor maintenance issues until they become major. And habitability laws will require you to make some repairs that you might otherwise have delayed.

If the property is already being rented, the departing owner is a valuable source of financial information. Ask for:

- a copy of the lease or rental agreement
- details on security deposits (location, amount, and whether the old owner will be returning them to tenants, in which case you'll need to recollect them)
- service contracts (such as for gardening—these can be canceled, but you might not want to if the seller is getting a good bargain)
- utility bills and maintenance and repair records for at least the last year (preferably longer), and
- all other paperwork relevant to the property.

And if the current tenant plans to stay, figure out which expenses you can cut out of your budget accordingly. Advertising and screening are the obvious ones, but you might be able to reduce the number of repairs and improvements you otherwise would have done before a new tenant moved in.

> **TIP**
> **If you want existing tenants to stay, encourage them.** During a transfer, tenants might worry that the new landlord will be difficult to work with and will raise the rent or change other lease or rental agreement terms as soon as legally possible. Some will start looking for a new place, just in case. As soon as you can, meet with the tenants to explain your policies and establish some personal rapport.

Our expense worksheet also includes some categories that you might not be able to estimate yet, such as gifts (for example, flowers to your tax accountant for dealing with your shoebox of receipts). Leave these blank if you can't imagine paying them—but use them as a reminder of possible unexpected expenses.

Monthly Property Expense Estimate	
Expense Description	**Amount**
Advertising and tenant screening	$
Local transportation	$
Out-of-city travel, meals, lodging	$
Cleaning and maintenance	$
Homeowners' insurance (if not included in mortgage payment)	$
Legal and other professional fees (accountant, property manager)	$
Mortgage payment (principal and interest, plus property taxes and insurance, if included)	$
Other loan payments	$
Repairs	$
Appliances and furnishings (irregular but major expenses, such as a refrigerator)	$
Supplies (for office and rental property)	$
Income tax	$
Property tax (if not included in mortgage payment)	$
Utilities and phone (if not covered by tenant)	$
Gifts and entertainment	$
Licenses	$
Homeowners' association dues (in condos and some developments)	$
Landlords' association dues, if you choose to join one	$
Educational publications, subscriptions, and memberships	$
Tools and equipment	$
Construction and improvements	$
Other, miscellaneous expenses	$
Total estimated expenses	$

> ⓘ **CAUTION**
>
> **Costs can mount if you're unable to make regular visits to the property.** Amy explains, "My property tax bill recently went up significantly, and I decided it wasn't worth the time and expense to fly from California to Texas to appeal it. But if more surprise costs like this come along, I'll probably have to either raise the rent or sell."

Estimate short-term profits

Continuing with the simple calculations, let's say you can afford to buy—or you already own—a house that's suitable for renting. Now you need to estimate whether the rent will cover your costs. Do that by filling in the chart below.

	Estimated Monthly House Profit or Loss	
A	Expected rental income (based on "Calculate rental income," above)	$
B	Estimated costs (based on "Monthly Property Expense Estimate" worksheet, above)	$
C	Profit or loss (A minus B, or expected income minus estimated costs)	$

This chart will tell you whether you stand to make money on such a property in the short term. If the income comes out ahead of the costs, great. But remember that if you're buying a rental property, you'll probably make a large down payment, and might eventually want to sell the place—so it's worth figuring out the ultimate return on your investment, which we'll discuss next.

If the property's expected income isn't enough to cover its costs and more, we recommend walking away (if you can—see our discussion for people trying to avoid foreclosure, below). Sure, the place might make a good long-term investment if and when property values rise, but that's a different ball game—we're assuming you picked up this book because you wanted to earn regular money as a landlord, not aim for one-time profits.

> ⚠ **CAUTION**
> **This calculation doesn't include tax benefits.** These benefits—
> depreciation and other tax deductions—can reduce your tax liability
> by thousands of dollars. If your calculations look borderline, skip ahead
> to Chapter 6, where you'll learn more about what these tax benefits are
> and how they help you increase your profits.

Another thing worth considering is the value of your own time. We
can't calculate that for you, but we will discuss some of the tasks that go
into being a landlord in this book.

Added financial concerns when renting in an attempt to avoid foreclosure

Some property owners get into the rental business in an effort to avoid
losing a home that has become unaffordable—perhaps one they can't
sell for what they owe on it. If you're in this situation, you might be able
to avoid foreclosure by renting the place to someone else while you rent
another (less expensive) place of your own until the situation changes.

In that case, you should continue your calculations as follows:

A	Profit or loss from rental (from above)	$
B	Cost of renting another house for yourself	$
C	A minus B = Total cash you'll need to spend on housing (after paying other bills)	$

> **EXAMPLE:** Samuel's monthly mortgage is $1,000, but after paying his
> other bills, he has only $800 left with which to make the payment.
> He discovers that he can rent out his house for $1,200. That amount
> covers the mortgage and other house-related expenses ($200 per
> month) so that he breaks even, neither profiting nor losing money on
> the rental itself. If he can find a smaller place to rent for $800 a month,
> he might be able to pay the bills and keep his house.

> ⓘ **CAUTION**
> **You might need to inform your tenants about defaults or imminent foreclosures.** Several states, including Oregon, Nevada, and Minnesota, require landlords to inform tenants, before signing a lease, if the property is subject to a notice of default or pending foreclosure.

Added financial concerns when buying for a college student

Buying a house for a college-bound child has become an increasingly popular option, with dorm costs often prohibitively high. The average annual room and board for public, four-year, in-state schools rose to $11,510 in 2019–2020 (up 2.9% over the previous school year), while private school room and board averaged $12,990 (up 3%). (Source: the College Board.) But before you assume buying a place for your college kid will be cheaper, make sure you'll truly come out ahead.

Step One is to find out what the actual room and board at your child's college will likely be. Then research both the rental and the real estate market in the area. If you're lucky, your child will be attending school in an area where average rentals are high enough to offset average mortgages and other costs (the reverse might be true, although the demand for housing in college towns has a tendency to drive up rents). By renting out some rooms to other students, you might come out ahead even before your child graduates.

Of course, citywide averages might not be enough. You'll need to look at property values right around the college, which will naturally be affected by student demand for housing. With a couple of sample home prospects in mind, run the profit-or-loss calculation described under "Estimate short-term profits," above, then compare it to how much you'd be spending on room and board. If it comes out about the same, then you should buy the property only if you like the idea of a long-term investment, or think it will bring in a high return when you sell (as discussed next).

What Will Your Long-Term Gain Be?

Whether you're an accidental landlord or are actively looking to buy a house to rent out, your research so far will help you analyze your house's worth as a long-term investment—taking into account up-front costs, ongoing costs versus income, property appreciation, and profits from the sale. Now you can:

- estimate the house's likely appreciation, or increase in value over time, and

- calculate the likely return on your investment (ROI), or the expected value of your investment in your property.

Appreciation: Will your rental property rise in value?

We've already discussed the general tendency for homes to rise in value over time. But to get a true picture of your home's prospects, you'll need to look at local home prices. Ask your real estate agent to calculate the change in median prices for the past ten or more years, or call or visit the town clerk or assessor. The more local your research, the better—one neighborhood's house values might rise or remain steady while another one's drop.

> *Parental home buyers are a campus trend!*
>
> *Many real estate agents see significant numbers of parents investing in homes for their children to live in while going to college. The top college towns in which to invest, according to a 2019 Redfin analysis of affordability, walking score, and the level of high-quality education relative to low tuition and fees are Binghamton, NY; Syracuse, NY; Buffalo, NY; Gainesville, FL; Athens, GA; Champaign, IL; Baltimore, MD; Tallahassee, FL; Cleveland, OH; and St. Louis, MO.*

If the price trend looks to be heading upward, you're probably on safe ground buying. If it's heading downward, you'll have to make a tougher decision—will you be getting a bargain just before prices tick upward again, or will you be entering a depressed housing market in which you'll have little choice but to hang onto the property for years trying to make the most of your rental income? Talk to your real estate agent and read the local media before making your decision.

Also remember that slow real estate markets sometimes increase demand for rental units, because people are skittish about buying, or have left a house due to foreclosure. If you can charge enough rent to offset the monthly costs from the beginning, it's a solid investment by any measure.

To figure out the actual amount by which your house is likely to go up in value year by year, take the appreciation rate that you researched above and use it to create an analysis like the one in the chart below. (It looks complicated at first, but is actually quite obvious when you follow it line by line.) The example shows the projected appreciation of a $400,000 house over a five-year period in an area with 5% appreciation.

Sample Projected Appreciation on $400,000 House									
Year	Current house value		Local appreciation rate		Appre-ciation amount		Current house value		Appreciated house value
1	$400,000	x	5% (or 0.05)	=	$20,000	+	$400,000	=	$420,000
2	$420,000	x	5% (or 0.05)	=	$21,000	+	$420,000	=	$441,000
3	$441,000	x	5% (or 0.05)	=	$22,050	+	$441,000	=	$463,050
4	$463,050	x	5% (or 0.05)	=	$23,153	+	$463,050	=	$486,203
5	$486,202	x	5% (or 0.05)	=	$24,310	+	$486,203	=	$510,513

Return on investment: How much will you get back?

Let's look years down the road, to estimate whether your total investment in the property will be worth it after paying all the associated expenses. The term to describe this is "return on investment," or ROI. It's usually expressed as a percentage. You can calculate ROI on other investments as well (such as stocks and bonds), and see how they're all doing relative to one another.

The basic idea is to take your estimated annual profits (including rents plus home appreciation—which are only paper profits until you sell, but that's okay), and divide it by your total investment in the property (down payment, annual costs, total mortgage principal paid that year, and anything you spent for major home improvements). That means filling in the following calculation (simplified to leave out tax deductions and depreciation):

Annual profit after expenses ($_____)
+ annual appreciation   ($_____)
= total annual gain or loss $_____
÷ annual investment   _____
=   _____ % ROI

EXAMPLE: Kira bought a house for $400,000 (putting $80,000 down), and began renting it out immediately. In her first year, she earned $2,000 in income (after expenses including mortgage interest, plus maintenance, utilities, and the rest), plus another $5,000 in home appreciation (paper profits until she sells). Dividing that by her investment amount (her $80,000 down payment plus $5,000 in mortgage principal payments over the year), her ROI would be approximately .082, or 8%.

So, what does the ROI percentage mean? It means that, continuing with our example, if Kira sold her home after the first year, she'd have earned an 8% return on her initial investment. She's probably doing pretty well compared to the returns on her stocks and other investments. Of course, we're using artificial numbers, and your returns might be far less.

At this point, we suggest you do the ROI calculation using projected numbers, for the first year as well as later years that you plan to own the property. If it's positive, that's another green light—but again, don't be too swayed by the prospect of home appreciation if your actual profits are negative. An ROI that's lower than you could get with other investments after several years might be a sign to look elsewhere.

Return to the ROI calculation once you have actual numbers, to see how reality compares with your projections. It could be a source of comfort if you're not earning a profit on your rents but home prices are appreciating—you might still come out ahead.

Setting Your Goals

It's decision time: Having explored some of the basics of owning rental property, you must decide whether it's truly right for you. To help you in this process, answer the following questions:

- **How committed are you to holding onto the property?** If you're hoping for, say, a year's trial run, it's safest if you already own the property. Buying a property that you might not keep for at least three to five years is a recipe for loss (especially because of the transaction costs: 5%–6% for the real estate agent's fees alone when you sell).

- **What are your short-term financial goals?** After running the calculations above, decide what amount of property income will make it worth your while to pursue this project. Balance this against your long-term goals, below.

- **What are your long-term financial goals?** At some point, you might want—or need—to sell the house. What amount of profits are you expecting or hoping to make? If your sales profits aren't likely to be high, then it's even more important that you're satisfied with the anticipated monthly rental income.

- **How much time are you willing to put into this project?** If being a landlord will take precious hours you can't spare, then it might not be worth making a priority right now.

Take a careful inventory of your objectives as a landlord and property owner, both in the short term and the long term. Discuss them with your family, especially if you expect them to help maintain the property, deal with your absences, or travel with you for that purpose. Then keep track of where you are vis-à-vis those goals from year to year. We'll help you track your profits and expenses, in Chapter 6. ●

So Happy Together: Landlording With Family or Friends

After evaluating all the pros and cons of being a landlord, you might feel like it's too much for any one person to handle. Good news! You don't have to do it alone. Many people successfully share the responsibilities and benefits of co-ownership with family members, friends, or professional associates.

In this chapter, we'll talk about investing together and divvying up the responsibilities of being a landlord, including:

- the pros and cons of co-owning rental property
- how to decide whether co-landlording is right for you
- ways to take title together, and
- what to cover in a co-ownership agreement.

Whether you're undertaking these responsibilities with a spouse, sister, longtime professional associate, or distant cousin with whom you've inherited a property, this information will help you decide how to manage the property and finances.

We use the term "co-owner" throughout this chapter, assuming that most people will be sharing landlording responsibilities with only one other person. But in some situations—for example, if you and three other siblings inherit your parents' house and decide to rent it out—you might have multiple co-owners. For practical, financial, legal, and emotional reasons, it's crucial that you have a carefully thought-out written agreement that specifies everyone's responsibilities, as well as how you'll divide expenses and profit and make key decisions. You might find that outside professional help—a lawyer, mediator, financial adviser, or even a family therapist, if needed—can help craft a plan that works for everyone.

Pros and Cons of Co-Owning Rental Property

Sharing the experience of being a landlord with someone else is like any situation with multiple cooks in the kitchen—some things are easier to do with the help of another person, and some things just seem to get more complicated. Here are some of the advantages you can expect:

- **Fewer responsibilities.** As we'll discuss in the next section, you and your co-owner could choose to divvy up landlording responsibilities according to your skills. Working on projects you're good at means you can hopefully accomplish them efficiently and quickly. You might be able to avoid—or at least share—tasks you don't like, if your co-owner is willing to do them.

- **Lower expenses.** You and your co-owner can share expenses, most likely in proportion to your ownership interest. For example, if you own 50%, you would pay only 50% of the replacement cost if the water heater broke.

- **Greater buying power.** You might be able to increase your buying power by co-owning with someone else. For example, by pooling resources you might purchase a more expensive and lucrative property, such as a multiunit building instead of a single-family house.

- **Lower risk of vacancy.** If a tenant doesn't pay the rent or the unit sits vacant for a month or two, the loss won't fall entirely on you— you'll share it with your co-owner.

But before you start scouting around for a co-owner, consider these drawbacks:

- **Lower income.** As nice as it might be to share the responsibilities of landlording, you also have to share the proceeds. If you each own 50% and split profits that way, you'll get half as much as you would otherwise. You'll also make less when you sell.

- **Less independence.** When you're the only landlord, you can decide who moves in, how much rent to charge, who will do repairs, and more. You'll probably lose some of this autonomy, and you and your co-owner could even disagree about some issues.

- **Less stability.** When you own with someone else, you must rely on that other person to do a designated share of the work—and pay a share of the bills. If your co-owner doesn't pay the appropriate share of the mortgage, for example, you might have to pay the whole thing or risk being foreclosed on.

- **Difficulty selling.** Depending on how you and your co-owner take title (discussed further below), you might each be free to sell your interest in the property at any time. But because there isn't a huge market in partial ownership shares, it could be difficult to sell only your share.

Having a Compatible Co-Owner

Whether sharing the risks and responsibilities of landlording is right for you depends on more than the objective pros and cons. The biggest predictor of success is your ability to actually work with a particular co-owner to accomplish your goals. You'll want to co-own with someone who sees things the same way you do.

Of course, your choice might have already been made for you, for example if you and your sister have jointly inherited a house, or you and your spouse are moving out of the house you already own but plan to rent. But in other situations, you might actively decide to buy together and co-own with someone else, perhaps even someone you don't know very well.

What to look for in a co-owner

If you're thinking about looking for a co-owner—or just want to know what to expect if you're planning to work with your spouse—carefully consider the following factors:

- **Finances.** You and your co-owner should be willing to share the minute details of your finances with each other, including the amount of money you have coming in and where it's currently being spent. The purpose is to make sure that, for example, a momentary cash crisis won't spiral into a bigger problem, such as ability to repay a mortgage on the property. You'll probably each want to know as much as you can about the past, current, and anticipated debts, income, and expenses of your co-owner.

- **Location.** It will be much easier to share the experience of land-lording if you're both living near the property in question. If you're both far away, you might want to discuss hiring a property manager, covered in Chapter 10.

- **Goals.** It's best if you and any co-owner have the same goals in mind. Do you want to buy a house your college kids can share, then sell it when they're done with school? Will it be okay if your son decides to stick around a few extra years? Or are you hoping to buy out the co-owner's share in a few years, so you can retire in the place? Make sure you are on the same page about both short- and long-term goals.

- **Personality.** You'll want to choose a co-owner who you're sure you can get along with professionally. That could mean that you don't discuss this possibility with a friend who's great with people but absentminded and never balances a checkbook.

Finding a co-owner

To find a co-owner, start by making your intentions known. If you have a particular co-owner in mind, you can approach that person with your proposition. It might be a vague idea about an eventual purchase or a specific plan to buy a property you've already identified. The more detail you provide, the more likely you are to look like—and find—a serious investor. If you don't have anyone in particular in mind, you can discuss your ideas more generally with people you know, getting the word out that you're looking.

If you're willing to work with someone you don't know, ask local real estate professionals and attorneys whether they know people interested in similar investments. Buying with someone you don't know is beyond the scope of this book, but suffice it to say that all the factors above—finances, location, goals, and personality—become even more important when the person isn't someone you're already acquainted with.

Sharing duties with your co-owner

Early on, you and your co-owner should talk about the various duties that co-owning a rental property will require, and who will do them. You might decide on a formal arrangement where each of you takes on certain tasks, perhaps using the "Landlording Duties" list, in Chapter 1. Or you might decide to be more flexible ("If you can handle maintenance problems on the weekdays, I'll take them on the weekends"). Married couples can take flexibility to the extreme, like Sarah, a San Francisco landlord, who explains, "I'll generally say to my husband something like, 'The doorbell's not working, do you wanna call Tom or shall I?'" In any case, it's a good idea to discuss different arrangements so you can decide how to proceed before you make a purchase together.

> *Spouses who co-own and jointly operate rental property have special tax options.*
>
> *Depending on how you run the business, you can opt to file a joint return and not be treated as a partnership for federal tax purposes. For details on qualified joint ventures, see IRS publication* Election for Married Couples Unincorporated Businesses *at IRS.gov.*

Once you've decided who will do what, each of you should stick to your responsibilities and give each other the freedom to handle the assigned tasks as desired (unless it's going to have major negative effects, such as decreasing the property value or subjecting the tenant to uninhabitable conditions). For example, while Amy attended school in Berkeley, California, her partner Phil remained in Texas for awhile, and agreed to help manage her rental property in Austin. However, Amy explains, "After a hailstorm, Phil said he'd take care of communicating with the insurance company and the roof repairperson. But I got so anxious, I kept stepping in, which only caused confusion. Finally Phil had to remind me of our agreement."

There might also be some tasks you handle together. Gordon and Connie, for example, who co-own a house in San Jose, California, always make a point of interviewing potential tenants together. They find they each recognize different flaws and strengths in the applicants.

Gordon, a lawyer, pays more attention to whether the applicants appear willing to abide by contractual obligations and can afford the rent. Connie tends to focus on whether people will pay on time regardless of whether they can afford it, and whether they'll care for the property as if it were their own. Working together, they're able to select better tenants than if they worked singly, and they are less apt to lay blame if one of the tenants doesn't work out.

How to Take Title

When you own property with another person, you'll need to decide how you take title—that is, how, in legal terms, you own the property together. This isn't a decision to procrastinate or flip a coin over, because it needs to be stated on your deed. Unless you're married, you have two main options for taking title in your own names: as tenants in common or as joint tenants. A third alternative is to form a business entity, such as an LLC, which will take title to the property in its name.

CAUTION

How you hold title affects your rights to use, rent, and sell the property. The information provided here will give you some basic information about your choices, but it's a good idea to talk to an attorney or tax adviser about your own situation before deciding which form of ownership is right for you.

Tenants in common

A tenancy in common (TIC) is probably the most popular way for unrelated co-owners to take title. As a tenant in common, you and your co-owner can own unequal shares of the property—for example, you could own 40% and your co-owner 60%. (You can also have more than one co-owner, with each of you owning different shares.) This is a big advantage if you have different amounts of cash to invest or are looking for different levels of return.

Owning a share doesn't mean you own a particular slice of the pie, however. Your portion is called an "undivided interest," which means all co-owners have the right to use and enjoy the entire property. Let's say, for example, that you and your friend decide to split your ownership 60/40, and you'd like to apply your 40% share toward ownership of the smaller downstairs part of the house, while your co-owner owns the more spacious upstairs. That's not going to work in terms of legal ownership rights. If you ever want to separate your ownership share and your co-owner disagrees, you'll have to request that a court "partition" the property—that is, legally split it into separate parcels, owned individually. Because physically dividing property isn't feasible in most cases, the usual result is that the property is sold and the proceeds split. It's a lengthy and expensive process, which you're better off avoiding.

Another potential problem with owning as tenants in common is that either you or your co-owner can transfer your interest at any time. That means that your friend might suddenly decide to sell that 60% interest in the property—and can legally do so without your consent, to any interested buyer.

And then there's the matter of what happens if one of you dies. In a tenancy in common, a deceased person's share passes under the terms of that person's will or, if there isn't one, the inheritance laws of the state. You could find yourself sharing with a new co-owner (your current co-owner's long-lost daughter in Indonesia, for example).

Perhaps even more troublesome, co-ownership gives owners the right to "encumber" the property, which means take out loans against it. If your co-owner takes out a large equity loan against the property and doesn't pay it back, your ownership interest might be at risk. You could get stuck making payments to stay out of foreclosure, even if your co-owner has taken the cash and skipped town.

Fortunately, you can draft an agreement to deal with some of these possibilities before they ever happen, which we'll discuss later in this chapter.

Joint tenants with right of survivorship

Another way to take title is as joint tenants with right of survivorship (JTWROS). Like tenants in common, joint tenants own an undivided interest in the entire property, and can't, for instance, draw a line down the middle. However, unlike tenants in common, joint tenants in most states must own equal shares—that is, if there are two of you, you each own 50%.

The other main difference between joint tenants and tenants in common is that if a joint tenant dies, the property immediately passes to the other tenant, even if the person's will says otherwise. That means you should choose to own property this way only if you want your co-owner to own the entire property if you die. This is a common way for married couples, domestic partners, and those in committed relationships to take title. It's probably an unsuitable option if you're buying with an unrelated investor.

Other options for married couples

In addition to the ownership methods described above, married couples have a few more options when it comes to taking title. In several states (Arizona, California, Idaho, Louisiana, Nevada, New Mexico, Texas, Washington, and Wisconsin), married couples (and in some states, registered domestic partners) can own community property. Alaska has adopted a community property system, but couples must opt in for these laws to apply—they can do so by executing a community property agreement or a community property trust. Couples who own property this way each own half the property, which they can pass to whomever they please through their wills. While living, they can't sell or give away their share unless the other spouse consents.

Finally, about half the states allow married couples (and sometimes, those in registered domestic partnerships or other "official" relationships) to take title as tenants by the entirety. In this case, you and your spouse or partner each own the entire property and can sell it only with the other's consent. In most states, if one of you is in debt, creditors can't come against that person's share of the property. Like joint tenancy, if one tenant by the entirety dies, the other gets the property without probate hassles.

Holding property as a business entity

One final option for co-owners is to form a separate business entity and take title in its name. All co-owners would, in turn, own shares or a membership interest in the business.

Probably the most popular choice for co-owners who form a business entity is the limited liability company, or LLC. An LLC combines some of the best features of corporations and partnerships, offering these advantages:

- **Limited liability.** The LLC protects your personal assets (your house, car, and such) from business debts. That means a creditor claiming to be owed money by the business (the rental property) won't be able to come after you personally. Similarly, if a tenant is injured on the property, the tenant will be able to recover only from the LLC, not from you.

- **Ease of tax preparation.** LLCs offer what's called "pass-through" tax status. That means the business's tax liabilities are paid directly by the members. You won't need to calculate or pay taxes separately for the entity itself.

- **Less formality than other business entities.** Relatively speaking, LLCs have to comply with fewer paperwork and meeting formalities than other business entities, such as regular "C" corporations.

- **No right of partition.** A property held in an LLC cannot be partitioned—the LLC owns it fully. You can decide in your operating agreement how any individual's membership interest can be sold, but you are protected from a partition action.

However, LLCs also have disadvantages, such as:

- **Complex partnership tax rules.** If you form an LLC with another person, you will be treated as a partnership for tax purposes. Tax rules governing partnerships are significantly more complicated than rules for individuals. You will need to hire a tax professional to help you deal with these complexities.

- **Cost.** Forming an LLC will take extra cash. You'll have to follow the process outlined in your state, and might spend several hundred dollars for filing fees alone. Costs will be even greater if you get help or advice from a professional.

Making It Work Over the Long Haul

Managing a property with a co-owner takes patience, understanding, and a longstanding relationship that is nurtured over time. Sergio Raddavero and his co-owner describe having owned a single-family home in Burlingame, California, for 20 years. Despite advice in books such as this one, they've managed to do this based only on an oral agreement that has never been put on paper. Sergio says the secret to their success is that "we understand each other and complement each other."

"He does more on the handyman side. I do more on the management side," says Sergio. "I'm better at managing the rentals, and I organize the finances. Every month, I print out a financial statement and send it to him. Keeping a partner informed and in the loop makes him feel comfortable and secure." The fact that they have had positive cash flow for most of those 20 years has also made it easier. They repaint the house every six years, put on a new roof every ten years or so, and have remodeled the kitchen once—always using a reserve account set aside for such repairs, and never having to dip into their own pockets.

The point is, while we highly recommend having a written co-ownership agreement, sometimes the mutual understanding and respect you have for each other is enough to create a good property management relationship. Regardless, being aware of your expectations before crafting an agreement, and having a clear understanding of each other's strengths and weaknesses, are keys to making the rental property business a success.

- **Formalities.** Although the formalities associated with forming and running an LLC are fewer than with a corporation, they're still more than with a simple co-ownership agreement between two people. For example, you must file paperwork to form the LLC (usually called the articles of organization), and then will want to prepare an operating agreement (covering a lot of the same topics a co-ownership agreement normally would).

- **Difficulty obtaining financing.** You might find it difficult—and more expensive—to find a lender willing to loan money to your LLC. Even if you find a willing lender, you'll probably have to provide a personal guarantee (undercutting the limited liability that made an LLC attractive in the first place). Some people get around this by taking title in their own names, then transferring title to the LLC. But most mortgages have a "due on sale" clause, making the mortgage fully payable when the property is sold. You risk the mortgagor "calling" your loan as a result of the transfer, forcing you to repay it in full or refinance the property.

> **Real estate contributes heavily to tax coffers.**
> About half of all partnerships filing tax returns are real estate and rental and leasing businesses. For fun (!) reading on tax statistics, check out www.irs. gov/taxstats.

For more information on various types of business entities, including state-by-state rules on forming an LLC or a corporation, see the Business Formation section of Nolo.com.

> ⓘ **CAUTION**
> **If you operate as a business entity, you might not be able to do a 1031 exchange.** A 1031 exchange, discussed further in Chapter 11, is a tax strategy that allows you to defer capital gains taxes when you sell investment property and purchase other investment property with the proceeds. If you think you might want to do a 1031 exchange in the future, discuss the possibility with your tax adviser.

Because limited liability is one of the primary benefits of forming an LLC, you should consider forming one if you are particularly concerned about protecting your assets. Another way to protect yourself is to purchase an umbrella insurance policy. Unless you own several rental properties, adequate insurance will probably be the more cost-effective way to deal with the risk of being sued. For more information on obtaining insurance, see Chapter 8.

If you've inherited property with family members and keeping the property in the family is a primary goal, you might also consider an LLC. In that case, an LLC can protect the property, because your co-owners won't be able to sell or encumber it. If interested, talk to your attorney about how to best convert ownership into an LLC.

> **RESOURCE**
>
> **Need to form an LLC?** Nolo's Online LLC formation service lets you do so quickly and easily. You complete a comprehensive interview online, and Nolo will create a customized LLC operating agreement and file your articles of organization with the state filing office. Your LLC will come into existence the day the articles are filed. See www.nolo.com/lander/entry/llc/llcname.

Creating a Co-Ownership Agreement

As we've explained, there are many day-to-day logistics involved in working with another person to co-own and manage rental property. Many of these details can be worked out—and potential problems can be avoided—if you and your co-owner start out with an agreement that specifies what each of you will be responsible for.

If you form an LLC, much of this will probably be covered in your organization's operating agreement. And if you're taking title in a form available only to married couples, you and your spouse might not face the same legal risks of other forms of shared ownership. Here, we're assuming you're taking title as tenants in common or joint tenants with a co-owner to whom you aren't married to. A good co-ownership agreement should address:

- **How you'll choose tenants.** As co-owners, each of you has a right to use the property. Technically, each of you could rent it out to whoever you'd like. But to avoid stepping on each other's toes, create a system for choosing tenants. You might set certain (nondiscriminatory) criteria (such as income, job stability, or lease length minimums), or provide a system for reviewing applications (for example, each person gets the right to veto one applicant who otherwise meets all minimum stated requirements).

- **Whether each of you will have the right to use the property personally.** Ownership as a tenant in common or joint tenant also entitles you to use of the property in question—if one of you occupies the place, the law won't assume that your possession is "adverse" to the rights of the other owner (in other words, your occupancy will be assumed legal). But neither of you wants your co-owner, or your co-owner's best friend, moving in rent free. Make sure the agreement specifies what happens if one of you wants to use the property personally.

- **Responsibilities each of you will handle.** As discussed above, you and your co-owner will want to lay out the exact duties each of you will be responsible for. The more detail you provide, the less there will be to disagree about later.

- **How you'll divide expenses and profits.** Make sure the agreement specifies that you'll split expenses and profits in relation to your ownership shares. (If you want another arrangement, discuss it with a tax adviser first—it could mean you're functioning as a partnership for tax purposes.)

- **Home improvements.** Unlike regular maintenance expenses, you might not be legally entitled to reimbursement from your co-owner if you make any improvements to the property. Address how you will decide to make improvements and how you will pay for them.

- **Responsibility for mortgage payments.** Usually but not always, co-owners purchase with a single mortgage. You must decide what to do if one of you does not pay the promised share. For example, you could agree that the nonpaying party must make up payments with interest and is not allowed to participate in decisions about managing the property until current.

> **TIP**
> **Look for an assumable loan.** If you have a joint loan and anticipate that one of you might sell before the loan is paid off, consider getting an assumable loan. You probably won't find one from a private lender, but might from a government agency such as the FHA or VA. Such a loan allows a subsequent purchaser to take the seller's place with the loan, meaning you won't have to refinance at that point.

- **Making sure the property is adequately insured.** Agree that you will always maintain adequate insurance so that you're not relying on each other's resources in the event of damage or a loss (discussed in Chapter 8).

- **The lease or rental agreement.** Your lease or rental agreement will contain many terms you choose—for example, whether you will allow pets, the amount of the security deposit, and how long a rental term the tenant must agree to (see Chapter 5). You might wish to discuss these terms with your co-owner first, then agree how you'll handle any changes.

- **What to do if one of you wants to sell.** To avoid getting stuck in business with a complete stranger (in a situation where the original owners have the right to sell the co-owner's interest to whomever they please), spell out what you will do if one of you wants to sell. For example, you might determine that each of you has the "right of first refusal"—that is, the right to purchase the other's share before it's offered to anyone else. You'll have to determine how to value the property if you go this route.

To keep things simple, you might agree to pay to have the property appraised, and for the purchasing party to pay the fair market value as determined by the appraiser.

- **What to do if one of you dies.** If you own property as joint tenants and one of you dies, the other will own the property. But if you are tenants in common, ownership will pass according to the terms of the deceased person's will or trust (or state inheritance laws, if there is no will or trust). In your agreement, you can specify that if either of you dies, the other has the right to purchase the deceased owner's share from the estate, and that each of you will add this to your will or trust documents.

- **How you will resolve disputes.** Even if it's hard to anticipate now, it's possible that you and your co-owner won't always agree. If that happens, you might want to try to resolve problems without going to court—by using mediation, for example. You can set up the requirements for this in your agreement.

As you can see, the issues you need to cover in a co-ownership agreement are many. Because these agreements can get complicated, we suggest hiring an attorney to help you draft one or review one you've drafted. Better to spend a little up front if it helps save money and hassle in the long term. ●

Preparing and Marketing Your Rental Property

Before you open the doors to prospective renters, you'll need to make sure the rental home is ready for showing. Particularly in competitive markets, your place should look as good as it can, to attract the best tenants at the best price. As John, who's been a landlord since 1975 explains, "It took me many years to discover that there's competition among landlords for the good tenants. The good tenants take away all your problems—they aren't breaking things and making up stories—and they let you stay ahead of the game."

This chapter explains the prep work involved, from scrubbing the toilet to painting the living room to making sure the house is fully up to code. Particularly if you're renting out a house that you or someone else has lived in for many years, you might have a lot of work to do.

This chapter also covers your choices for advertising and marketing your rental house and how to deal with renting out property that's still occupied. We'll also discuss why it's important to make a number of key decisions—such as how much rent you'll charge or whether you allow pets—before you run your first ad or talk with potential tenants.

Make Sure Everything Is Up to Code

Your first order of business is to make sure your house complies with all local and state housing codes. Chapter 7 discusses your legal duty to rent out habitable housing and your repair and maintenance obligations, and explains how to research the extent of your responsibilities.

If you recently bought the property, you doubtless obtained an inspection report, which hopefully chronicled the structure's condition and repair needs. But if you're about to rent out a home that hasn't been inspected recently, you might not be sure what kind of shape it's in or what repairs it could use. It's worth hiring a professional inspector—just like you'd do when buying a house—to check the place out and identify potential problems, such as a leaky roof or faulty electrical circuits.

Look for an inspector who will give you a written, narrative report that helps you understand which issues need immediate attention and which you'll need to follow up on in the future. Common and significant code compliance issues include insufficient smoke or carbon monoxide detectors, and the absence of ground-fault circuit interruption (GFCI) outlets.

RESOURCE
More information on home inspections. The Real Estate section of Nolo.com includes many useful articles on home inspections. Also check out the website of the American Society of Home Inspectors (ASHI) at www.homeinspector.org.

Should You Make Major Repairs or Improvements?

If your property is in really bad shape (perhaps you've inherited your parents' 75-year-old house), it might be easier to sell it than to turn it into a rental. At the very least, preparation for renting means making sure that the house is safe and habitable. And, particularly in competitive markets, you might need to spend some big bucks on optional upgrades (such as on modernizing the kitchen or bathroom) before finding a renter. Unless you have the cash to pay for such upgrades, you might end up having to add repayments on a home equity loan to your monthly expenses—making it even less likely that the rent will cover the costs.

Start by talking to contractors and getting cost estimates. Then look again at the calculations in Chapter 1, to see how your short-term profits and long-term investment prospects will shake out. If you'll be going deep into debt with no hope of profiting until years later when you sell, putting the place up for sale now might make more sense. (See Chapter 11 for tips on selling your house.)

But what if you can't or don't want to sell right now, or think the property won't sell without some improvements anyway? That might change the analysis. After all, a renter might be willing to pay more once the place is improved. And in competitive markets, you'll feel the pressure to bring the place up to par: If competing rentals (particularly in a planned unit development where units look alike) offer more amenities such as built-in dishwashers, you might need to install one, too.

Do your homework, however, before deciding which improvements to make. Major home improvements almost never return 100% of their value. Remodeling a kitchen or adding a deck tends to do the most to boost a sales price, but you're still unlikely to recoup the entire amount spent. The National Association of Realtors® frequently reports on the financial pros and cons of remodels (visit www.realtor.org and search for "remodeling impact").

Prepare the Rental for Showing

First impressions count, and when interested renters first lay eyes on your rental house, you want their reactions to be positive. No amount of, "I'm going to take care of that … and that … and that … in the next few weeks" will dispel the negative impression left by dirty windows, peeling paint, or an unkempt front yard. Basic cleanup doesn't cost much, but it can make all the difference to prospective tenants.

If you're too busy to do the work yourself, it's possible that hiring a handyperson or cleaning service will pay for itself by cutting down the amount of time your place is vacant.

> **TIP**
> **Keep your receipts.** Much of your prep work will be tax deductible, as discussed in Chapter 6.

Clean up the outside

The true first impression is made while your prospective tenants are getting out of their car or walking up to your property. If it looks run-down or bedraggled, some people will just turn around and leave. Make sure your property looks welcoming and demonstrates your attention to at least basic maintenance by:

- Sweeping the sidewalk and clearing paper and debris from the yard, porch, driveway, and entryways.
- Mowing the lawn, pruning the shrubs, and pulling weeds.
- Washing all the windows.
- Checking that the doorbell works.
- Ensuring that the property is well lit, and the address is visible from the street. Replace the porch light bulbs, and consider adding lights with sensor detectors that go on automatically when someone approaches the house.

> ### Updating landscaping has big payoffs
>
> Outdoor projects (such as reseeding a lawn or adding flower beds), typically offer more than 100% return at resale.

- Adding greenery, such as flowering potted plants that you can place strategically.
- Putting out a nice welcome mat or add other decorative touches, such as a bench on the porch or a birdhouse in the tree.
- Painting the exterior of the house if it's faded or peeling.

Spruce up the inside

No matter how good the outside looks, tenants will ultimately focus on picturing their daily life inside your property. Here's how to create a clean, tidy, and attractive interior:

- Make sure all rooms (especially the bathroom and kitchen) are germ-free and spotless (including all appliances, cabinets, and fixtures).

- Sweep or vacuum the floors or carpets. Replace any flooring that's torn, badly stained, or mildewed. Remove slippery throw rugs.

- Make sure everything works—from the shower to the ceiling fan to the front door lock.

- Replace burnt-out light bulbs. If the current bulbs work but are a mismatch of types and brightness (for example, some are LEDs, some are CFLs, while others are halogen), consider replacing all of them with the same type of bulb (LED is usually best). Also, make sure that the bulbs are the same color temperature—for example, you don't want a mix of "daylight" and "soft white" bulbs.

- Replace the window coverings if they're in bad shape, and leave coverings open when prospective tenants visit, to let in lots of light.

- Repaint all rooms, especially if it's been a year or two since the last paint job.

- Get rid of ants, spiders, flies, and any other pests buzzing or roaming around the rental.

- Cover electrical outlets, especially if families with small children will be visiting the place. Coil long electrical or phone cords to get them out of the way. Block off or child proof any dangerous areas for kids, such as pools and stairways.

- Check that smoke detectors, carbon monoxide detectors, and fire extinguishers are in place (and in working order).

- Bring in a few nice pieces of furniture, including a chair or two that will give people a chance to sit down and imagine what it's like to live there. A coffee table with flowers and a few magazines or books will make the living room appealing.

- Put a new shower curtain—a neutral one without a crazy pattern is usually best—in the bathroom.

- Remove old soap bars, towels, or cleaning supplies that are lying around.

- Put a pot of spiced apple cider on the stove, a tried-and-true trick to make the house smell good.

"The rental property should be absolutely spotless," says Sharon, who owns a rental property in Chico, California, and also manages two other properties in Sonoma County. "There should be no litter, no trash that needs to be emptied, no dust, no mildew, no paint that doesn't look fresh, and no lawn that needs mowing. In short, it should look like the kind of place you would live in!"

> **TIP**
> **Do the work now.** No matter how anxious you are to get new tenants moved in, take the time to repair and refurbish first. By waiting to deal with things like a ratty carpet or a bad paint job, you'll just end up paying more later, when the job has gotten bigger. Plus, you'll irritate or inconvenience your tenants.

Set the Rent and Other Important Terms

You'll need to make a number of key decisions before you place your first ad, talk with prospective tenants, or prepare your lease or rental documents. Cross off these to-dos first:

- Decide how much rent you're going to charge (see Chapter 1).

- Set your requirements for tenants' minimum income and credit scores.

- Determine how much security deposit you're going to collect.

- Figure out the maximum number of occupants you'll accept.

- Fine-tune your pet policies (if you're going to allow pets, what kind? Will you limit size?).

> ⚠ **CAUTION**
>
> **Check with your insurance company before deciding your pet policies.** Your insurer might charge you a higher premium (or deny coverage altogether) if you allow dogs the insurer considers a higher risk (in terms of biting or injuring people). Doberman Pinschers, Siberian Huskies, and Rottweilers are among the dozen or so dogs typically found on insurance companies' "vicious/aggressive breed" list.

- Pin down whether you'll offer a fixed-term lease or a month-to-month tenancy.
- Set the date the rental will be available.
- Evaluate what utilities (if any) you can and will pay for. And,
- Finalize any other policies and rules that will apply to the rental, such as whether you'll allow a home business, require a cosigner on the lease, or prohibit smoking in the unit.

Good rental policies are a combination of the practical ("What will work for this property?") and the legal ("May I legally require or forbid this?"). Showing your rental property (or even having an initial phone conversation) without a firm idea of how to answer questions about the issues above is a mistake that will waste everyone's time. Plus, you might face legal trouble, such as a fair housing complaint, if you offer certain terms to some potential tenants, but not to others.

Setting your rental priorities dovetails with writing your lease (a topic we'll cover in Chapter 5).

Get to Know the Neighbors

While you're puttering around the property, take the time to introduce yourself to neighbors in the surrounding houses. Some of them might be concerned about the house becoming a rental, given the widespread reputation that renters have for taking worse care of a property than homeowners do.

Reassure them that you're doing your best to find excellent tenants and plan to maintain regular oversight of the property. Sometimes just knowing that the landlord is a real person goes a long way toward making neighbors feel comfortable.

> ⓘ **CAUTION**
> **Let neighbors know how to reach you with complaints about your tenants.** Laura, a Bellevue, Washington, landlord, for example, says: "I like to meet the neighbors, give them my phone number, and say, 'If you have a problem, give me a call.' That happened with a Bellevue property—in fact, I wish they'd called me sooner. The tenants were leaving garbage on the back deck, and the neighbors had to look at dirty diapers and stuff. I went and talked to the tenants: Problem solved." (If a tenant later does cause trouble, our advice in Chapter 9 will explain how to act swiftly.)

Come on Down! Advertising Your House for Rent

A little word-of-mouth among your friends or colleagues, and posting on Facebook and other social media, might be all you need to find the perfect tenant, particularly if the market is tight and you have a competitively priced rental. For example, Laura describes how she found one of her best tenants: "The existing tenant (who needed to get out of the lease early), placed an ad in her mom's club's newsletter. I've also heard of landlords offering tenants money if they bring in a good replacement tenant."

For wider choice, however, you'll need to advertise publicly. Possible ways to do that include:

- using Craigslist (craigslist.org), or other local online services you find

- putting a "House for Rent" sign in front of the property or in one of the windows
- posting flyers on neighborhood bulletin boards
- hiring a property management company (discussed in Chapter 10) that will advertise your rental as part of the management fee
- posting a notice with a university, alumni, or corporate housing office
- advertising in a local newspaper, and/or
- working with a local real estate broker who handles rentals.

The method of advertising that will work best depends on your particular rental (its rent, size, amenities, and location), your budget, the saturation of the market, the type of renter who will likely be your tenant (such as students versus families), and whether you're under time pressure to rent your place out. If, for example, your rental is near a popular park or shopping area, a For Rent sign in the window is a must. In many markets, Craigslist is the only way to go. Longtime landlord Dennis has found that, "What does work is Craigslist. I don't use the newspapers anymore. You don't get many calls from the paper."

> **TIP**
> **A picture really is worth a thousand words.** One of the great advantages of online advertising services is that you can post digital photos, and often videos, of your rental, inside and out.

Your ads should contain a clear (and accurate) description of the property, including basic details, such as:

- rent
- size—particularly number of bedrooms and baths
- location—either the general neighborhood or street address, including proximity to public transportation and shopping areas and the school district

- whether you're offering a fixed-term lease or a month-to-month rental agreement
- the date the rental is available if you are positive it will be ready for a new tenant
- special features—such as fenced-in yard, view, washer/dryer, fireplace, remodeled kitchen, furnishings, garage, parking, hardwood floors, wall-to-wall carpeting, or security system
- any important rules, such as no pets, and
- your phone number and/or email for more information, or the date and time of any open house.

> ⚠ **CAUTION**
>
> **Avoid discrimination complaints—or a lawsuit.** Be sure your ad never mentions sex, race, religion, national origin, disability, or age (unless your property meets the legal requirements of senior citizens housing). See Chapter 4 for a discussion of antidiscrimination laws.

How to Show Your Property

Prospective tenants will likely start phoning as soon as you've advertised your vacancy. Be ready to tell them how they can come for a visit. You have three basic choices:

- individual appointments, in which you meet at the property and conduct personal tours
- private open houses attended by multiple prospects who have been invited by you, or
- public open houses, where anyone who has seen your ad, a sign, or otherwise knows of the vacancy can show up.

During that first phone call, provide complete details on the property and your policies. Some prospective tenants will say "No thanks" on the spot, but that's fine—and might even be a good thing. You'll avoid wasting your time showing your rental to someone who wouldn't have been interested in it anyway (or won't meet your requirements). Also, as John, an experienced California landlord, reminds us, "Give prospective tenants clear, simple driving directions, so they're not feeling frustrated by the time they arrive—if they find their way there at all."

Your decision whether to show your rental by appointment or by open house depends on market factors and your own time and preferences. For example, in a soft market, where good tenants are hard to find, you'll need to schedule appointments at the prospective tenant's convenience. In a hot market, with lots of interested applicants, one or two open houses should do the job. If you hold an open house, be sure it's at a convenient time, such as during two or three hours on a Saturday afternoon.

> **TIP**
> **Prepare the rental unit for a secure showing.** If you'll be allowing strangers into a rental house that no one is currently living in, consider bringing at least one other person with you. If you'll be holding an open house and expect a mob scene, sign up a few helpers—ideally people who can answer questions and enthusiastically promote your rental. If someone is still living on the property, ask that they hide, secure, or remove all valuables and prescriptions.

As you show your rental to prospective tenants, be polite and responsive to everyone, even those whom you're pretty sure are not in the running. For example, after hearing someone's laundry list of needed cosmetic upgrades, you could fairly cross that applicant off your list. Still, while it's fine to tell the person that you won't be making those upgrades anytime soon, beware of doing so in a way that might cause offense. For one thing, you need to preserve (or begin creating) your reputation as a businesslike landlord. Perhaps more importantly, you never want to give a disappointed prospect an opening to accuse you of a fair housing violation, as might happen if the demanding prospect concludes that your tone and demeanor had more to do with race, religion, sex, or another protected characteristic than it did with your unwillingness to go along with the demands.

Pardon Those People: Renting Property That's Still Occupied

Many first-time landlords buy or inherit property with tenants in place. Hopefully, yours will be a good tenant who wants to keep renting. But what if the tenant plans to leave, or you decide not to renew the lease or rental agreement for a tenant who is less than ideal? If possible, it's almost always best to wait until the current tenant moves out to show a rental unit to prospective tenants. (This is especially a good idea if your elderly parents are the current residents and they're leaving their long-time home for a nursing home or assisted living.)

Waiting until the place is vacant gives you the chance to spruce it up. It also avoids problems such as promising the house to a new tenant, only to have the existing tenant not move out on time or leave the place a mess.

Nevertheless, to comply with a lease that's still valid for many weeks or months, or to eliminate any gap in rent, you might need to show your property while its current tenants are still there. Follow these suggestions to minimize the disruptions to current tenants and maximize your chances of having a successful showing:

- **Communicate.** Before advertising, discuss your plans with outgoing tenants so you can be as accommodating as possible.

- **Warn tenants about showings.** Give current tenants as much notice as possible before entering and showing the rental. In all states, you have a right to show the still-occupied property to prospective tenants, but your current tenants are still entitled to a reasonable level of privacy and appropriate notice (typically 24 hours—for details, see the discussion of the notice-of-entry clause in leases and rental agreements in Chapter 5).

- **Don't overdo showings.** Try to limit the number of times you show the house in a given week, and make sure your current tenants agree to any evening and weekend visits.

- **Offer something in return.** Consider offering existing tenants a restaurant gift certificate or another perk. As a last resort, for situations where showing the rental will be a major imposition or the tenants refuse to cooperate, you might reduce the rent slightly.

- **Avoid putting a sign on the rental property itself.** This almost guarantees that your existing tenants will be bothered by strangers. If a sign seems like a necessary advertising method, make sure it clearly warns against disturbing the occupant and includes a telephone number for information. An ideal sign might say something like, "For Rent: Shown by Appointment Only. Call 303-555-1700. Do Not Disturb Occupants." If you're using a real estate agent to help with the renting and showing, make sure that the agent has procedures in place to prevent unannounced (and likely illegal) property showings.

> **TIP**
> **A prospect who violates the "Do not disturb" sign won't be a good tenant.** Catherine, a Berkeley landlord who rents a cottage behind her own house, looked out her window one day to see a woman wandering through her backyard. Catherine says, "It turns out she was a prospective tenant who just chose to ignore the sign. I figured this didn't bode well for her ability to follow my rental agreement terms, so of course I didn't rent the place to her."

If, despite your best efforts, the current tenants are uncooperative or hostile, avoid hassles and wait until they leave before showing the rental. Also, if the current tenant is a complete slob or has damaged the place, you're better off applying paint and elbow grease before trying to rent it again. Never advertise or rent a unit in which the current tenant is ignoring a termination notice or, worse, fighting an eviction. Better to clear the decks before embarking on your search for a new tenant.

> **CAUTION**
>
> **Showing your property in extreme situations.** As this book goes to publication, COVID-19 is creating a situation where certain areas have shelter-in-place orders or active outbreaks, making in-person showings of rentals challenging—or even illegal. Whether you're dealing with COVID-19, an impending hurricane, or another evolving public health or safety threat, heed government-issued orders and precautions. Even when there is no official advice in place, use common sense to protect the safety of everyone involved in a showing—yourself included. ●

Screening and Choosing Good Tenants

Afterall your work preparing, showing, and marketing your new property, the day will come when a prospective tenant looks around and says, "It's great, I'd like to rent it." Is that your cue to set a move-in date and watch the rent checks start to roll in? Not so fast.

Choosing tenants is the most important decision you'll make. A bad choice can result in damage and lost rent. And tenant turnover is invariably expensive: By the time you factor in lost rental income (depending on how long the property sits vacant), advertising and screening costs, and the value of your time to plan and run the whole tenant selection show, one change of tenants can easily cost two to three times the monthly rent. And nothing can destroy a profitable year more quickly than an eviction lawsuit, even one that you ultimately win.

All the landlords we talked to in preparing this book were eager to tell us horror stories about tenants who didn't work out—and how they then learned to find the best tenants (and avoid legal hassles) through a fair and thorough screening process. This chapter shows how your common sense, coupled with a clear understanding of the law, will keep your rental income steady and safe. It will help you meet the all-important goal of finding (and keeping) good tenants who pay their rent on time, take good care of your property, and are considerate neighbors.

Hate to Choose? A Property Manager Could Handle This

Many landlords contract with property management companies to handle a number of landlording tasks, such as advertising their rentals, screening tenants, collecting rent, handling tenant complaints, arranging repairs and maintenance, and evicting tenants (usually for an additional fee). But not all management companies deliver on their promises—like prospects, they too have to be researched and screened. See Chapter 10 for details.

> ⓠ **TIP**
> **Lesson learned the hard way: Nice guys aren't always what they seem.** As Darla in Seattle found, "When I tried to rent my house out, I had plenty of people interested. One guy seemed really nice, and looked good on the application he filled out. So I didn't bother to do a financial background check. Bad move—he was a total loser, with a lousy credit record and past evictions. I wound up with a big utility bill after I evicted him for nonpayment of rent."

Creating a Rental Application

If you were to ask a group of landlords whether their "gut reactions" to prospective tenants have always panned out, you'd likely find a few whose instincts have never failed them—but at least as many whose gut misled them. That's why you should ask each prospective tenant to fill out a rental application that includes:

- information about the applicant's employment, income, credit, and rental housing history
- up-to-date references from landlords and employers
- identifying information, such as a Social Security number (SSN), a driver's license number, a passport, or an Individual Taxpayer Identification Number (ITIN) (a number issued by the IRS to persons who are required to file income taxes but who can't obtain a Social Security number), and
- details on past bankruptcies, evictions, or criminal convictions (you'll also get much of this information from a credit report, as discussed below).

You can either hand over the blank rental application in person when showing your rental, or email a copy to interested applicants. If more than one person plans to live in the unit or property, each one over the age of 18 needs to fill out a separate application. This is true whether you're renting to a married couple or unrelated roommates, complete strangers, or the cousins of your current tenant.

CAUTION

Don't pick and choose who gets a rental application. After explaining the basic terms of the tenancy (such as the length of the rental, the rent, deposit, maximum number of occupants, and pet rules), give a rental application to anyone who appears to be qualified and interested—even if you think they can't afford your place. Be sure applicants understand that they must fully complete the application in order to be considered.

Your prospect's signature at the bottom of the rental application is crucial. It authorizes you to verify the information and references and to run a credit report. (Some employers and banks require written authorization before talking to you about a person.)

RESOURCE

More information on rental applications. The Rental Applications and Tenant Screening area of the Landlords section of Nolo.com offers more information on how to screen and select tenants based on a rental application and credit report (discussed below). A sample rental application published by Nolo is shown below. (Source: *Every Landlord's Legal Guide*, by Marcia Stewart, Janet Portman, and Ann O'Connell (Nolo).)

TIP

Information on the rental application will also help you track down a tenant who later skips out. This doesn't happen often, but it happened to Thai, a first-time landlord. He explains, "Eight months into a one-year lease, the tenant just picked up and left. She changed her phone number and didn't respond to my emails. Now I'm much more careful to get references, and ideally a family member's address, which can work like a 'permanent address.'"

Renting to Section 8 Tenants

"Section 8" is a federally run and financed housing assistance program of the Department of Housing and Urban Development (HUD). (It comes from Section 8 of the U.S. Housing Act, 42 U.S.C. § 1437f.) Tenants pay a percentage of their income to the landlord; the local housing authority makes up the rent balance.

Landlords have traditionally been able to opt out of the Section 8 program. However, as the U.S. government's ability to provide low-income housing diminishes, this is changing in some localities. In New Jersey, for example, if an existing tenant becomes eligible for Section 8 assistance, you must participate in the program as to this tenant, at least. (*Franklin Tower One, L.L.C. v. N.M.*, 157 N.J. 602; 725 A.2d 1104 (1999).) In Connecticut, Maryland, and Massachusetts, landlords may not refuse to rent to existing or new tenants paying with Section 8 vouchers. (*Comm'n on Human Rights and Opportunities v. Sullivan Assoc.*, 250 Conn. 763; 739 A.2d 238 (1999); Mass. Gen. Laws ch. 151B, § 4(10); *Montgomery County v. Glenmont Hills Associates Privacy World at Glenmont Metro Centre*, 936 A.2d 325 (2007).)

Some states have required landlord participation in Section 8 by banning source-of-income based discrimination ("SOI"). Such states make Section 8 vouchers protected sources, and include California, Connecticut, Maine, Massachusetts, New Jersey, New York, North Dakota, Oklahoma, Oregon, Utah, Vermont, Wisconsin, and the District of Columbia. Localities within other states may pass similar laws.

There are pluses and minuses to participating in Section 8. Although many landlords are leery of accepting tenants whose ability to pay the rent is already marginal, Phil, a first-time landlord who shares his Berkeley triplex with two Section 8 tenants, says, "The fact that they're getting a rental subsidy helps them pay on time. Plus, it's a good deal for them and they want to keep it that way, so if anything, they're more responsible than regular tenants might be."

Rental Application

A separate application is required from each applicant age 18 or older.

Date and time received by Landlord _____

THIS SECTION TO BE COMPLETED BY LANDLORD

Address of property to be rented: _____ 178 West 81st St., Apt. 4F _____

Rental term: ☐ month-to-month ☑ lease from __3/1/20xx__ to __2/28/20xx__

Amounts Due Prior to Occupancy

First month's rent..	$ 3,000
Security deposit	$ 3,000
Credit-check fee...	$ 38
Other (specify): Broker's fee	$ 3,000
TOTAL..................	$ 9,038

Applicant

Full Name—include all names you use or have used in the past: __Hannah Silver__

Home Phone: _609-555-3789_ Work Phone: _609-555-4567_ Cell _609-555-6543_

Email: _hannah@coldmail.com_ Social Security Number: _123-00-4567_

Driver's License Number/State: __D123456/NJ__

Other Identifying Information: _____

Vehicle Make: __Toyota__ Model: __Corolla__ Color: __White__ Year: __2018__

License Plate Number/State: __NJ1234567/New Jersey__

Additional Occupants

List everyone, including minor children, who will live with you:

Full Name	Relationship to Applicant
Dennis Olson	Husband

Rental History

FIRST-TIME RENTERS: Attach a description of your housing situation for the past five years.

Current Address: __39 Maple St., Princeton, NJ 08540__

Dates Lived at Address: _May 2017–date_ Rent $ _2,000_ Security Deposit $ _4,000_

Landlord/Manager: __Jane Tucker__ Landlord/Manager's Phone: _609-555-7523_

Reason for Leaving: __New job in NYC__

Previous Address: _1215 Middlebrook Lane, Princeton, NJ 08540_

Dates Lived at Address: ___6/2008–5/2017___ Rent $ _1,800_ Security Deposit $ _1,000_

Landlord/Manager: _Ed Palermo_ Landlord/Manager's Phone: _609-555-3711_

Reason for Leaving: _Better apartment_

Previous Address: _____

Dates Lived at Address: _____ Rent $ _____ Security Deposit $ _____

Landlord/Manager: _____ Landlord/Manager's Phone: _____

Reason for Leaving: _____

Employment History

SELF-EMPLOYED APPLICANTS: Attach tax returns for the past two years

Name and Address of Current Employer: _Argonworks, 54 Nassau St., Princeton, NJ_

_____ Phone: _609-555-2333_

Name of Supervisor: _Tom Schmidt_ Supervisor's Phone: _609-555-2333_

Dates Employed at This Job: _2000–date_ Position or Title: _Marketing Director_

Name and Address of Previous Employer: _Princeton Times_

13 Junction Rd., Princeton, NJ Phone: _609-555-1111_

Name of Supervisor: _Dory Krossber_ Supervisor's Phone: _609-555-2366_

Dates Employed at This Job: _2/2000–8/2020_ Position or Title: _Marketing Associate_

ATTACH PAY STUBS FOR THE PAST TWO YEARS, FROM CURRENT EMPLOYER OR PREVIOUS EMPLOYER(S).

Income

1. Your gross monthly employment income (before deductions): $ _8,000_

2. Average monthly amounts of other income (specify sources): $ _____

   Note: This does not include my husband's income. $ _____

   See his application. $ _____

   TOTAL: $ _8,000_

Bank/Financial Accounts

	Account Number	Bank/Institution	Branch
Savings Account:	1222345	N.J. Federal	Trenton, NJ
Checking Account:	789101	Princeton S&L	Princeton, NJ
Money Market or Similar Account:	234789	City Bank	Princeton, NJ

Credit Card Accounts

Major Credit Card: ☑VISA ☐MC ☐Discover Card ☐Am Ex ☐Other: _____

Issuer: City Bank _____ Account No. 1234 5555 6666 7777

Balance $ 1,000 _____ Average Monthly Payment: $ 1,000

Major Credit Card: ☐VISA ☐MC ☐Discover Card ☐Am Ex ☑Other: Dept. Store

Issuer: City Bank _____ Account No. 2345 0000 9999 8888

Balance $ 2,000 _____ Average Monthly Payment: $ 500

Loans

Type of Loan (mortgage, car, student loan, etc.)	Name of Creditor	Account Number	Amount Owed	Monthly Payment

Other Major Obligations

Type	Payee	Amount Owed	Monthly Payment

Miscellaneous

Describe the number and type of pets you want to have in the rental property: _____
None now, but we might want to get a cat sometime

Describe water-filled furniture you want to have in the rental property: None _____

_____

Do you smoke? ☐ yes ☑ no

Have you ever: Filed for bankruptcy? ☐ yes ☑ no How many times _____

Been sued? ☐ yes ☑ no How many times _____

Sued someone else? ☐ yes ☑ no How many times _____

Been evicted? ☐ yes ☑ no How many times _____

Been convicted of a crime? ☐ yes ☑ no How many times _____

Explain (include dates) any "yes" listed above: _____

_____

References and Emergency Contact

Personal Reference: ___Joan Stanley___ Relationship: ___Friend, coworker___

Address: _785 Spruce St., Princeton, NJ 08540_

_____ Phone: _609-555-4578_

Personal Reference: ___Marnie Swatt___ Relationship: ___Friend___

Address: _82 East 59th St., #12B, NYC_

_____ Phone: _212-555-8765_

Contact in Emergency: _Connie & Martin Silver_ Relationship: _Parents_

Address: _7852 Pierce St., Somerset, NJ 08321_

_____ Phone: _609-555-7878_

Source

Where did you learn of this vacancy? _Ryan Cowell, Broker_

_____

I certify that all the information given above is true and correct and understand that my lease or rental agreement may be terminated if I have made any material false or incomplete statements in this application. I authorize verification of the information provided in this application from my credit sources, credit bureaus, current and previous landlords and employers, and personal references. This permission will survive the expiration of my tenancy.

Hannah Silver _February 15, 20xx_

Applicant Date

Notes (Landlord/Manager): _____

_____

_____

_____

_____

_____

_____

_____

_____

_____

Check References and Run a Credit Report

If you're lucky, your initial ads might turn up one or more potential tenants whom you like personally, and whose written applications look good. Should you sign one of them up yet? Sorry, not yet—those completed applications can lie or cover up a rental or financial history that would make the applicant a poor risk. Even after 20 years as a landlord, Dennis says, "It's hard to judge people just by meeting them—are they going to pay bills, are they going to take care of property, are they going to be a nuisance to the neighborhood?" So your next step is to choose your top two or three applicants and confirm the representations on the application.

> **TIP**
> **Best thing I ever did: Weed out tenants by charging first and last months' rent.** Kyung bought a three-family house in New Haven, Connecticut, and lived in one of the units (the two rents paid the entire mortgage). "But," she explains, "because we had a small child, and were going to be sharing the driveway and laundry area, we needed tenants we could trust. We not only interviewed people carefully, but we asked them to sign a one-year lease, plus put down first and last months' rent. That ruled out a lot of people who didn't have money or were bad risks. We decided we'd rather go months with no one living there than regret saying yes to someone. It worked out great; we found good, long-term tenants."

Check with previous landlords

Who better to tell you about a tenant than the person's past landlords? In particular, a former landlord has no reason to paint a deceptively rosy picture of a problem tenant in order to unload that person onto you. When you call, ask targeted questions such as:

- Did this person pay the rent on time (and, if not, what were the circumstances)?

- Did the person ask for repairs when appropriate (but not every time there was a minor problem)?
- How easy was it to communicate with this person?
- Was the former tenant considerate of neighbors (no loud parties)?
- Did the person take good care of the property?
- Would you rent to this person again?

Assuming you're dealing with a candid, businesslike landlord, you want to hear positive answers to your questions. But what if you sense that you're talking to an unreasonable landlord, whom even you wouldn't want to rent from? If so, or if your prospect has alerted you to this possibility, consider the landlord's statements, but be sure to contact other past landlords to get a more complete picture.

Collect Holding Deposits Carefully

Eager applicants will often ask you to accept a holding deposit pending your review of their rental application. (A holding deposit is supposed to guarantee that applicants will get the rental if their credit and references check out.) These tenants want you to know that their money is where their mouths are—if their rental, employment, and credit histories meet your satisfaction, they'll move in.

Holding deposits should be accepted warily and handled with care. Some states impose disclosure requirements on landlords who collect them, by requiring you to explain the circumstances in which you'll keep or return the money (or credit it toward the first month's rent). Beyond these technicalities, however, consider the added bookkeeping. Are you prepared to keep track of these deposits? It's normally a bad idea to require holding deposits—many tenants who are otherwise perfectly good candidates will not have cash available to sideline into a holding deposit.

TIP

Check out pets, too. If the prospect has a dog, cat, or other pet, ask landlord references whether the pet caused any damage or problems for other tenants or neighbors. It's also good to meet the pet, so you can make sure that it's well groomed and well behaved. That will avoid situations like the one Gordon, with property in San Jose, California, faced: "One tenant told us they had a small dog, and they didn't, they had a big one. And the dog basically killed all the grass in the backyard and destroyed the landscaping." You must, however, accommodate an applicant with a legally recognized disability whose pet serves as a support animal—no matter what your pet policies otherwise might be.

Verify income and employment

You no doubt want a tenant who will pay the rent each month. That's why you need to find out whether, in raw numerical terms, the tenant has the income with which to do so. Call the prospective tenant's employer to verify income and length of employment. (The employer might require written authorization from the employee, which you'll have on the rental application or on a separate, stand-alone consent form—digitally send either one to the employer.) You can also ask the prospective tenant to document other sources of income, such as Social Security, disability payments, workers' compensation, welfare, child support, or alimony. Ask self-employed applicants to provide copies of recent tax returns.

How much income is enough? Think twice before renting to tenants where the rent will take more than one-third of their income, especially if they have a lot of debts or financial obligations, if their job is seasonal or gig-based, or they have a history of switching from job to job.

> ⓘ **CAUTION**
>
> **Boring tenants can be better than ones you'd want to hang out with.** As Sarah, a San Francisco landlord, explains, "We've rented to people we wanted to give a break to—we identified with them, because they were young and having trouble finding a place. Of course, being young, their plans changed, and they moved on quickly, and broke the lease. If we could do it all over again, we'd choose the boring tenants with the more stable financial situation."

Check credit reports

A handy way to check prospective tenants' financial circumstances (in particular, their debt load) and on-time payment record is to get each person's credit report from at least one credit reporting agency (CRA). John, who's been a landlord for decades, puts it another way: "If you don't run credit checks, you're crazy."

A good credit report contains a gold mine of information, such as the person's history of paying rent or bills late, past bankruptcies, some criminal convictions, and sometimes past evictions. (A landlord's legal right to get information on evictions, however, varies from state to state.) Credit reports also give you a FICO score—a number between 300 and 850. A low number indicates a poor risk; most landlords will reject applicants with scores under 550 or 600.

Credit reports usually cover the past seven to ten years. To obtain one, you'll need a prospective tenant's name, address, and Social Security number or ITIN. Technically, as long as you're requesting the report for a valid business reason, which includes evaluating the credit risk of a prospective tenant, you don't need the prospect's consent. But, because many people believe that you need their okay, it's simpler to ask for it (for convenience's sake, get it in writing).

Three CRAs have cornered the market on credit reports:

- Equifax (Equifax.com)
- Experian (Experian.com), and
- TransUnion (TransUnion.com).

However, you can't order a credit report for someone else directly from one of these big three. Instead, you'll need to use one of the credit bureau's tenant screening services on their websites (you'll receive similar information to what you would receive in a standard credit report). Many property management websites, such as Cozy (Cozy.co), Avail (Avail.co), and TurboTenant (TurboTenant.com), provide similar online tenant screening services (do an online search for "tenant screening" or "credit report").

It's legal in most states to charge prospective tenants a fee for the cost of the screening report and your time and trouble. Any credit check or report fee should be reasonably related to the cost of the screening itself—$20 to $50 is common. (And you must really run the report— you can't just pocket the fee.) Check your state law for any limits and rules as to what you must do when accepting credit check and application-screening fees.

> **TIP**
>
> **Keep good records.** Take notes of all your conversations with applicants and references and keep them on file, along with applicants' credit reports. (See our advice on record keeping, in Chapter 5.) You'll need these records in order to survive a fair housing challenge if a disappointed applicant files a discrimination complaint. Take special care to store credit reports in a safe place, such as a locked filing cabinet, where only you and those who "need to know" can access them. Under the "Disposal Rule" of the Fair and Accurate Credit Transactions Act of 2003, you must destroy the report when you no longer need it.

Check Database of Sex Offenders

Not surprisingly, most landlords don't want tenants with criminal records, particularly of violent crimes or crimes against children.

Checking a prospective tenant's credit report is one way to attempt to find out about a person's criminal history, but not all convictions will show up on a credit report. Self-reporting is another: Rental applications typically ask whether the prospective tenant has ever been convicted of a crime.

"Megan's Law" databases can also be a useful source of information. Named after a young girl killed by a convicted child molester who lived in her neighborhood, this federal disclosure law charges the FBI with keeping a nationwide database of persons convicted of sexual offenses against minors and violent sexual offenses against anyone. (42 U.S.C. §§ 14071 and following.)

Every state has its own version of Megan's Law, requiring certain convicted sexual offenders to register with local law enforcement officials, who keep a database on their whereabouts. Search online for your state's database, and note the restrictions on your use of information derived from it.

Check college transcripts

If you'll be renting to college students, the credit reports might not show much—they could be only now signing up for their first credit cards! But you can ask to see a copy of a recent school transcript. (If they're freshmen, a high school transcript will do.)

A transcript can reveal a lot. If it shows no "incompletes," a full load, and good grades, you're probably looking at a person who can follow through with a commitment. Even so, you might want to consider requiring a cosigner (as discussed in Chapter 5) if the student depends on parents for substantial support.

Avoiding Illegal Discrimination

Although you can exercise personal choice in deciding who lives in your rental house, there are limits on the reasons for which you can exclude someone. Federal, state, and local laws specify illegal reasons to refuse to rent to a tenant, and limit what you can say and do in the tenant selection process. The federal Fair Housing Act and Fair Housing Amendments Act (42 U.S.C. §§ 3601–3619, 3631) prohibit discrimination on the basis of race or color, religion, national origin, gender, age, familial status (pregnancy or children), and physical or mental disability (including recovering alcoholics and people with a past drug addiction). These are called protected classes. Many states and cities also prohibit discrimination based on marital status, military status, sexual orientation, gender identity, and/or source of income.

The federal antidiscrimination laws mentioned above don't apply to owner-occupied rental housing of four units or less, but they do apply to single-family home rentals, unless you go without advertising or the services of a real estate broker. Don't fasten onto this exception without considering the practicalities involved: Rarely will you be able to rent the home without some sort of advertising or help from a broker. And even if you end up continuously renting via word of mouth, your state or local antidiscrimination laws might cover this loophole in the federal rules. It's far more efficient to comply with fair housing laws from the get-go and not open yourself up to a charge of discrimination which, even if you prevail, will cost you plenty in time, money, and a sullied reputation.

To minimize the chances that you'll need to answer to a fair housing charge, treat all applicants more or less equally. For example, don't set tougher standards (such as a higher income level or a credit score) for renting to a member of an ethnic minority or a single parent. Base your decisions on where you advertise, what you say, and how you screen and choose tenants on sound business reasons, devoid of stereotypes or your personal feelings.

Renting to Undocumented Immigrants

It's not against the law to rent to someone who is in the United States illegally. Then again, it's not against the law *to refuse* to rent to someone who is here illegally. Some landlords recognize that many undocumented immigrants have been here for years, hold stable jobs, and are unlikely to become the target of immigration raids. Others assume, whether rightly or not, that people who are here without proper documentation, and subject to deportation, are more likely to skip out on a rental than others.

If you decide to rent to legal residents only, you'll need to advise all applicants that they must supply proof of legal residence. Asking only those who appear to be "foreign" will open you up to a charge of discrimination based on national origin, race, or color.

Next, you'll have to review and understand the documents that applicants give you. You'll quickly discover that the various visas, work permits, receipt notices, and other documents issued by the Department of State (DOS) or United States Citizenship and Immigration Services (USCIS) are indecipherable, to say the least. And that's before you deal with the possibility of fake documents. Short of being shown a U.S. passport, many landlords throw up their hands.

In recent years, several localities around the United States have passed ordinances making it illegal to rent to people who aren't legal residents. Every such ordinance has either been withdrawn or struck down by a court. Landlords in California and New York City must heed their state and local rules forbidding landlords from demanding proof of legal residence, but if the landlord learns of an applicant's illegal status through any other means, the landlord may decline to rent on that basis.

For further protection, keep a paper trail (such as copies of all credit reports and references from previous landlords) for all applicants. Be organized about filing the applications and other materials and notes on prospective tenants, and keep these for at least three years after you rent a particular unit.

> **CAUTION**
> **You can't use your property's inaccessibility as an excuse not to rent to a tenant with a disability.** The Fair Housing Amendments Act requires all landlords to accommodate the reasonable needs of tenants with disabilities, in many cases at the landlord's expense. (42 U.S.C. § 3604(f)(3)(B).) You're expected to adjust your rules, procedures, or services in order to give a person with a disability an equal opportunity to use and enjoy the house, dwelling unit, or a common space (such as a walkway or yard area). Accommodations include such things as providing a close-in, spacious parking space for a wheelchair-bound tenant (if you provide parking). You aren't, however, required to make accommodations that would pose an unreasonable expense for you. For more on the rights of a tenant with disabilities to make alterations, see Chapter 5.

> **RESOURCE**
> **More information from HUD and state agencies.** For information on the rules and regulations of the Fair Housing Act, contact HUD's Housing Discrimination Hotline at 800-669-9777 or check HUD.gov. For information on state and local housing discrimination laws, contact your state fair housing agency. You'll find a list on the HUD website (click the link for "State Information").

Can You Reject a Prospective Tenant Based on Information From a Google Search?

Many landlords, following the lead of countless employers, do a Google search on rental applicants as part of the screening process. Depending on how active the person is online, you could find a wide variety of personal information; particularly on someone who posts regularly in social media such as Facebook, Twitter, Pinterest, or a personal blog. You might even discover things that you couldn't legally have asked a prospective tenant—such as the person's sexual orientation, race, ethnicity, or religion.

If, however, you use information found online to reject someone who is in a legally protected class and is otherwise a qualified tenant, you could face a discrimination lawsuit. (See "Avoiding Illegal Discrimination," above.)

On the other hand, if you learn that your applicant lied on the rental application (for example, by answering "No" to a question about previous evictions, but posting a request for apartment leads because her former landlord evicted her), you can factor that into your decision. Material misrepresentations on an application are sound business reasons to reject an applicant. To protect yourself, be sure your rejection is based on a legitimate business reason, such as in the example above, and document it (print out the webpage and attach it to your applicant's file).

That said, it remains risky to reject an applicant even for legitimate business reasons, when that applicant is a member of a protected class; for example, has a mental disability. Say you learn about the disability on the person's Facebook page, but reject him because of less-than-stellar landlord references. If challenged by the rejected applicant, you'll be on the defensive, trying to convince a fair housing judge that you ignored the legally irrelevant information (the applicant's mental disability) and focused solely on the proper information (negative references).

Can You Reject a Prospective Tenant Based on Information From a Google Search? (continued)

Many landlord attorneys, taking a cue from their employer-side attorney counterparts, counsel landlords not to do a Google search, period. An "old-fashioned" screening process will uncover most of the information you'll need, and you'll have unassailable sources, such as a poor credit history, to back up your reasons for rejecting. See "Whom to Reject," below.

Is This the One? Characteristics of the Perfect Tenant

Armed with the information you've collected, it's time to see how your top pick or picks match up against the "Checklist of Ideal Tenant Qualities," below.

Of course, intangibles will also come into play. If you communicate well with one prospective tenant and not with another, it makes sense to choose the one whose phone calls you won't soon come to dread. That's doubly true if you're sharing the same property, for example in duplex units.

If you're lucky, you'll find someone who meets all of these criteria and will likely be a good, long-term tenant. Or maybe none of your prospects will seem acceptable—all might have either a troubling rental history, insufficient income, or some other quality (such as immediate and unreasonable requests for upgrades) that would lead most any landlord to reject them. We advise against just swallowing your misgivings and picking the least objectionable.

Checklist of Ideal Tenant Qualities
Any tenant you accept should meet all or most of these criteria:

- ☐ ability to meet your basic rental terms, such as number of people living in your space or length of the rental term
- ☐ sufficient income to pay the rent (the industry standard is a monthly gross income that's triple the monthly rent)
- ☐ satisfactory credit report (debt level and bill-paying history)
- ☐ solid to high credit score
- ☐ positive references from other landlords
- ☐ positive references from current employer
- ☐ no recent terminations or evictions
- ☐ clean criminal record, and
- ☐ complete and accurate rental application.

TIP

Best thing I ever did: Choose a known tenant, despite possible overcrowding. Don, who lives in Philadelphia, says, "When I upgraded to a three-bedroom condo, I decided to rent out my original two-bedroom unit, which included a small den. A hard-working janitor I knew was having trouble finding a place he could afford for his family of five. I let them rent my condo, despite the cramped quarters (they converted the den to a nursery). They were so thrilled, they've taken better care of the place than anyone else would have."

No matter how urgently you want the rent stream to resume, remember that a bad pick can cost you dearly. Go back to the well, and perhaps advertise in different media, drop the rent, spiff up the rental to make it more attractive, or do something else to enlarge the pool of promising applicants.

But once you've identified a good applicant, your next step is to convey the good news to the lucky person and set a date to sign the lease or rental agreement (discussed in the next chapter).

When None of Your Prospects Look Financially Solid

Depending on your rental and the market, the pickings could be slim. If you've held off long enough and simply can't find a financially stable tenant, consider requiring a creditworthy cosigner on the lease. (This approach is often used by landlords renting to college students.) If you're renting to someone with bad credit, be extra sure that their references check out. And consider charging a good-sized deposit—as much as you can collect under state law and the market will bear. For more information on security deposit agreements and cosigners, see Chapter 5.

Whom to Reject

You'll probably have people applying for your rental whom you simply don't want to rent to, even if they're the only applicants. You're legally free to reject people for the following reasons (called your "legitimate business interests"):

- poor credit history
- income that you reasonably regard as insufficient to pay the rent

- negative references from previous landlords indicating problems—such as property damage or consistently late rent payments—that make someone a bad risk

- convictions for criminal offenses of any kind (however, you cannot reject someone with a conviction for drug use; you can, however, reject a person who was convicted of manufacturing or selling drugs, or who currently uses illegal drugs)

- inability to meet the legal terms of a lease or rental agreement, such as someone who can't come up with the security deposit or who wants to keep a pet and your policy is no pets, or

- more people than you want to live in the unit—assuming that your limit on the number of tenants is clearly tied to health and safety or legitimate business needs. (See the discussion of occupancy limits in Chapter 5.)

These are the candidates whom you may safely and legally reject. If you have a bunch of equally qualified applicants and need to pick one, it's safest to choose the person who applied first. You can also apply tie-breaking criteria that are less hard-and-fast. You might, for example, pick the one you feel you'll communicate best with, or who appears to have the skills necessary to take care of your house and garden. But be sure to examine your motives to make sure your preference for one applicant over another isn't based on discriminatory assumptions about people who are in a protected class.

If your reasons for refusing to rent to someone are, in fact, based on information in a credit report or tenant-screening report, you can't just say "Sorry, I found a more qualified tenant." In that case, you must give the applicant the name and address of the agency that reported the negative information or furnished the report. You must tell the applicant that he or she has a right to a copy of the file from the agency, by requesting it within the next 60 days, or by asking within one year of having asked for their last free report.

You must also tell the rejected applicant that the credit reporting agency didn't make the decision to reject the person and can't explain the reason for your rejection. Finally, you must tell such applicants that they can dispute the accuracy of their credit reports and add their own consumer statement to their reports. These notices are known as "adverse action reports" and are a requirement of the federal Fair Credit Reporting Act (FCRA). (15 U.S.C. §§ 1681 and following.)

RESOURCE
More information on rejecting tenants. For details on when and how to prepare an adverse action report, see the article, "Using Consumer Reports: What Landlords Need to Know," on the Federal Trade Commission's website Business Center at business.ftc.gov. (Under "Credit & Finance," click "Credit Reporting," then scroll down.)

Tenant Screening Checklist

Did you:

☐ Deal with current tenants fairly and respectfully?

☐ Know and comply with fair housing laws, and act consistently?

☐ Give every applicant over age 18 a rental application to fill out?

☐ Thoroughly check out the information on the applications of your top most-likely tenants (check references, get credit reports, and so forth)?

☐ Keep good records documenting your decision to choose (or reject) a particular tenant?

Preparing a Lease and Getting the Tenant Moved In

Many landlords believe that if they've checked a tenant's credit and references, any additional paperwork isn't all that important. So they spend a few bucks to buy a one-size-fits-all lease from an office supply store and feel they're covered. Or worse, they simply shake hands with a cheerful, "See you on the first!"

This casual approach couldn't be riskier. "Getting it in writing" might seem formal and unfriendly, but it's the only way to really run a profitable business and avoid problems on both sides. Many of the disputes between landlords and tenants—over rent, deposits, repairs, roommates, pets, or rights to entry—have little to do with whether the tenant is a decent person and everything to do with whether the basic rules of the tenancy were covered in a lease or rental agreement.

"If the lease spells out what can and can't happen, most people are responsible," says Dennis, a longtime landlord from Petaluma, California. And because state law (and in a few instances, federal and local law) dictates many aspects of the landlord-tenant relationship, it's crucial that your rental document include them, so that both you and the tenant understand the rules of the game.

This chapter will get you started by explaining the key provisions to include in your lease or rental agreement, including the state laws that come into play. And we'll guide you through handling other paperwork and records, such as a move-in checklist inventorying the condition of the rental house, and payment and repair records (to form a paper trail should disputes surface later).

CAUTION
Watch out for mass-produced, preprinted leases and rental documents. Many ignore state-by-state differences, use illegal or unenforceable clauses, or are poorly written and full of hard-to-understand legal language. For a solid lease or rental agreement that's valid in your state and easy to create, check out "Helpful Nolo Resources for Landlords," further described in the introduction to this book.

Is the Property Already Rented?

If you've recently bought or inherited rental property, you might acquire existing tenants. If they have a lease, you'll need to wait until it expires before changing any of its terms, such as the rent. If they have a rental agreement, you can make changes (such as increasing the rent) with appropriate notice (typically 30 days), following your state rules and any rent control restrictions.

Purchasers. If you're a purchaser, be sure the last owner gives you copies of the lease or rental agreement, plus details on deposits (more on this below), house rules, maintenance and repair records, and all other relevant paperwork.

Inheritors. If you've inherited the property, work with the former owner's executor or trustee (the person in charge of winding up the owner's affairs) to see if the information and documents can be found.

Take special care that the security deposit is accounted for. In some states, landlords must segregate the funds, provide tenants information as to their location, and periodically pay interest. Some states require sellers to either refund the deposit, letting the new owners collect them anew, or transfer the deposits to the new owners, with notice to the tenants.

Even if your state doesn't specifically set forth the procedure for handling deposits, it makes sense to do one of the two things described above, even in an inheritance situation. If the deposit isn't properly transferred or returned when you take over, and the tenant later looks to you, the current owner, for its return, you'll probably be stuck returning it, even if you never got it in the first place.

Which Is Better, a Lease or a Rental Agreement?

Here's a key question to ask when making your first decisions about renting out your property: For what length of time will you and your tenants be mutually committed to your rental arrangement? Do you want to lock both of you in for a year (or more), or do you want to give both sides the ability to call it quits after giving approximately a month's notice?

Leases and rental agreements have a lot in common: Both cover basic issues, such as rent, security deposits, and who can live in the rental unit. The primary difference between them is the length of the tenancy they create—leases typically last for a year, while rental agreements normally go month to month. Often, but by no means always, your choice will depend on how long you want a tenant to stay. But, because other factors can also come into play, carefully read what follows before deciding.

> **TIP**
> **Use a written agreement, even if you're friends.** When Amy first moved to California and began renting out her Austin, Texas, home, she thought she had the perfect tenant: the roommate she'd been living with all along, plus a friend of his. She says, "We agreed orally that the two would pay a certain rent each month and give 30 days' notice before moving. So I was pretty surprised when I got an email saying he'd be moving in ten days, and then discovered they expected me to go without half the rent until the other tenant's girlfriend moved in two months later. I eventually got most of the rent covered, but the friendship hasn't fared so well."

How a rental agreement works

A written rental agreement commits you and your tenant to a short rental period, typically a month. It automatically renews each month, unless you give the tenant the proper amount of written notice. State laws usually require 30 days' notice to change a term of (such as rent) or to terminate a rental agreement (subject to notice requirements and any restrictions imposed by local rent control ordinances and anti-retaliation and discrimination laws). The tenant can also terminate the agreement on short notice (typically 30 days, although this varies).

How a lease works

A lease obligates both you and the tenant for a set period—usually a year, but sometimes longer. With a fixed-term lease, you can't raise the rent or change other terms of the tenancy until the lease runs out. The only exception is when the lease itself allows specific future changes (such as, "The monthly rent will increase by $100 on October 1, 20xx"), or if the tenant agrees in writing to the changes.

Although a lease offers the security of a long-term tenancy, it can be frustrating to landlords who discover they'd be happier if the tenant departed early. Under ordinary circumstances, landlords can't ask a tenant to move out or convince a court to order an eviction before the lease term expires. There are exceptions here too, however, such as when the tenant fails to pay the rent or violates another significant term of the lease, or breaks the law, such as by repeatedly making too much noise, damaging the rental unit, or selling drugs on your property. (We'll explain how to deal with such situations, in Chapter 9.)

Which is better for you?

If you're balancing landlording with a full-time job, you're probably best off looking for high-quality, long-term renters who will sign a lease for a year or more. While leases restrict your flexibility, they offer big pluses. For one, tenants are likely to think hard and make a serious personal commitment before entering into a long-term lease, in part because they think they'll be liable for several months' rent if they leave early. (They're not entirely correct in that fear, but we'll get to that later.) And people who plan to live in the property for a long time have an incentive to treat it well.

Many landlords also prefer long-term leases in order to avoid the hassles and expenses of regular turnover, such as cleaning, advertising, showing the unit, checking out applicants, and possibly spending months with no rental income. As Sergio, with rental property in Burlingame, California, puts it, "We look for long-term strong tenants who will pay the rent on time and take care of the place. We're not aggressive at raising rents at the end of the year's lease term."

If your area has a high vacancy rate or local landlords have trouble finding tenants during certain seasons of the year, a lease can be especially good protection. For example, if you're renting near a college that's in session for only nine months a year, or in a vacation area that empties out during summer or winter months, you're far better off with a year's lease. This is especially true if you have the market clout to charge a large deposit, so that a tenant who wants to leave early has an incentive to find someone to take over the tenancy.

> ### Do Tenants Break Lease Terms?
>
> *According to a 2019 survey, over 25% of renters admit to having broken the terms of their lease in some way. (Source: Porch.com.) And 48.7% of landlords have had tenants ask to break the entire lease early.*

Other landlords prefer month-to-month rental agreements, precisely because they offer flexibility, allowing the landlord to increase the rent or end the tenancy on relatively short notice and without giving a specific reason. Kathy, with property in Florida, says, "We don't use a lease, since tenants often need to break it anyway." And Catherine, a Berkeley landlord, explains her preference, "I'm using a month-to-month rental agreement because I used a tenant-matching service and wasn't sure they'd found me someone I'd like to keep over the long term. I've been burned before, by tenants whose life circumstances took a turn for the disastrous."

Also, a month-to-month arrangement might be preferable if you're hoping to sell the property within the coming months. Prospective buyers may be put off by the presence of long-term tenants, especially if they hadn't been planning on renting out the property, or if the tenants are paying less than market rental rates. (The new owner takes on the obligations of the previous owner, including leases.) A rental agreement might also be a better choice if your house is in a tight rental market where new tenants are easily found and rents are trending upward.

> **CAUTION**
> **A lease guarantees less income security than you'd think.** As experienced landlords know, it's usually not hard for a determined tenant to break a lease and avoid paying the remaining rent. A few states allow this without penalty in specific circumstances, such as a tenant's need to move to a health care facility. And nationwide, tenants who enter military service are entitled to break a lease. Most states also require landlords to "mitigate" (minimize) their losses—meaning that if a tenant moves out early, you must use reasonable efforts to find another suitable tenant at the same or a greater rent. If you rent the place immediately (or if a judge believes you could have done so with a reasonable effort), the lease-breaking tenant is off the hook—except, perhaps, for having to pay for the few days or weeks the unit was vacant plus your costs of renting it again.
>
> For your state's law, see the chart in the "Landlord's Duty to Rerent When a Tenant Breaks a Lease" article, under State Landlord-Tenant Laws in the Landlords section of Nolo.com.

Why a Verbal Agreement Isn't Really Enough

Legally speaking, oral leases or rental agreements are perfectly valid for both month-to-month tenancies and for leases of a year or less in most states. You and your tenant could, in theory, sit down over coffee and say, "A one-year lease at $1,000 a month, okay?" "Okay." And if you got into a legal spat about the rent, a judge could rule for one of you based on oral evidence alone.

But while oral agreements are easy and informal, using one is never wise. As time passes, people's memories (even yours) have a funny habit of becoming unreliable. You can almost count on tenants claiming that you made, but didn't keep, certain oral promises—for example, to repaint the kitchen or to not increase the rent. Tenants might also forget their own key agreements, such as no subletting. And you probably won't even think to cover certain other issues, such as how deposits can be used. Oral leases are especially dangerous, because they require both of you to accurately remember one important term—the length of the lease—for a considerable length of time.

If something goes wrong with an oral rental agreement or lease, you and your tenants are all too likely to end up in court, arguing over who said what to whom, when, and in what context. This doesn't mean your written agreement needs to be multiple pages long, especially if you know and trust your tenant. But at least get the basic terms written down, including the rent, the length (or term) of the rental, when and where rent is due, and other important matters you've agreed on, such as whether pets will be allowed.

State Laws to Know When Preparing a Lease or Rental Agreement

As described below, conscientious landlords spell out details in their leases or rental agreements regarding matters governed by state law, such as:

- late rent fees
- bounced check charges
- security deposit limits and uses, deadlines and procedures for returning deposits, interest requirements, and other rules (including types of properties that are exempt from state law)
- a tenant's rights, such as to withhold rent if you fail to make necessary repairs
- a landlord's notice requirements to enter rental property
- notice by tenant required to end a tenancy, and
- required landlord disclosures, such as for mold, recent flooding, or details on where the security deposit is being held.

You can find these and other key state laws relevant to preparing a lease or rental agreement, getting a tenant moved in (and out), and running a rental business under State Landlord-Tenant Laws in the Landlords section of Nolo.com.

Typical Provisions in Leases and Rental Agreements

Most leases and rental agreements contain a standard set of rental provisions or clauses, often set out as numbered paragraphs. This section explains common terms you should include in your lease or rental agreement, and notes where state laws come into play. For the most part, leases and rental agreements will contain the same basic clauses, but there are key differences regarding the term of the tenancy that warrant using one rather than the other, depending on your situation.

Names and addresses of landlord and tenants

Every lease or rental agreement should identify the tenant and the landlord or property owner—called the "parties" to the "agreement." (Agreement is a synonym for contract and can refer to either a lease or a rental agreement.) "Lessee" is a term used commonly to refer to a tenant, and "Lessor" is used commonly to refer to a landlord. However, we recommend using "Tenant" and "Landlord" for clarity. If a property manager or company is authorized to receive notices and legal papers for you, your lease or rental agreement should also include its name and address. It is perfectly fine to refer to a property manager or company as "Landlord" in your lease or rental agreement.

All adults who will live in the rental house, including both members of a couple, should sign the agreement. This underscores your expectation that each tenant is legally responsible for the rent (the whole rent, even if roommates have left), for the use or misuse of the property, and all terms of the agreement (a concept known as "joint and several liability").

> **TIP**
> **Gathering signatures is extra important when renting to unrelated roommates.** As Laura, who owns properties in three states, explains: "It can be a hassle when people want to switch roommates—inevitably, one of them takes a job somewhere else, while the other wants to stay. I make sure the lease says I need to preapprove the new person. I also make clear that the remaining tenants need to keep paying the entire rent, and that I'm not going to refund the security deposit if one roommate leaves early. If you're renting to college students, be ready for a lot of this."

If you're signing the lease together with your spouse or other co-owners, you might want to put both names on the lease, particularly if both of you plan to actively participate in managing the property.

Number of occupants

Most leases and rental agreements will specify that the rental property will be the residence of only the tenants and their minor children. Well-drafted agreements should also let the tenants know that they may not move anyone else in as a permanent resident without your consent.

Most of the time, leases and rental agreements will also include a limit on the number of people who can live in the rental property. In setting a maximum occupancy, however, you must tread carefully: You are not free to set unreasonably low occupancy figures (for example, permitting no more than three people for a three-bedroom house) in order to maintain a "quiet atmosphere" or to reduce wear and tear. Federal law requires landlords to allow two persons per bedroom unless you can point to legitimate business reasons justifying a lower number. (Some states are more generous: California, for example, allows two per bedroom plus one more. New York City has a unique "roommate law" that allows current tenants to add roommates.)

Also check your state and local health and safety codes, which probably set a maximum number of tenants based on the size of the property and the number of bedrooms and bathrooms.

> ⓘ **CAUTION**
> **You can't discriminate against families with children.** Legally establishing reasonable space-to-people ratios is okay, but you can't use overcrowding as an excuse for refusing to rent to tenants with children, especially if you'd rent to the same number of adults. Discrimination against families with children is illegal, except in housing reserved for senior citizens only.

Rental home address and furnishings

The property address is often called "the premises," in leases and rental agreements. The section of your agreement dealing with the premises should include details on any furnishings, parking space, storage areas, or other extras that come with the property.

If a particular part of the rental property that a tenant might reasonably assume to be included is not, such as a garage you wish to use yourself, be sure you explicitly exclude it from your description of the premises.

Term of the tenancy

The term is the length of the rental. Your agreement should include the beginning date (when the tenant has the right to move in) and whether it's a month-to-month tenancy or a lease. If it's a lease, the ending date should also be specified.

Rent

Your lease or rental agreement should provide specific details on the rent, including:

- **Amount due each month.** Unless you're in a rent-controlled area, you can legally charge as much rent as you want (or, more practically speaking, as much as the market will support). Chapter 1 includes a discussion of how to set rent.

> **TIP**
> **Raising the rent.** If you sign a lease, you won't be able to raise the rent until it expires. You'll have more flexibility with a month-to-month rental agreement.

- **When and where rent is due.** This is your choice, but traditionally rent is due by the first of the month and is mailed to you. If the first falls on a weekend or legal holiday, then rent is usually due the first weekday after that.
- **Acceptable forms of payment.** Specify personal or cashier's check, or other form of payment, such as money order or electronic funds transfer. Accepting cash is a bad idea, because it's risky to regularly handle large amounts of cash.

- **Late fees when rent isn't paid on time.** Late fees can motivate your tenant to make on-time payments. The amount must closely approximate the actual losses you suffer when your tenant pays late, not act as a penalty for late rent. These losses can include the value of your time (or your employee's time) in dealing with the late rent, such as preparing and delivering the notice, plus the interest you're losing because the rent isn't in your bank account (probably minimal). But they can't include indirect consequences, such as late fees on your car payment because you couldn't pay it without receiving the rent check. Also check into (and follow) your state's laws, which might place a legal maximum on the amount of the late fee, and dictate when you can impose it. If your state hasn't set rules, you'll be on solid ground if you: (1) don't apply the late fee until at least three to five days after the due date; (2) charge no more than 4%–5% of the rent; and (3) keep the increases moderate if you want the late fee to increase each day the rent is late (cap them with an upper limit). An acceptable late charge on rent of $1,000 per month would be $10 for the first day rent is late, plus $5 for each additional day, up to a maximum of 5% of the rental amount.

> **CAUTION**
> **Don't try to disguise excessive late charges by giving a "discount" for early payment.** When the "discount" is substantial, it's simply a roundabout way of charging an excessive late fee, which will make it illegal if challenged.

- **Grace period (if any) before you charge a late fee.** Many landlords don't charge a late fee until two or three days after rent is due, but in most states, you can legally impose the late fee on the due date (that is, you don't need to give a grace period).
- **Bounced check charges.** If your state's law doesn't say how much you can charge, plan on charging what your bank charges you, probably $15–$35 per returned check, plus a few dollars for your trouble.

See Chapter 9 for advice on dealing with tenants who pay rent late or violate another lease term such as moving in extra roommates.

Rent Control

State and local laws in an increasing number of areas limit the amount of rent landlords may charge, and how and when rent may be increased. While it used to be true that rent control laws (also called rent stabilization, rent regulation, or a similar term) were in place mostly in large cities, this is no longer the case. Oregon and California have enacted statewide rent control laws, and it's likely that other states will soon follow suit.

Rent control laws commonly regulate much more than rent. For example, owners of rent-controlled properties must often follow specific "just cause" eviction procedures. And, rent control ordinances might require that your lease or rental agreement include certain information—for example, the address of the local rent control board. Most rent control laws exempt certain properties, such as those with rents over a specified amount and single-family homes.

If you own rental property in a state or city that has rent control, get your hands on a current copy of the law and any regulations interpreting it. You can count on tenants knowing the rules, and you'll be at a severe disadvantage if you're not up to speed. Check with the applicable rent control board or city manager's or mayor's office for information.

TIP
And now, for an atypical lease clause: Rent-to-own provisions. In a rare but increasing number of cases, landlords agree to grant tenants an option to buy the property, sometimes at a preset price, at some point during the rental period. See Chapter 12 for details.

Security deposit

All states allow you to collect a security deposit when a tenant moves in, and hold it until the tenant leaves. The general purpose is to ensure that the tenant pays rent on time and keeps the rental unit in good condition. Rent that you collect in advance for the first month is not considered part of the security deposit.

It's easy to get into legal trouble over deposits, because they're strictly regulated by state law, and sometimes also by city ordinance. In some states, single-family rentals are exempt from certain aspects of the security deposit rule, such as a requirement to pay interest on the deposit, or to hold it in an account separate from the landlord's personal funds. To avoid disputes, your lease or rental agreement should include details on deposits, including:

- **Dollar amount.** Many states limit the amount you can collect to a maximum of one or two months' rent, with the limit sometimes higher for a furnished rental.

- **Restrictions on tenant use of deposit for last month's rent.** Some statutes forbid the tenant from using the deposit as last month's rent. This way, a tenant won't leave you with insufficient funds to cover necessary cleaning and repairs at the end of the tenancy.

- **Where you must keep the deposit and whether you must pay interest.** Several states and cities (particularly those with rent control) require you to put deposits in a separate account and pay the tenant interest. Some states require you to put deposits in a separate "trust" account, rather than mix the funds with your personal or business accounts. Even if you aren't required to keep separate accounts, it's a good idea, as we discuss in Chapter 6.

- **When you must return the deposit.** When a tenant moves out, you'll usually have a set amount of time (in most states, 14 to 30 days) to either return the tenant's entire deposit or provide an itemized statement of deductions and refund any deposit balance.

- **The deductions you may impose.** You can generally withhold all or part of the deposit to cover unpaid rent, damage to the rental property and cleaning costs (outside of "ordinary wear and tear"), or other tenant financial obligations (such as payment of utilities). Expect to make use of this clause; very few landlords end up returning the entire deposit.

> **CAUTION**
> **Be careful about charging nonrefundable fees.** While some states allow landlords to collect a fee that's not refundable (such as for pets or cleaning), most state laws are muddled on the subject. And a few states, such as California, specifically prohibit landlords from charging any nonrefundable fee or deposit. To avoid the legal uncertainties, just factor in the expenses you're worried about when setting the rent, or charge a higher security deposit.

- **How deposit deductions must be itemized when the tenant moves out.** Some states set specific rules and procedures for move-out inspections and preparing itemized statements of security deposit deductions for the tenant.

> **CAUTION**
> **Watch out for liquidated damages clauses.** This item (often found in fixed-term leases) means that a tenant who moves out before the lease expires is supposed to pay the landlord a predetermined amount of money (perhaps the whole security deposit) to replace whatever amount of rent will go unpaid. In most states, liquidated damages clauses are unenforceable—which doesn't mean that the tenants can take off scot-free, just that they will be liable only for the landlord's actual damages, which the landlord must prove in court.

How High a Deposit Should You Charge?

Normally, the best advice is to charge as much as the market will bear, within any legal limits (many states limit the deposit to two to three times the monthly rent). The more the tenant has at stake, the better the chance your property will be respected—a particular concern in high-risk situations, like when a tenant has shaky credit or comes with a large pet. And, the larger the deposit, the more financial protection you'll have if a tenant leaves owing you rent. When renting a single-family home, where damage can be more expensive to remedy than similar damage in an apartment, it makes sense to set the deposit as high as you can.

But a high deposit means that prospects need to come up with a large amount of cash that's tied up throughout the tenancy, which might be unattractive to otherwise qualified renters. Here are some alternatives to a high deposit:

- **Higher rent.** Many acceptable, solvent tenants have a hard time coming up with several months' rent, especially if they're still awaiting the return of a previous security deposit from their last rental. These tenants might rather pay a slightly higher rent than an enormous deposit.

- **Installment payments.** You might gain a marketing advantage by allowing a deposit to be paid in installments, rather than as one lump sum.

- **Renters' insurance.** As a term of the lease, in most states you can require the tenant to buy renters' insurance to cover certain damage by the tenant or guests, as well as injury to other people (this typically includes injuries such as dog bites caused by a tenant's pet).

Utilities

Your agreement should state who pays for what utilities. Normally, landlords pay for garbage and sometimes for water, particularly if there's a yard. Tenants usually pay for other services, such as gas, electricity, cable TV, and Internet. In single-family rentals, tenants often pay for everything.

Tenant's repair and maintenance rights and responsibilities

A carefully written lease or rental agreement will include a statement that makes tenants responsible for:

- keeping the rental premises clean and in good condition (but not for major maintenance, which should remain your responsibility as a landlord)
- reporting defective or dangerous conditions to you, and
- reimbursing you for the cost of repairing damage caused by their abuse or neglect.

Many leases and rental agreements also tell tenants what they can't do in the way of repairs or alterations—such as painting walls, rekeying locks, or adding built-in bookshelves without your permission. Chapter 7 covers landlords' and tenants' rights and responsibilities regarding repairs and maintenance.

What happens when the rental is partially or totally damaged

You might want to lay out what will happen in the event that part or all of the property is damaged by fire, flood, or some other disaster. When a rental is totally destroyed, many leases and rental agreements give the landlord the option of either continuing the tenancy in full effect, but reducing rent or providing an alternate residence for tenants, or terminating the tenancy with a certain number of days' notice.

Step Aside: Tenants Might Be Allowed to Make These Repairs or Alterations

In certain narrow situations, tenants can alter or repair the premises regardless of what your lease or rental agreement says. Examples include:

- **Alterations by a person with a disability.** Under the federal Fair Housing Act, a disabled person may, with your prior approval, modify living space if needed to make it safe and comfortable. For example, the tenant might need to have the countertops lowered to wheelchair height. However, if the modifications will make the unit unacceptable to the next tenant, the disabled tenant must agree to undo them before leaving. Ask for a reasonable description of the proposed modifications, proof that they'll be done in a skillful and efficient manner, and evidence that the tenant is obtaining any necessary building permits. If you'll need to undo the modifications when the tenant leaves, you can insist that the tenant place enough money to cover the estimated restoration costs in an interest-bearing escrow account (the interest belongs to the tenant).

- **Use of the "repair and deduct" procedure when landlords fail to act.** As explained in Chapter 7, tenants in many states may repair defects or damage that make the premises uninhabitable or substantially interferes with its safe use or enjoyment, and subtract the cost from next month's rent.

- **Installation of satellite dishes and antennas.** Federal law gives tenants limited rights to install wireless antennas and small satellite dishes.

- **Specific alterations allowed by state statutes.** Some states allow tenants to install energy conservation measures (like removable interior storm windows) or burglary prevention devices without the landlord's prior consent.

When a rental is partially destroyed, many leases and rental agreements require the tenant to give the landlord a certain period of time to fix the damage, and, if the work is not completed within that timeframe, either party may terminate with a certain number of days' notice.

The section regarding partial or total destruction should also make it clear that when the tenant or the tenant's guests cause the damage, the landlord may terminate the tenancy at any time, and the tenant will remain responsible for all of the landlord's—and tenant's—losses.

Renters' insurance

Renters' insurance covers losses to the tenant's belongings resulting from fire or theft, as well as injury to other people or property caused by the tenant's negligence. Besides protecting the tenant from personal liability, renters' insurance benefits you, too: You want damage caused by the tenant to be covered by the tenant's policy—not yours, as a claim will likely increase the cost of the insurance.

In most states, you can require tenants to carry renters' insurance. Note that some states do restrict how and when you can require it, so be sure to check your state laws before including a renters' insurance clause in your lease or rental agreement.

If you decide to require renters' insurance, require tenants to obtain at least a certain amount of coverage during the entire tenancy, and require that tenants provide you with proof of insurance on at least an annual basis. Consider having the tenant name you as an "additional insured" on the policy, so that you are alerted if the tenant cancels or changes coverage at any point during the tenancy.

When and how landlords may enter rental property

Nearly every state clearly recognizes the right of a landlord to enter the premises while a tenant is living there, under certain broad circumstances, for example, such as to deal with an emergency or when the tenant gives permission. Your agreement should set forth and explain this right.

Many states have access laws specifying other circumstances under which landlords may legally enter rented premises, such as to make repairs (for example, fix a broken oven), inspect the property, and show the property to prospective tenants and purchasers. State access laws typically specify the amount of notice required for such entry—usually 24 hours (unless impractical—for example, in an emergency). A few states simply require the landlord to provide "reasonable" notice, often presumed to be 24 hours.

Extended absences by tenant

Some leases and rental agreements require tenants to notify the landlord in advance if they'll be away for a certain number of consecutive days (often seven or more). Such clauses can give you the right to enter the property while the tenants are gone for needed maintenance and to inspect for damage. This type of clause is usually most appropriate for rentals in cold-weather places where landlords want to drain the pipes to guard against bursting.

You Can't Ask Tenants to Sign Away Their Rights

Most states have passed tenant-friendly laws covering subjects such as landlords' access to rental property, the amount and use of security deposits, and tenant rights to a livable home. Tenants also have important legal rights under federal law (particularly in the area of discrimination).

You can't get around these rights by asking tenants to waive them—for example, by including a lease clause saying that the premises are acceptable "as is," or not warranted as fit, safe, secure, or in good repair. Most states will not uphold a clause that diminishes tenant rights to habitable property.

Limits on tenant behavior and illegal activity

A good lease or rental agreement will contain a clause forbidding tenants from using the rental property or adjacent areas, such as the sidewalk in front of the house, in a way that violates any law or ordinance, including laws prohibiting the use, possession, or sale of illegal drugs. These clauses also prohibit tenants from intentionally damaging the property (called "committing waste," such as by punching holes in the wall), or creating a "nuisance" by annoying or disturbing other tenants or nearby residents—for example, by continuously making loud noise or allowing garbage to pile up.

Basically, you can set any kind of restriction you want—as long as it's not discriminatory, retaliatory, or otherwise in violation of the law. For example, you may prohibit smoking in the rental property as well as on the deck, patio, or front porch.

We'll discuss some common restrictions involving pets, home businesses, sublets, and guests in the following sections.

Pets

You have the right to prohibit all pets, or to restrict the types allowed—for example, forbidding dogs or cats, but allowing birds, or prohibiting certain breeds of dogs (if required by your insurance company). However, you must allow assistance animals (also known as "service" or "support" animals) used by people with physical or mental disabilities (protected by the fair housing laws).

Not every landlord wants to prohibit pets. Allowing them can attract a wider range of tenants. And it offers benefits if you're sharing the property, as Catherine in Berkeley explains: "I had one great renter who had a dog—we took care of each other's dog when we traveled, shared poop patrol, and more."

No matter what you decide, spell out your pet rules—for example, the type and number of pets allowed (such as one cat or one dog under 20 pounds). Also state that the tenants will keep the yard free of all animal waste and keep the dogs on leash and under control (no excessive barking that bothers the neighbors).

See Chapter 8 for a discussion of landlord liability for dog bites and other animal attacks.

> **TIP**
> **You might want to waive your no pets policy.** That's what Sarah, a San Francisco landlord of a single-family home, has done in many instances. She explains, "We've said 'No Pets,' but if we find a good tenant, we'll meet the pet and take it case by case. Dog owners in particular seem to be very responsible, maybe because they already have to walk their animals every day. One dog we let move in chewed some stuff up, but the owner was completely willing to pay for it without question." But be careful about waiving your rules when you own a multifamily property. The last thing you want is for a tenant to observe that you're waiving the rules only for some people because of race, nationality, or another protected characteristic.

Renting to Pet Owners

The San Francisco Society for the Prevention of Cruelty to Animals (SPCA) is one of several humane societies across the country that offers animal guidelines for landlords and tenants, including sample documents, such as a pet agreement. For additional information, see the national Humane Society's website at HumaneSociety.org and search "renting with pets."

Also see the Dogs in Rental Housing articles in the Landlords section of Nolo.com, for more information on renting to pet owners.

Restrictions on home businesses

Are you at all worried that your tenant might run a business from your rental property—potentially burdening neighbors by increasing local traffic, and exposing you to liability if a customer or business associate gets hurt? If so, you can prohibit this with a clause in your lease or rental agreement specifying that the premises are "for residential purposes only." For more on the subject, see "Home Businesses on Rental Property," below.

Home Businesses on Rental Property

If a tenant wants to run a business from your rental home, be sure to spell out all the details in your lease or rental agreement. First, you'll need to check local zoning laws for restrictions on home-based businesses, including the type of businesses allowed (if any), the amount of car and truck traffic the business can generate, and other rules about outside signs, on-street parking, number of employees, and percentage of floor space devoted to the business. And if your rental is in a planned unit or a condominium development, check the CC&Rs of the homeowners' association.

Also consult your insurance company as to whether you'll need a different policy to cover the potential liability of tenants' employees or guests. In many situations, a home office for occasional use won't be a problem. But if the business will involve people and deliveries coming and going, such as a therapy practice, jewelry importer, or small consulting firm, seriously consider whether to expand or add coverage.

You might also want to insist that the tenant buy certain types of liability insurance, so that you won't wind up paying if someone gets hurt on the rental property—for example, if a customer trips and falls on the front steps.

Finally, be aware that a residence used as a commercial site might need to meet the accessibility requirements of the federal Americans with Disabilities Act (ADA). You can insist that the tenant pay for any modifications. For more information on the ADA, see ADA.gov.

CAUTION
What if a tenant wants to run a day-care operation in your rental? You might not be able to stop it. Some states give licensed day-care owners the right to conduct business in a rental. However, landlords in California and New York, for example, may limit the number of children. Also, the business must comply with state fire and health regulations regarding minimum facility size and fire exits. If the property won't pass inspection, and making the property compliant (for example, by adding exits or stairways) is not something you're willing to do, the tenant won't be able to get a permit and won't be able to run the facility.

Restrictions on assignments or sublets

Most leases and rental agreements prohibit "assignments," which happen when your tenant moves out permanently and brings in a replacement tenant for the remainder of the lease. Your rule on prohibiting assignments should state that you won't unreasonably refuse to rent to a proposed newcomer. (That simply reflects your obligation, in most states, to use reasonable efforts to find a replacement once the original tenant leaves.) When you think about it, it's actually to your advantage to have a lease-breaking tenant do the work of finding a suitable replacement.

Your agreement should also prohibit tenants from temporarily renting their (and your) space to someone else (called a sublet), without your written consent. If you want to prohibit a tenant from letting someone stay in the rental while the tenant is on vacation or renting out a room on Airbnb, be sure your agreement explicitly says so. And even if you allow a tenant to rent out space on Airbnb or a similar service, local laws or homeowners' association covenants might restrict these kinds of short-term rentals. See "Legal Restrictions to Renting Your Home on Airbnb or Other Rental Services" and related articles in the Real Estate section of Nolo.com.

Limits on guest stays

It's common for leases to limit overnight guests. For example, you might allow a guest for no more than ten days in any six-month period, with written approval required for longer stays. The idea is to keep long-term guests from gaining the status of full-fledged tenants, who haven't been screened or approved or signed the lease or rental agreement.

Attorneys' fees and court costs in a lawsuit

In case of a dispute over the meaning or implementation of a part of your rental agreement or lease, the agreement can specify who will pay the costs of a lawsuit. For example, disputes about rent or security deposits are common. This clause can act as a nice deterrent—even with several properties, Laura says, "I have something in the lease saying the prevailing party will have their legal costs covered, and I've never had a tenant threaten to sue." Attorneys' fee clauses don't, however, apply to disputes that don't stem from the lease or rental agreement—for example, lawsuits over alleged discrimination.

Grounds for termination of tenancy

This important clause states that any violation of the lease or rental agreement by the tenants, or by their guests, is grounds for terminating the tenancy according to the procedures established by state or local laws. Chapter 9 provides an overview of how tenancies can be ended.

Lead-based paint and other disclosures

Federal, state, or local laws might require you to disclose certain things about the property before a new tenant signs a lease or rental agreement or moves in, including the presence of lead-based paint (a federal law requirement discussed in Chapter 8). State laws might require other disclosures, too, such as the presence of mold, shared utility arrangements, or recent flooding. And rent control ordinances often require disclosures, such as the name and address of the government agency or elected board that administers the ordinance.

Some states require landlords to inform tenants of the name and address of the bank where the security deposit is being held, and the name and contact information of the person authorized by the owner to receive legal papers. Check your state and local laws for details on these and other disclosure requirements.

If your property contains a hidden (not obvious) problem that could cause injury or substantially interfere with your tenant's safe enjoyment and use, and the problem is impossible to fix, you're better off legally if you disclose the defective or dangerous condition before the tenant signs the lease. Examples include naturally occurring dangers, such as loose soil, and human-made dangers, such as steep stairs.

Tenant rules and regulations

If your property has more than one unit—even if it's a duplex you share—think about what you might want to require of tenants concerning shared areas like the yard, garage, driveway, or even a pool. Be clear about your rules on smoking, parking, and pets. Also give details on what's considered excessive noise.

There's no need to cover every detail of daily living, however. Landlords of single-family rental houses often find it easier to discuss things like recycling or maintenance tips in a move-in letter, discussed below. To make sure you have some clout, include a clause in the lease or rental agreement giving you the right to terminate the rental arrangement if the tenant repeatedly and seriously violates house rules.

CAUTION
Watch out for conflicts with community association rules. If you're renting out a condo or another property governed by a community association, check to make sure that none of the terms of your lease contradict the CC&Rs or association rules. If, for example, your lease says pets are allowed but the CC&Rs say they're not, your tenant will not be allowed to keep a pet.

Signing a Lease or Rental Agreement

Once your lease or rental agreement is completely drafted, make an appointment with your new tenant(s) to review and sign this important document. Bring two copies to your meeting (one for you and one for the tenant(s)). Of course, this assumes that you're not interested in negotiating any of the terms. In a soft market, or when you're dealing with prospects whom you really want and might be willing to bend the terms for, you might want to negotiate selected issues before your signing meeting.

Before you even think about signing the lease, start with this very important step: Ask for the money, and to be extra careful, don't accept a personal check. Until you have the tenant's cash, certified check, or money order for the first month's rent and security deposit in hand, signing a rental commitment is a recipe for trouble. Starting with the second rent payment, of course, you might prefer to accept checks (insisting on cash is inadvisable), and you'll have to trust that your careful tenant-screening process weeded out those tenants who would have given you checks that bounce.

Next, encourage tenants to ask questions about anything that's unclear on your lease or rental agreement. "Make sure you sit down with each tenant before they move in and go over the lease, so you both have a good understanding from the beginning about what you expect from each other," says Dennis from Petaluma.

CAUTION

Don't sign until all terms are final and mutually understood. All of your expectations should be written into the lease or rental agreement before you and the tenant sign. Never sign an incomplete document assuming last-minute changes can be made later. If you've altered a preprinted form by writing or typing in changes, you and the tenant should initial and date each change when you sign the document.

Should You Ask for or Accept Cosigners?

Some landlords require cosigners on rental agreements and leases, especially when renting to students who depend on parents for much of their income. The cosigner signs the rental agreement or lease or a separate document, agreeing to cover any rent or damage repair costs the tenant fails to pay.

In practice, a cosigner's promise might have less legal value than you'd think. Suppose your tenant doesn't pay the rent, and the cosigner doesn't step up. Most landlords will simply evict the tenant, because the alternative (suing in small claims court to force the guarantor to honor the promise) is too much trouble (and is practically impossible if the cosigner lives in another state).

Still, a tenant who thinks you can (and will) notify and sue a cosigning relative or friend might be less likely to default on the rent. Similarly, a cosigner asked to pay the tenant's debts may persuade the tenant to pay, or might (as many parents will) come to the tenant's rescue.

Because of the practical difficulties associated with cosigners, many landlords refuse to consider them, which is legal in every situation but one: If a tenant with a disability who has insufficient income (but is otherwise suitable) asks you to accept a cosigner, you must at least investigate the proposed cosigner's suitability. If that person is solvent and stable, federal law requires you to accept the cosigner, in spite of your general policy.

If you decide to accept a cosigner, you might want to have that person fill out a separate rental application and agree to a credit check—after all, a cosigner who has no resources or connection to the tenant will be completely useless. If the tenant and prospective cosigner object, you should probably wonder how serious they are about the arrangement. Once you're satisfied that the cosigner can genuinely back up the tenant, add a line at the end of the lease or rental agreement for the dated signature, phone, and address of the cosigner.

Be sure all adults (18 years of age and older) who will live in the rental unit—including both members of a couple—sign the lease or rental agreement. Doing this makes everyone who signs responsible for all terms, including the full amount of the rent. As Gordon, a landlord in San Jose, California, says, "If you have to evict your tenants, you can evict the guy who signed the lease, but the others might not move out. A smart attorney can get around that, but you can avoid the problem from the get-go if they all sign the lease."

After everyone signs, give one copy of the signed lease or rental agreement to the tenant(s) and keep the other one for your files.

Getting the Tenant Moved In

A clearly written and easy-to-understand lease or rental agreement is critical to starting a tenancy. But there's more that can be done to help establish a positive relationship. On or before the tenant's move-in day, set up a time to go over your house rules and important information about the rental, walk through the house, and hand over the keys. Bring a welcome gift, such as a bottle of wine or a gift certificate for a local bakery. Be cordial and allow enough time to answer all the tenant's questions.

Give new tenants a move-in letter and house rules

A good move-in letter will provide all kinds of valuable information for the new tenants, such as:

- your phone numbers (during the day and after hours), email, and emergency contacts
- how and where to report maintenance and repair problems
- location of garbage cans, trash pickup days, and available recycling programs
- maintenance dos and don'ts, such as how to avoid overloading circuits and use the garbage disposal properly

- where to find appliance manuals, water shut-off valves, smoke detectors, and other important information
- homeowners' association rules (if any), and
- any other useful information about the property and neighborhood.

Many landlords highlight important lease terms in their move-in letter, such as their policy regarding late fees and adding a roommate or pets.

> **TIP**
> **Renting out a condo or house in a common-interest development (CID)?** Remember to give the tenant a copy of the community association rules (often called CC&Rs), and emphasize that failing to comply with them might give you no choice but to evict.

Inspect and photograph the rental property

To ward off future arguments, it's absolutely essential that you and your tenant (ideally, together) check the place over for damage and obvious wear and tear before the move-in (but after your own prepping of the property, discussed in Chapter 3). You and the tenant should document what you find with a checklist describing the general condition of each room (and any furnishings), backed up with photos or video, and signed by both (or all) of you.

Write down, in as much detail as is practical, both serious problems, such as a broken heater, and minor flaws, such as a stained kitchen counter, dirty drapes, or chipped paint. Ideally, you'll have fixed all major problems before the tenant moves in, but if not, now's the time to do so (especially any habitability or security problems).

This checklist will protect both you and your tenant when the tenant moves out and questions why you withheld all or part of a security deposit. Coupled with a system to keep track of the rental property's condition (as discussed in Chapter 7), your checklist will also be extremely useful if a tenant withholds rent, breaks the lease and moves out, or sues you outright, claiming the unit needs substantial repairs.

Besides just being useful, a checklist is sometimes mandatory. Many states require landlords to give new tenants a written statement on the condition of the rental premises at move-in, including a comprehensive list of existing damages, and give tenants the right to inspect the premises to verify the accuracy of the list and note any problems.

> **RESOURCE**
> **Where to find a room-by-room inventory and relevant state laws.** Nolo's book, *Every Landlord's Legal Guide,* includes detailed forms for inspecting and inventorying the rental property at move-in and move-out and making security deposit deductions, as well as state laws in these areas. Nolo also publishes an online Landlord-Tenant Checklist for documenting the condition of the rental (and any furnishings) at the beginning and end of the tenancy. See Nolo.com.

Organizing Your Rental Records

Making written notes of key events in a tenant's rental history, and organizing your rental documents, will come in very handy if you and your tenant disagree, perhaps in court, about what happened and when. For example, suppose you terminate the tenancy of a tenant who chronically paid rent late. If that tenant claims that your real reason was illegal (say, discrimination on account of race), your records, including late fee notices, requests for rent, and bank records will help you establish your true motive. You never want to be in a position where the only evidence before a judge is your word against the tenant's.

Start by setting up a file folder for the following documents (it's also a good idea to keep electronic copies):

- tenants' contact information, including phone numbers (home and work, plus emergency contacts), plus vehicle make, model, color, year, and license plate number
- a copy of your tenant's rental application, references, and credit report

- your copy of the signed lease or rental agreement
- deposit information, including the location and interest rate terms of your deposit, and
- move-in checklist and photos or video of the condition of rental unit at the beginning of the tenancy.

After your tenant moves in, add these documents to your file:

- your written requests for entry
- rent increase notices and late fee notices
- records of tenant repair requests and how and when they were handled, and
- any other correspondence with your tenant.

Chapter 6 provides advice on keeping important financial and tax records. ●

Manage Your Rental Income to Maximize Tax Deductions

Do you know how to give an accountant a supersize migraine? Put the rental payments from your tenants right into your family bank account, dip into the same account when you need to buy things for the property, don't bother saving receipts or keeping records, and let your kids use the maintenance and office supplies you originally bought in connection with the rental property.

This will guarantee that, at the end of the year, you and your accountant tear your hair out trying to figure out whether your rental property business made or lost money, which expenses will be tax deductible (important if you did make a profit), and whether you were even active enough as a landlord to claim business owner deductions. In the worst-case scenario, you could end up in an IRS audit, perhaps having to pay back taxes and penalties for disallowed deductions.

But wait, there's a better way: Treat your rental property as a business from the beginning, even if it's only half of your duplex or a spare room in your house. That includes:

- drawing a clear line between your business and personal finances
- taking steps to shield you and your family from personal liability for business debts
- learning what tax deductions you're allowed as someone actively running a business (instead of a passive investor), how to conduct business so you can claim them, and how to prove you deserve them
- keeping your income and expense records in good order
- making sure you're actually earning a profit, and
- getting professional help when needed.

We'll show you how to do all these things in this chapter. You should read it even if you don't expect to turn a profit—that picture could change, and it's worth developing good habits, and keeping clear records, from the start.

TIP
Good financial management translates into a good credit record. Because you're probably operating as a sole proprietor, your ability to pay business bills on time and repay loans is as important to your credit record as how you handle your personal credit card. A good credit record will make it easier to take out loans—which you might need for property improvements or to weather a rough patch. Conversely, a poor credit record will hurt your ability to not only take out loans at reasonable interest rates but accomplish other life goals, like getting a new job. For more on the hows and whys of keeping up a good credit score, see the Debt Management section of Nolo's website (Nolo.com).

Keeping Your Business Finances Separate

It's not hard to keep your personal finances separate from your rental property finances—but it gets harder the longer you wait to create an appropriate system.

Opening and using a separate bank account

Choose your favorite local or online bank and open a separate checking account. If you incorporate your business activities or form an LLC (as discussed below), open the account in the name of that business. If not, just use your own name. (In theory, you could register a separate business name with your state or county government—often called a "DBA," for "doing business as"—but there's little point, because the laws will probably require you to include your last name in your DBA anyway.)

> **CAUTION**
> **Shop around for bank rates.** Look for a low-cost or even free checking account, and read the fine print regarding extra fees for things like going below a certain balance or bouncing a check. Avoid using the word "business" when asking about accounts—some banks immediately raise their checking account rates for businesses, no doubt imagining the massive profits you'll bring in.

Because you'll probably have to spend money on your property before it earns a dime, it's good to seed your checking account with start-up cash ("capital contributions") from your personal account. Once you start earning rental income, deposit it into your business account and pay all expenses out of that account (after charging expenses to your business credit card, if you have one). Repay yourself for those capital contributions by writing a check to your personal account. When writing checks, always use the memo line to write what the money is being spent on.

> **CAUTION**
> **Landlords in certain states must put tenants' security deposits into a separate bank account.** Adding them to a separate, business account won't do it in these states. (However, your property manager, if you hire one, might take care of this for you.) Check your state's security deposit laws, summarized in the Landlords section at Nolo.com.

Opening and using a separate credit card account

For convenience, you might want to open a separate credit card account for your business. Credit cards are convenient, sometimes offer benefits like cash back, and allow you to store money in a place other than your checking account, which is relatively easy prey for identity thieves.

> ### TIP
> **Already have more than one personal credit card account?** You could simply pay one down to a zero balance and start using it exclusively for your business.

Be scrupulous by making business purchases on your business credit card only, even if you find the perfect plants on sale and forgot to bring the right card. If you must make an exception, save the receipt and write a memo for your files as soon as you're home, then repay your personal account out of your business account.

Do your best to pay off the entire credit card debt month by month —mounting interest can quickly undercut your profits. Credit card interest rates are typically the highest of any type of loan.

> ### TIP
> **What if you buy something for mixed use?** For example, suppose you pick up a tray of ground cover that you'll use partly for business and partly for your home. One option is to ask the cashier to divide the bill between two credit cards. Another is to pull out both your business and personal checkbooks and use separate checks to pay. If you must use only one credit card, go with your personal one, then make a note for your files and repay the proportional share from the business checking account. (After-the-fact conversions of property from personal to business raise eyebrows at the IRS.)

Sharing property between your home and business

There's no need to rush out and buy two sets of everything—a new lawn mower, power saw, or computer, for example. If you already have or need to buy something at home, you can use it for your business, too. The catch is that, if you want a tax deduction, you'll need to keep track of what percentage of the property's use is dedicated toward your business.

With "listed property" (described later in this chapter), that percentage must be greater than 50% for the IRS to recognize the business use. The same is true for property you want to deduct under Section 179 (described below).

Telephones are a separate case—the first landline into a home is always considered personal, so you can't deduct its cost no matter how much you use it for work (though you can deduct additional lines used solely for business, plus long-distance calls, if charged separately for them; use the "Utilities" section of your tax return).

With other property that isn't "listed," however, you can simply take a proportional amount of the applicable tax deduction based on your percentage of business use. That's true of cellphones, too; you could keep logs and deduct a percentage of your use, or ask your provider for an itemized bill and add up the business-related calls.

A related issue is whether you'll actually decide to create a separate office within your home in order to qualify for the home office deduction. We'll discuss that below under "Deducting for use of a home office."

Shielding Yourself From Liability for Business Debts

We're assuming you're currently operating as a sole proprietorship, meaning you haven't done anything special or filed any papers with your state. You create a sole proprietorship simply by going into business by yourself. The same goes for partnerships (two or more people going into business together create a partnership). There's no need to register with the state or sign a partnership agreement.

Starting out as a sole proprietorship or partnership is certainly convenient, but there's a catch: As a sole proprietor or partner, you and your business are legally one and the same when it comes to debts and liability. It won't matter how hard you've worked to keep your books and finances separate. If someone claims you owe them money— perhaps a contractor whom you've refused to pay for shoddy work, or your tenant who sues you for medical costs after slipping on the badly lit back porch—your own assets could be on the line.

That's why some businesses that start out as sole proprietorships or partnerships eventually decide to convert to separate legal entities, usually a limited liability company (LLC) or a corporation.

> **CAUTION**
> **No business structure can completely shield you from all liability.** Even if you operate as a corporation or an LLC, a creditor can go after your personal assets if, for example, you personally guarantee a loan or lease (which many banks require of landlords); your business owes federal or state income, payroll, or other taxes; or you fail to abide by corporate rules (for example, you mix corporate and personal funds and don't keep records of meetings and shareholders).

Pluses and minuses to forming a corporation

Incorporating means that you formally declare that your business is a separate legal entity from you, its owner. Once you incorporate, the corporate entity becomes responsible for your business's debts and liabilities instead of you (with certain limitations).

The process of incorporating can be a bit involved, however. It involves choosing a name, filing articles of incorporation with your state, paying filing and other fees (often hefty), adopting bylaws, appointing a board of directors (most states allow just one director, who can be you), and issuing shares (probably to yourself).

Running a corporation is also more complicated than running a sole proprietorship or partnership. You'll need to comply with federal and state securities laws concerning record keeping, corporate taxation, and more.

The upshot is that forming a corporation might require more time and expense than you want to invest. For many landlords, the personal liability issue can be dealt with in other ways. See "Alternative ways to minimize your risk," below.

Pluses and minuses to forming an LLC

Limited liability companies, or LLCs, are less complex to form and run than corporations. Yet, just like corporations, the owners of an LLC are not personally liable for business debts (with similar exceptions).

To form an LLC, you need to file articles of organization with your state, pay filing and other fees, and draft an internal operating agreement. Although you'll have to pay annual fees, you won't have to deal with many of the other ongoing requirements that corporations face, such as holding regular board meetings and keeping minutes. And your taxes will be much more straightforward, because you can choose to pay them through your individual tax return. Again, however, you might want to look for simpler alternatives.

Alternative ways to minimize your risk

Forming a separate legal entity isn't the only way to deal with unexpected events that require you to dip deeper into your own pockets than you can handle. Another cautionary measure is buying adequate insurance to protect yourself (see discussion of insurance in Chapter 8).

Also, simply behaving in a responsible manner will help forestall problems—for example, by signing written agreements with contractors to help head off disputes, following health and safety codes, and making repairs and taking other preventative safety measures on your property before a tenant gets injured (as discussed in Chapter 7). See Chapter 2 for more on the pros and cons of LLCs.

Spent a Lot of Money? Take More Tax Deductions!

A surprising number of landlording expenses can be turned into tax deductions. When Lisa first began renting out the Berkeley, California, house she formerly lived in, she says, "I had no idea how much I'd save in taxes—enough that, once I ran the numbers, I went straight to my HR director's office and changed my wage withholding so I could start enjoying the benefits with my very next paycheck."

Apart from your day job, you'll hopefully have some new income from the property as well, so you've got every interest in offsetting it with some deductions.

The basic formula works like this:

- Add up your gross income (mostly rent received over the year).
- Deduct your start-up expenses.
- Deduct your operating expenses (mortgage interest and property tax included).
- Deduct your depreciation and amortization expenses.
- Deduct any Section 179 expenses. (This deduction is much more limited for landlords than other business owners.)
- Deduct 20% of net business income, assuming you qualify for the "pass-through" deduction that's available between 2018 and 2025.
- The result is your taxable income, or the amount the IRS will ask for a bite of (after you report your profits and losses on Schedule E).

Let's take a closer look at the various federal tax deductions available to landlords, and how you can make the most of them. Most states also impose income taxes, which you'll have to research on your own—but state income tax laws tend to mimic the federal system. Our goal here is not to provide every legal detail or prepare you to fill out a tax form, but to raise your awareness of likely tax-reducing strategies—and dead-end tax traps.

> **TIP**
> **We're assuming you'll really be acting like a business owner.** Mere property "investors" don't have access to as many tax deductions. For example, if you're lax about placing ads, and the property sits vacant for months at a time, the IRS could classify you as an investor (and make you pay penalties and back taxes if you claimed

business-owner deductions). The key is to strive to earn a profit by actively running a business, working at it regularly, systematically, and continuously. Hiring a property manager to take over much of the activity still counts, for IRS purposes. There's also a general "safe harbor," by which the IRS assumes you're a business, if you work at least 501 hours per year. Also, for purposes of the pass-through deduction, spending at least 250 hours per year on work connected to the rental property puts you into a "safe harbor," so long as you keep separate books and contemporaneous records showing your rental income and expenses and don't live in the property for more than 15 days a year or 10% of the time. Fortunately, neither of these safe harbor rules prevent you from qualifying as a business even after doing fewer hours.

Who Gets the Deductions If You Co-Own?

If you share ownership of your property with someone other than your spouse, you can share the tax deductions, as well. For example, if you take title to the property as tenants in common, you'll have to list each of your percentage ownership interests (60%/40%, for instance), on your property deed, and the IRS will expect you to share the expenses and tax deductions in equal proportions.

If you've placed ownership of the property into a partnership or an LLC, the deductions will pass through to its partners or members. The deductions can then be allocated among you as you wish, subject to IRS "substantial economic effect" rules (which let the IRS disregard allocations of losses done only to avoid taxes).

This is a complicated area of tax law, so see a tax expert to work out the details.

It's entirely possible—especially if you recently bought the property—that you'll be able to wipe out all your taxable rental income with your expenses, and not have to pay any tax at all on the rental income. Of course, you'll need to keep good records of every penny spent in order to do this. And, unfortunately, one of the most valuable contributions you'll be making to your rental property is your own time—and that's not tax deductible.

If your Schedule E actually shows a tax loss on the property, you might be able to deduct at least a portion of the loss from other income, but this gets more complicated. It's governed by what are called the passive-loss and at-risk rules, which we don't cover in this book.

If you do expect a profit of over $1,000 per year, however, get ready: The IRS will expect you to file "estimated taxes" four times per year, starting on April 15. There's a way around this, if you have a day job. Ask your HR department to withhold extra from your pay—enough that your total withholding adds up to less than 90% of the total tax you expect to owe that year. The "Tax Withholding Estimator" on the IRS website will help with this. Also see IRS Publication 505, *Tax Withholding and Estimated Tax*.

RESOURCE
For in-depth information on all the topics in this section, see *Every Landlord's Tax Deduction Guide*, by Stephen Fishman (Nolo). It also covers some topics not discussed here, such as the tax implications of employing your children, and how to deduct business losses. For personalized advice, consult an accounting or tax professional—you can deduct that expense, too.

Deducting start-up expenses below $5,000

You can deduct up to $5,000 of your start-up expenses the first year you're in business. Start-up expenses are any expenses you incur before offering your property for rent, so long as they're related to getting your business up and running. Once you're in business (that is, after you've placed an ad or otherwise started offering the property for rent), all your expenses are considered operating expenses, which we'll discuss below.

> **TIP**
> **You might need a business license.** Some cities or localities require that all landlords—or at least those whose properties have more than a minimum number of units—pay an annual license fee and possibly undergo a property inspection. Check with your city for details.

Examples of possible start-up expenses include:

- costs of researching and investigating the rental market
- educational information, including how-to books (like this one), classes, or seminars
- attorney and accounting fees (except legal and other fees paid to complete the purchase of the rental property)
- licenses
- insurance premiums
- if you have to travel overnight to get the property ready to rent, lodging as well as meals, though only at 50% of the meals' cost
- repairs to get the property ready to rent
- office supplies, such as telephone, paper, and notebooks (but not equipment and other long-term assets)
- printing bank checks
- advertising your property for rent (such as ads and signs), and
- any other operating expenses that you paid before offering the property for rent, such as landscaping and gardening costs, property maintenance, and utilities (excluding utility connection fees).

What's absent from the above list? Some pretty big-ticket items, actually. Not only is the cost of the property itself excluded, but all equipment, furniture, appliances, and other property that's expected to last more than one year. These items are considered long-term assets, and are deductible only in limited amounts per year, via depreciation. Also absent from the list are any expenses directly related to the purchase of the property, such as closing costs, escrow fees, attorneys' fees, travel expenses related to the purchase, title insurance, and transfer taxes. These costs are added to the property's tax basis and depreciated over time, as described below.

Deducting start-up expenses over $5,000

What if your start-up expenses add up to more than $5,000? You can deduct the additional expenses in equal amounts over the first 15 years you're in business. However, this is a long time to wait to get the full deduction value of your expenditures. One useful strategy is to put the property on the rental market as soon as possible, so that you never run through the $5,000. That automatically triggers the switch into the realm of operating expenses (upon which there's no set limit).

Putting the property on the market doesn't mean you have to do an advertising blitz. Starting with a simple "For Rent" sign on the property will do. Keep proof of your first ad in case of an IRS audit—a date-stamped picture of the "For Rent" sign is all you need.

Another problem with spending more than $5,000 during your start-up period is that if your expenditures end up exceeding $50,000, you won't get to use the full $5,000 start-up deduction. Your allowable deduction is reduced by any amount you spend over $50,000 on start-up expenses. For example, if you spend $54,000 in startup expenses, you'll lose $4,000 of your first-year deduction. That means you'll get a $1,000 first-year deduction and you'll have to spread out (amortize) the remaining $53,000 worth of deductions over the next 15 years.

Deducting operating expenses

The operating-expense deduction is sort of a catchall for the many day-to-day costs you'll face as a landlord, for things like upkeep, supplies, taxes, and fees. But it doesn't cover everything you might think of. For one, it excludes long-term capital expenses (such as equipment purchases), which we'll discuss below. For another, it excludes entertainment, or any expenses that might be considered excessive or personal. In IRS-speak, you can claim a tax deduction only if an operating expense is ordinary and necessary, current (likely to be used, or used up, within a year), directly related to your rental activity (not for your personal benefit), and reasonable in amount (sorry, no luxury hotel stays, golf games with mentors, or paying your ten-year-old $100 an hour to sweep the deck; and watch out when trying to deduct meals, as this gets you into legally iffy territory).

Here are examples of expenses the IRS recognizes as ordinary and necessary to a rental business:

- **Interest payments on mortgage loans, other loans, and credit cards.** (Discussed below.)
- **Property and other taxes.** (Discussed below.)
- **Professional fees.** For example, included are attorney, accounting, property management, and rental broker fees.
- **License renewals.** If you must register your rental with a local government, these fees are deductible.
- **Ongoing insurance premiums.** This includes not only homeowners' insurance, but a portion of your car insurance if you regularly use the car for your landlord business.
- **Homeowners' association dues.** If your property is a condo, townhouse, or in a community development, you'll be paying association dues, which cover repairs and maintenance.
- **Local transportation expenses.** For example, you might travel from your home office or other office to make regular property visits, shop for supplies, or transfer garbage to the dump. You can

deduct either an IRS amount based on mileage, or actual costs of owning and operating your car. If you don't work from home, trips from your home to your landlord-business office or place of business are considered nondeductible commutes.

> CAUTION
> **Got a traffic or parking ticket while on landlord business?** Don't try to deduct it. For public policy reasons, taxpayers can never deduct government fines or penalties.

- **Out-of-town travel costs.** You might have to travel overnight and outside your city limits to spend time at the property or attend to related business matters (for example, to attend a real estate seminar or visit an attorney). Transportation, hotel, and related expenses like Internet access, phones, and laundry are fully deductible. Meals and beverages are deductible at 50% of their cost. As an alternative to actual meal expenses, you can deduct a standard daily meal allowance, or "per diem" (which varies depending on your destination, and is adjusted by the IRS annually). If you plan to mix vacation time into your trip, the value of your deduction might be reduced depending on the percentage of time you spent on rental activities—spending at least four hours a day on rental activities will protect you.

- **Keeping up the property.** Upkeep costs can include repairs, maintenance, cleaning, environmental remediation of problems that arose after you bought the property and in the ordinary course of business operations, and gardening. They don't include improvements, or work that makes the property better than it was before —these must be deducted via depreciation, as discussed below.

- **Disability access.** You can deduct the costs of making your property accessible to the elderly or disabled according to the federal Americans with Disabilities Act (ADA) standards (limited to $15,000). This is a special deduction, because such changes would normally be considered "improvements," and subject to depreciation.

- **Office supplies.** You can deduct the cost of supplies you use in your office, including software, paper, postage, and notebooks (but you can't deduct equipment and other long-term assets).

- **Education and information.** Books, magazine or newsletter subscriptions, classes, or seminars are deductible.

- **Advertising and tenant screening.** Unless you rent via word-of-mouth and skip any screening of potential tenants (a risky step), you'll need at least a "For Rent" sign, and will probably pay for classified ads and prospective-tenant credit checks. (Of course, if you charge the tenant for the cost of pulling a report, you cannot also deduct this expenditure.)

- **Utilities.** If you (not your tenant) pay the gas, water, garbage, electric, or other utility bills, you can deduct them.

- **Business meals.** If, for example, you take the head of the local landlord association to lunch to get some free advice, and the food or beverages aren't lavish or extravagant, these costs are 50% deductible. Unlike in past years, however, there is no deduction for entertainment, amusement, or recreation expenses.

- **Business gifts.** These are limited to $25 per gift recipient per year (however, if you give a gift to all the employees of a business, such as a holiday fruit basket delivered to your gardening service, you may deduct the entire cost, as long as it's reasonable). Incidental costs such as shipping don't come under the limit.

- **Membership fees.** Joining a landlords' association would be considered reasonable. But don't try deducting fees for country, social, or athletic clubs.

- **Home office expenses.** You may deduct these, but it's tricky—see the discussion below before deciding to take the home office deduction.

> 💡 **TIP**
> **Renting a unit that's attached to your home?** If, for example,
> you live in half of a duplex, or have a cottage on your property, you'll
> need to figure out what portion of the property expenses are personal,
> and what portion can be called rental operating costs. The easiest way
> to do this is to calculate the percentage of square footage occupied by
> the rental unit, then apply that percentage against your overall costs
> for household operating expenses like insurance, utilities, mortgage
> interest, landscaping, and repairs and maintenance. Of course, some
> items can be separately calculated. For example, if you have separate
> yards with a fence in between and the gardener charges separately for
> each, or separate utility meters, use these figures.

Deducting mortgage and other loan interest

In most cases, interest you pay on loans taken out to pay expenses on
your rental property are tax deductible. By contrast, if you took out
a loan using your rental property as security, but spent the money on
personal things, the interest wouldn't be deductible.

Unless you've inherited a paid-off property, or converted a house you
lived in for many years, the mortgage interest on your rental property
might be among your biggest expenses. Your monthly mortgage
payment is composed of principal (a direct repayment of what was
borrowed) and interest, or the amount you pay the lender for the
privilege of using its money. You can't, unfortunately, deduct your
principal payments as an operating expense.

However, your interest payments are tax deductible in the year you
pay them. The same goes for any private mortgage insurance (PMI)
premiums that your lender requires—likely if you made a low down
payment, to protect the lender against your default. If, however, you
prepay PMI premiums for more than one year in advance, for each year
of coverage you can deduct only the part of the PMI payment that will
apply to that year.

You may not deduct, at least for the current year, the points you paid to get your mortgage (unlike the rules for primary homes); these must ordinarily be spread out over the term of the loan before you can deduct them.

Will you be taking out a loan to improve the property (for example, add a room or remodel)? Your interest payments on this loan are also deductible.

Loans you take out to repair the property, such as a home equity loan, are treated slightly differently. In these cases, you may deduct not only the interest paid, but the principal amount during the years that you repay it.

Finally, interest paid on your business credit card can be deducted (but remember, you should be paying your card off monthly, except in emergencies). You can also deduct interest on a car loan if you use your personal car for business—just figure out what percentage of the time you use the car for business, and then deduct that percentage of the loan interest.

Deducting property tax payments

Although the United States has no federal property tax, your state, local, and municipal governments might all be poised to extract property taxes from you—in the thousands of dollars. Fortunately, you can deduct these as an operating expense, so long as the tax is based on the property's assessed value (and not, for instance, an added amount for local improvements).

The availability of a tax deduction will offset only a fraction of the full cost, so always check whether you're being overcharged. Your state will allow you to appeal the assessment within a certain time period, which is worth following up on if the amount is demonstrably off base. Unfortunately, you can't count on your assessment going down when house values do.

Deducting for use of a home office

If you use part of your own home regularly and exclusively for your rental property business, you might be able to deduct a portion of the related home expenses—such as your mortgage interest, utility bills, cleaning, and home repair costs. And the home office deduction would let you deduct the full amount of any expenses that are solely and directly connected to your home office, such as painting the room and adding a carpet. Office furniture, like a desk or chair you use for your rental business, is deductible whether or not you qualify for a home office deduction.

But there's a major catch to this deduction. Unless you can really set aside space and equipment in your house for exclusive business use, you'll have trouble qualifying for the deduction. It doesn't have to be a whole room. If you can at least set off part of a room for exclusive use, you might yet qualify—but you'll get less of a deduction, due to the small size of the area identified as your home office. And even in a small section of a room, you might need the same desk area and computer to manage your landlord business as to handle personal bills, not to mention handle personal matters online—so you couldn't meet the exclusive-use test.

If you sell your house, you'll have to pay capital gains tax on the profit earned from the area used as a home office within the last two years. Normally, without your home office, the capital gains tax exclusion of $500,000 for married couples filing joint returns and $250,000 for singles would shield a nice chunk of your profits. But if, for example, you claimed one-fifth of your home as a home office, you'd lose the benefit of that exclusion for one-fifth of your sale profits, which would become fully taxable.

Deducting for depreciation

Depreciation deductions can be complicated—but lucrative enough to be worth spending time learning about. In any case, depreciation is not an optional deduction. Even if you choose to ignore it, the IRS will dock you when you sell the property (in effect, by adding the depreciation you should have claimed to your sales profits, upping your capital gains tax bill).

The basic concept of depreciation is that the cost of certain assets are not everyday operating costs—yet deserve some sort of tax deduction—because the asset will:

- last for over a year
- get worn out or used up over time
- remain in your hands as owner for more than one year, and
- be used in your rental business.

Examples of common depreciable assets for landlords include the rental building and its structural components, personal property bought for the rental property (such as appliances, furniture, and carpets), and personal property bought for use on the rental property, such as tools and equipment. Not the land itself—it doesn't wear out.

However, the IRS says that you may currently deduct any item you purchase for your rental activity that costs $200 or less, even if is a long-term asset. For example, you could currently deduct a $50 lamp you buy for your rental activity, even though it is a long-term asset that will last longer than one year. But you can deduct even more—property that costs up to $2,500—using the "de minimis safe harbor" discussed below (see "IRS Regulations on Deducting Repairs and Improvements").

> **CAUTION**
> **Receipts aren't always enough.** For certain types of depreciable property, called "listed" property, the IRS will want to see documentation showing that you actually used it for your business, not for your personal life. Listed property includes cars and other vehicles, motorcycles, boats, airplanes, and property used for entertainment, recreation, or amusement, such as cameras and stereos. You'll need to keep a log book showing when and how the property is used. (One exception to the record-keeping requirement is for computers—as of 2018, they are no longer considered listed property.)

You can either combine the depreciation of your rental property (all buildings, components, and improvements) with the personal property assets inside it (such as appliances), or depreciate them separately. Separating them is harder, but can give you higher deductions in the early years of ownership.

In fact, through 2023, something called "bonus depreciation" can allow you to deduct, in just one year, 100% of the cost of personal property that you bought and had available for use either within the rental property itself or for your rental business (at least 50% of the time if it's "listed property"). There's no upper dollar limit! Bonus depreciation can also be used for $8,000 of what you spend on a business vehicle. The bonus depreciation option applies whether you buy the property new or used. However, the item's total useful life must be 20 years or less, as set by the IRS (see discussion of recovery periods, next). In future years, bonus depreciation will continue to help landlords, but at progressively lower percentages through 2026.

How long the depreciation period lasts. Instead of deducting asset costs in the year you pay them (as with a regular deduction), you will normally spread out the deductions over a certain number of years (the "recovery period"). The IRS provides preset recovery periods, based on which of its depreciation "systems" you choose, and on how much time the IRS thinks will pass before the asset wears out or gets used up.

The IRS offers more than one possible method for divvying up the total depreciation amount for each year. We're not going to get into the details here; you can find more information in *Every Landlord's Tax Deduction Guide*, by Stephen Fishman (Nolo), and in IRS Publication 946, *How to Depreciate Property*.

In the case of residential real estate and structural components, the deduction is typically spread over 27.5 years—by which time the buildings are assumed to have "worn out." Of course, because land can't be depreciated, you have to subtract its value from your purchase price before taking the depreciation deduction.

This is true even for condo owners. Despite the fact that you don't personally have title to any land, you still own an interest in commonly held land, the size of which should be listed on your deed.

Other assets have a much shorter recovery period, in most cases five or seven years, and only three years for software. The shorter the recovery period, the sooner you get the full value of your deduction. Do some research before deciding how to claim your deduction. You'll soon realize there's a history of arguments between taxpayers and the IRS about issues like whether a fake floor to cover wiring is personal property or a structural component, which could make a huge difference in the recovery period.

When the recovery period ends prematurely. If you sell your property before the recovery period is up, you can't continue to take the deduction. In fact, you must stop taking depreciation for any asset that you either sell, destroy, dispose of, or stop using for your rental business before the recovery period ends.

> ⃝!⃝ **CAUTION**
> **Buying art, collectibles, or antique furniture for your rental?** Don't expect to depreciate it. Although such items might eventually wear out, the fact that they're increasing in value in the meantime make them ineligible for depreciation.

How to calculate each depreciable asset's true cost. As mentioned earlier, the cost of buying a house is more than its purchase price. You can add in attorneys' fees, closing costs, transfer taxes, and the cost of making later improvements to the property. Added together, these are called the property's "basis." The full basis of a piece of property can be depreciated.

What if you inherited the property, and so didn't pay a dime for it? You're still expected to claim depreciation deductions for it. Because you obviously can't use its purchase price as your starting point, your "basis" is instead its fair market value at the time of the previous owner's death. Of course, you still need to subtract the value of the land.

Rather than buying or inheriting property that they decide to rent out, some owners convert a property that they previously lived in to rental use. In this case, your basis for depreciation purposes is either the property's fair market value on the date of the change, or your own adjusted cost basis in the property on that date, whichever is less.

RESOURCE
See IRS Publication 551, *Basis of Assets*, for more detail on calculating cost basis.

You must separately depreciate additions, new structures, and improvements: for example, if you add a new room, replace the roof, remodel, replace major appliances, add fences or other structures, or install new plumbing or wiring. A simple repair (that returns the property to the condition it was in before the problem arose that required fixing) is not an improvement. Interestingly enough, certain changes to the land itself can be depreciated, such as landscaping in preparation for renting out. However, the recovery schedule will likely be less than for the main property.

Figuring out which work constitutes an improvement and which constitutes a repair can be tricky—and it's in your interest to classify as much as possible of the work as repairs, so that you can immediately deduct their costs. You can plausibly claim that some parts of a project are repairs and some are improvements. For example, you might have your kitchen floors redone after the dishwasher floods (a repair) and also install a new dishwasher (an improvement). See the list of examples of improvements below.

Depreciation exception: Section 179

A piece of the tax code called Section 179 lets business owners deduct the entire cost of certain long-term personal property in one year, rather than having to depreciate it. This is an alternative to using "bonus depreciation," and usually a less advantageous one. The allowance is subject to a maximum annual limit, which can change periodically. For 2020, the limit was $1.04 million. This deduction is also limited to the total of your profit from all your businesses and your salary (if you have one).

IRS List of Examples of Home Improvements

Additions
Bedroom
Bathroom
Deck
Garage
Porch
Patio

Heating & Air-Conditioning
Heating system
Central air-conditioning
Furnace
Duct work
Central humidifier
Filtration system

Plumbing
Septic system
Water heater
Soft water system
Filtration system

Lawn & Grounds
Landscaping
Driveway

Walkway
Fence
Retaining wall
Sprinkler system
Swimming pool

Interior Improvements
Built-in appliances
Kitchen modernization
Flooring
Wall-to-wall carpeting

Insulation
Attic
Walls
Floors
Pipes and duct work

Miscellaneous
Storm windows, doors
New roof
Central vacuum
Wiring upgrades
Satellite dish
Security system

IRS Regulations on Deducting Repairs and Improvements

Complex IRS regulations govern how to determine whether a business expense is a building repair that is currently deductible in a single year or an improvement that must be depreciated over many years.

An expense a landlord incurs for a rental building must be depreciated if it makes the building as a whole, or any one of eight separate building systems, materially better than before, adapts it to a new use, or restores it to operating condition after it has fallen into disrepair.

The regulations also contain three "safe harbor" rules, enabling landlords to currently deduct rental building expenses even if they would have to be depreciated under the regular rules.

For a detailed discussion of the IRS repair regulations, refer to *Every Landlord's Tax Deduction Guide*, by Stephen Fishman (Nolo).

What's more, you can use Section 179 only for personal property not contained in your rental property, such as computers, office equipment, office furniture, and business vehicles. And the property must be used for your business more than half the time, plus you must have purchased it in the year you claim the deduction.

Deducting 20% of net profits

In 2017, the Tax Cuts and Jobs Act (TCJA) created a new income tax deduction that benefits many landlords. By qualifying for this "pass-through deduction" you can potentially deduct up to 20% of your profits, if any (net rental income). The deduction won't last forever, however—it's scheduled to go away after the year 2025.

You'll need to show the IRS that you:

- are truly in business as a landlord (though not necessarily full time)
- own the property being rented, either personally or through a limited liability company (LLC), partnership, or other pass-through entity
- actually earned a profit from your year's rental activity, after subtracting expenses from gross revenue, and
- that your total taxable income from all sources is on the plus side, rather than amounting to a loss after you subtract deductions.

This deduction is meant to make your (or your tax-preparer's) life easier, but if it doesn't do that for you, it's also legally okay to skip it.

Proving What You've Spent: Record Keeping

To save yourself from stress next time taxes are due, track your income and expenses as they arise. That will give you a clear picture of your rental property's profitability, and help you claim the maximum in tax deductions. For example, without a paper trail, you won't be able to easily convince the IRS that the cleaning supplies you bought on a certain date were not for use in your home, but were used to prepare your vacant rental for an open house (and are, therefore, deductible).

TIP
How long should you keep financial records? The IRS expects you to keep any receipts and other records concerning a property's purchase and capital improvements for as long as you own the property. (And because repairs and improvements can be hard to distinguish, it's worth keeping repair records around, too.) The rest should be kept for three to five years, depending on local law. But, in case a child is ever injured on your property, keep those records permanently, because the claim could arise years later.

According to Kathy, who rents out a duplex in Seffner, Florida, "At first, when we bought our duplex, the mortgage payments wiped out all our rental income, so I didn't bother much with keeping track of expenses for tax purposes. But now, 28 years later, with the place paid off, you can bet I record everything—like my mileage when I go to the property, or my mileage to the bank when I make a deposit. It all goes into a ledger I keep."

Here's how to begin; and if at some point you own more than one rental property, follow the same system to separately track your expenses for each:

- **Buy a receipt book.** Some states require you to give tenants a receipt, but it's a good practice in any case, especially if they sometimes pay with cash. The receipts should list the tenant's name, amount paid, date paid, and mode of payment (including check number).

- **Create files for expense receipts, or invest in a bookkeeping program. If you're just starting out, you might find old-fashioned paper easier to use, and thus ultimately more accurate.** Each file should be labeled with one expense category, for example "Start-Up Expenses," "Operating Expenses," and "Depreciable Property Expenses." Also keep separate files for your bank and credit card statements, filed in chronological order.

- **Make sure your expense receipts make it into the files.** Receipts are important—the IRS won't necessarily accept, for example, a canceled check alone as proof of what you purchased, because it contains no independent verification of what you spent the money on. If you order online, print out the receipt page. You won't, however, always be near your filing cabinet when making a purchase. Some landlords like to keep a separate envelope in their purses, wallets, or glove department, making it easy to slip a printed receipt in right after buying something. Write on the receipt what the item was, why you bought it, and, if you paid by check, the check number. Transfer these regularly to your file.

- **Track your cash spending.** A handful of quarters into the parking meter, a couple bucks for highway tolls, a few more dollars for cleaning fluid—it adds up. Your purse or glove compartment makes a handy place to keep a little notebook, in which you record every cash purchase, including the amount, date, and business purpose. If the cash came out of your personal account, repay yourself from your business account using a check, to create an automatic record. Like any normal human, you might sometimes forget to follow all these practices, so try to avoid using cash whenever possible.

- **Ask servicepeople for detailed and, in some cases, split-up invoices.** An invoice that states what was done, and preferably describes it in terms of "repairing, patching, replacing," and so forth, will help show whether the expense was for a repair or an improvement. Or if an electrician both repairs the wiring in your rental property and adds new wiring to a new porch on that property (an improvement), asking for separate invoices will allow you to deduct for the repair this year while depreciating the improvement cost. Invoices help in mixed-use situations, too. For example, if you're renting out one unit of the duplex you live in and a roofer redoes the shared roof, asking for separate invoices will allow you to pay one from your business account and one from your personal account.

- **Keep a log showing use of listed property.** As mentioned earlier, cars and other modes of transport, and any other listed property, can be claimed as tax deductions only if you can show you used them for your business, not personal use. Keep track of the dates and uses of these items.

- **Track use of your personal car on rental business.** As a first-time landlord, you're probably not going to invest in a new business car. That will likely mean logging a lot of miles in the family car. That expense notebook in the glove compartment? Use it to log the date, destination, before-and-after odometer readings, and purpose of your car trips (for example, to the rental property, the hardware store, or the bank). If you wish, you can stop doing this after 90 days (or after one week each month), call that your "sampling period," and use the results to extrapolate your rental mileage for the entire year. If a trip is for mixed purposes—for example, you drive from your home office to the dump with garbage from both your home and rental property, you can call it a business trip.

- **Keep business property separate or identifiable after you've bought it.** Whenever you buy things with your business account —perhaps new paint, a screwdriver, or office supplies, like postage stamps and a printer and paper—keep them in a separate place, label them as business property, or do whatever else will remind you not to convert them to personal use.

- **Keep notes on tenant complaints.** If a tenant raises an issue that leads to a repair, having a record will help establish that the work was indeed a regular operating expense, not part of a larger improvement.

- **Make calendar notations about your business activities.** Both when you're at home and when traveling for rental reasons, having notes in your calendar regarding what you did and who you met with will help support your expense deduction claims.

- **Save paperwork.** Don't throw away correspondence (including email) related to your rental property. Hang onto relevant business cards. Agendas from seminars or conventions you attend are also valuable pieces of your paper trail if you're ever audited.

Are You Rich Yet?
Tracking Income and Expenses

Take another look at the projections you made regarding annual income and expenses in Chapter 1. You'll want to run the same type of numbers once you're in business, on a monthly basis—using real (not projected) numbers. The idea is to pull information from your bank and credit card statements and files of invoices and receipts, keep tabs on whether your income and expenses are balancing out as expected, and find out what's actually left in the till. If you're using a property management company, it should send you monthly financial reports—and you should review them carefully and raise any relevant questions.

You can do a bare-bones analysis the old-fashioned way, using the Monthly Income/Expense Worksheet below, a pencil, and a calculator. Of course, some months will be odd ones, for example if you paid your estimated taxes or bought a large piece of equipment. The purpose is not to create an average, but to get regular snapshots of your expenses and your cash on hand. As you look back over these worksheets, you'll be able to spot which months you need to plan ahead for.

Unfortunately, a simple analysis like this one leaves out many factors, like the impact of tax deductions. And handmade worksheets are hard to work with at tax time. (We put more categories below than you'll find on Schedule E, to make sure you didn't forget anything.) That's why many landlords find it worthwhile to invest in an accounting software package, such as *QuickBooks* (for general small-business use).

You can also hire an accountant to put all your rental data together and produce financial reports. You'll have to decide whether the cost is worth the reduced effort on your part.

Monthly Income/Expense Worksheet	
Month: _____ Year: 20_____	
EXPENSES	
Advertising and tenant screening	$
Local transportation	$
Out-of-city travel, meals, and lodging	$
Cleaning and maintenance	$
Homeowners' insurance (if not included in mortgage payment)	$
Legal and other professional fees (accountant, property manager)	$
Mortgage payment (principal and interest, plus property taxes and insurance, if included)	$
Other loan payments	$
Repairs	$
Supplies (for office and rental property)	$
Income tax	$
Property tax (if not included in mortgage payment)	$
Utilities (if not covered by tenant)	$
Business gifts	$
Licenses	$
Homeowners' association dues (in condos and some developments)	$
Educational publications, subscriptions, and memberships	$
Tools and equipment	$
Construction and improvements	$
Other miscellaneous expenses	$
TOTAL EXPENSES	$
INCOME	
Rental income	$
Other income (such as late fees, interest on security deposit, or damage reimbursements; landlords of multiunit properties may also charge for items like laundry or parking)	$
TOTAL INCOME	$
RESULTS	
Net income this month (total income − total expenses)	$
Cash remaining from last month (get from last month's worksheet)	$
Total cash on hand this month	$

At the other end of the spectrum is the minimalist approach espoused by Phil, a landlord in Berkeley, California, who says, "We're somewhat accidental landlords, with only two units, and I just put all my records and receipts into one folder and use *TurboTax* at the end of the year. We don't even have an accountant—*TurboTax* has a premier version that addresses rental real estate." If you take Phil's approach, at least be scrupulous about running all expenses through your business checking account, and reviewing your monthly statements to make sure your balance is as expected.

How Much Cash to Keep in Reserve

As soon as you start turning a profit (which could take months or years), think about setting some of it aside for a rainy day. (We're assuming you're already setting aside enough to cover irregular expenses like property taxes and insurance.) It's simply bad business practice to spend everything in your business account and leave nothing to fall back on. That means resisting the temptation to either churn your profits back into property improvements or make them your weekend play fund.

Instead, take a portion of your business profits and transfer them to an interest-earning savings account. (This is comparable to the "emergency fund" that financial advisers suggest people keep for family, with three to six months of living expenses, in case of a job loss or another emergency.)

How much should you keep in your reserve fund? As with your main property, it's best to set aside enough to pay for unexpected events like the roof starting to leak or a flood in the basement. Experts recommend saving the equivalent of 5% of a home's purchase price (or current value) each year to cover maintenance and repairs. Also keep enough to pay the mortgage and other monthly costs if the tenant unexpectedly moves out. This should cover as many months as are appropriate given the local average vacancy rate.

What to Do When Expenses Exceed Income

What if you're still not making any business profits and are perhaps struggling to cover the rental property's expenses? This can be both a short-term problem, in terms of how you pay the bills, and a long-term concern if your goal is to hold onto the property for a certain length of time. Here are the first steps toward dealing with the situation:

- **Figure out whether the problem is short or long term.** It's not uncommon to get into a temporary cash crunch—for example, because a tenant moves out unexpectedly and the place needs repainting before you rent it again. Your approach can involve temporary, stopgap measures—unlike situations where the monthly rent never covers monthly expenses. Also, if the tenant has simply stopped paying rent, see Chapter 9 for a discussion of how to restart the flow.

- **For short-term problems, look for sources of financing.** Can you loan cash to the business from your personal funds? That's a rational approach, as long as you can spare the money and you keep records of the transfer. However, it might mean shifting money that's currently held in stocks, bonds, or other investments. Talk to your financial adviser about whether, given the comparative rates of return between your real estate investment and others, this shift would be wise. If not, or if you don't have any personal sources of cash to draw upon, consider a home equity loan or line of credit from a bank. Use credit cards only for minor expenses or as a last resort, due to their high interest rates.

- **Look at your largest outflows for areas to cut.** For example, can you cut expenses by refinancing your mortgage, shopping around for cheaper homeowners' insurance, or (if you're paying utilities) performing energy-saving repairs like sealing cracks?

> **TIP**
> **Make sure you're in good communication with your tenant.**
> Some cash crunches come about because the tenant isn't in the
> habit of calling you about minor maintenance issues before they turn
> into expensive emergencies. Such a situation often develops when
> landlords aren't responsive to tenants' early calls. And you need to stay
> on top of things like collecting late rents or terminating a tenancy for
> nonpayment.

- **Look into raising the rent.** Unfortunately, you can't do this every
  time cash is tight. If your tenant has a lease, you'll have to abide
  by its terms until the expiration date (though you could offer
  to buy the tenant out). And you'll have to comply with state
  and local laws governing rent increases, not to mention take
  into account local market conditions. See Chapter 1 for a full
  discussion of when and by how much you can raise the rent.

- **Prioritize your debts.** Put off paying your bills until close to their
  expiration date, and talk to creditors about accepting even later
  payments where possible. But whatever you do, don't miss a
  mortgage payment. If the problem is serious enough that you'll
  have trouble paying the mortgage, talk to your lender about
  workout options. For details, see the Foreclosure section of Nolo's
  website, at Nolo.com.

- **For long-term problems, reexamine the numbers.** Go back to
  the analysis you did in Chapter 1 and reconsider whether the
  property is likely to sufficiently appreciate in value to make
  your current losses worthwhile. Also talk to your tax or financial
  adviser about whether the losses will help you shelter other
  income (a complex area requiring individual advice). If keeping
  the property no longer looks worthwhile, see Chapter 11 for
  advice on selling.

Finding Professionals to Help You

Plenty of first-time landlords get by without professional advice, relying instead on software programs for bookkeeping and tax preparation. But hiring a professional can make your life easier, and potentially help you save money in the long run. Below are the most likely categories of pros to help you. Notice that the list doesn't include so-called "tax preparers" of the sort you'll see in storefront offices during tax time. In most states, no licensing is required to be a tax preparer, so we don't advise taking your chances on them. Pros you might consult include:

- **Enrolled agents (EAs).** With at least five years of experience and licensing from the IRS, these are a reliable choice for tax advice and tax return preparation.

- **Certified public accountants (CPAs).** These provide sophisticated accounting and tax work, and are licensed and regulated in each state.

- **Licensed public accountants.** These are also reliable, though not as highly regarded as CPAs.

- **Tax attorneys.** If you get into serious trouble with the IRS or another tax agency, an attorney can provide legal representation. But for most tax advice, consulting a CPA will be more cost-effective.

Here are some tips for choosing a qualified professional:

- **Get recommendations.** Ask friends, business associates, or your local landlord association.

- **Look for experience in assisting landlords.** You're dealing with sometimes unique issues and tax considerations, so it helps to have an accountant or tax pro who's familiar with them.

- **Interview two or three prospects.** Choose the one who is not only reasonably priced, but seems knowledgeable and easy to communicate with. ●

Keeping Things Shipshape: Repairs and Maintenance

Everyone wants a nice place to call home, including your tenant. And while you need not to turn the place into a palatial estate, you are responsible for keeping it in good repair and in a habitable condition. Besides, if someday you want to move back into this home, or retire in it, undoing years of poor maintenance will be a major bother.

To show you what maintenance entails, this chapter will cover:

- your legal responsibilities, and the tenant's responsibilities, for keeping the property livable
- how to prevent and respond to problems, and
- whether to hire the tenant or someone else to help you meet some of your repair and maintenance obligations.

Keeping your property in good repair requires some up-front work, but it will help keep your tenants happy—and happy tenants will likely complain less and stay longer, reducing turnover and interruptions to your income stream. If you end up with a tenant whose repair demands are unreasonable (asking for cosmetic upgrades, not genuine repairs), having a fundamentally safe and sound rental will also let you confidently decline such requests.

Finally, regular attention to upkeep might prevent major (and expensive!) problems later, because you'll hopefully catch issues in their early stages. In the long run, being diligent will save you money, reduce the chance of injuries, and ultimately translate into lower insurance premiums.

CAUTION

Don't invade the tenant's privacy just to make repairs. Landlords in many states must give notice of entry when making repairs or doing inspections. You'll need to research and comply with your state's rules. Find yours in the chart in the "State Laws on Landlord's Access to Rental Property" article in the Landlords section of Nolo.com. Then make sure your lease or rental agreement mentions these entry rules and your own policies, to minimize disputes with those tenants who feel landlords never have the right to enter their property.

Dealing With the Legalities: Your Repair and Maintenance Obligations

Your obligation to keep the property in good shape is imposed by law. But how do you know what's expected of you? And what does the tenant have to do? Here are some guidelines.

What are you responsible for?

Your responsibility to repair and maintain the property is based on several different legal principles. If you're worried about meeting all your obligations, start by learning and complying with the basics. First, figure out any repair and maintenance requirements imposed by your local housing codes. For example, many cities require landlords to install smoke and carbon monoxide detectors in residential units, or security items such as viewing devices in doors that open onto a hallway. Your local building or housing authority and health or fire department can provide this information.

Also get a copy of and carefully read your state's housing laws, which should lay out rules for repair, maintenance, and many other landlording responsibilities. Again, your local building or housing authority should be able to point you to the appropriate code sections, usually available online. To find a direct link to your state's statute, visit www.nolo.com/legal-research and select "How to Find a Law."

Keeping your property habitable

According to a legal concept called the "implied warranty of habitability," you're required to offer and maintain livable premises. This means you must make sure the property meets minimum requirements (sometimes spelled out in local building codes), generally including:

- maintaining electrical, plumbing, sanitary, heating, ventilating, air-conditioning, and other facilities and systems
- supplying water, hot water, and heat in reasonable amounts at reasonable times

- providing trash receptacles and arranging for their removal, and
- maintaining any common areas in a safe and clean condition.

Every state but Arkansas has, by judicial decision or statute, adopted the implied warranty of habitability (and even in Arkansas, many local laws require that rental housing be habitable). Your city or county might specify additional habitability requirements, especially when certain features or services, like storm doors or shutters, are essential in some areas, but virtually useless in other parts of the state.

Common Myths About Repairs and Maintenance

Many landlords (and tenants) are under the mistaken impression that every time a rental property turns over, certain cosmetic changes, such as a new paint job, are required. But ugliness isn't a habitability problem—it's the actual condition of the rental property that determines what's needed in terms of repair and maintenance. Some changes might be called for during the tenancy, rather than at the end.

Paint. No state law requires you to repaint the interior at any point (local ordinances might, however), as long as the paint isn't creating a habitability problem—for example, it's so thick it seals a window shut. Lead-based paint, however, can create legal problems.

Drapes and carpets. So long as drapes and carpets aren't so damp or mildewed as to constitute a health hazard, and carpets don't have dangerous holes that could cause someone to trip, you aren't legally required to replace them.

Windows. A tenant is responsible for a broken window only if the tenant or a guest intentionally or carelessly broke it. If a burglar, vandal, or neighborhood child broke it, though, you're responsible for the repair.

Keys. You might need to change the locks and rekey the property for each new tenant. Even if it's not legally required, it's a good idea.

Legal requirements won't always be listed somewhere obvious like building codes: Often, it's the courts that decide what makes a place habitable. But you can assume that if an aspect of a dwelling (such as a weatherproof roof) makes it a fit place to live, you're probably responsible for maintaining it.

> **CAUTION**
> **Don't try to evade your responsibility to keep the place habitable.** Some landlords have tried advancing one of these two theories:
> • "The tenants saw the place when they moved in, so it's not fair for them to complain now." (In other words, by moving into an unfit rental, the tenant effectively agreed to accept those conditions, and waived the protections of the implied warranty.)
> • "The tenant signed a lease saying I won't provide habitable housing, and is bound by that signature."
>
> Nice try, but courts almost always reject these theories. You're better off making sure your property is in good shape.

Keeping the property useable

Landlords have another legal responsibility with an obscure name: the "covenant of quiet enjoyment." As courts define it, this amounts to an implied promise that you won't act (or fail to act) in a way that interferes with or destroys the ability of the tenant to use the rental property and conversely, that you'll act in a way that enables peaceful use.

For example, if your failure to fix a leaky roof or eliminate a major rodent infestation means the tenants can't use the kitchen, you've failed to meet your obligations under the covenant. When tenants can't live in the rental, you have for all practical purposes evicted them (called "constructive eviction"). Constructive eviction lets tenants wave goodbye to your property, without having to pay any rent as of the time you should have fixed the problem.

Keeping your promises

Your property might have nonessential features like a washing machine, swimming pool, or dishwasher. Although keeping these things in working order might not affect the habitability of the place, you're likely still legally required to repair and maintain them. Usually, either your lease or rental agreement expressly makes you responsible, or your actions have impliedly promised that you will maintain these features—for example, because you've repaired the item in the past or advertised it as part of the property. After all, if you advertise a "hot tub in the backyard," the tenant can reasonably expect that the hot tub works under normal use, and that you'll keep it that way for the duration of the tenancy.

Minor repairs

Your most frequent tenant calls are likely to be about minor problems —leaky faucets, temperamental appliances, worn carpets, or noisy heaters—not about major problems that make the house unlivable. Most of the time, these minor repairs are your responsibility.

One exception is when the tenant or one of the tenant's guests caused a minor repair problem. When that happens, the tenant needs to either take care of the repairs, or (if your lease or rental agreement prohibits the tenant from doing so) pay you to deal with them.

You can also draw the line at fixing up ordinary wear and tear. It's not your job to keep the rental premises looking just like new, just to stop deterioration. Nevertheless, if a tenant that you're happy with asks for a basic spruce up—replacing some shabby-looking but still functional blinds, for example—it might be worth making the upgrade. You'll probably have to make the changes when the tenant moves out, anyway.

TIP

Best thing I ever did: Establish good communications with our tenants. Phil, who owns a triplex, explains, "I work full time, and I probably could be more proactive about things like checking whether the rental units' roof needs fixing, or improving the landscaping. But we at least make sure to keep good dialogue going with our tenants, so that we know if something needs immediate attention, and they know we'll see to it quickly."

Relocating Your Tenants During Renovations or Repairs

Most repairs to your rental property will be quick and won't inconvenience your tenants much. For example, fixing a clogged toilet, replacing a lighting fixture, or even laying new carpets mostly require your tenants to stay out of the way and perhaps move belongings aside so workers can do their jobs. In these situations, you need not compensate tenants for the very temporary loss of the use of their home, and you certainly don't have to move them out (and pay for alternate lodging) while the work is being done.

Tenants might need to move out, however, if repairs are lengthy or involve chemicals that no one should be exposed to. Whether you or your tenants pay for the nights away depends on why the work is being done. If it's to maintain the rental in a fit and habitable condition, or you simply want to spiff the place up, you pay. But if you're doing cosmetic upgrades at the tenant's request, or the work is needed as a result of the tenant's negligence, it's fair to expect the tenant to cover the temporary relocation expenses.

For instance, your tenants can't live in a unit while it's tented for termite fumigation. Because maintaining a fit home is your responsibility, and tenants can't be blamed for the presence of termites, you'll need to pay for the cost of their temporary living quarters.

What if you decide to refinish the hardwood floors? Most contractors will advise occupants to remain away from the home for at least three days, both to allow the finish to dry and to avoid the very toxic odors. Whether you have to pay for alternate lodging depends on the reason for the work: If it's because a pipe burst and flooded the room, chances are it's not the tenant's fault, and you should pay for the hotel stay. But if the refinishing job is really a cosmetic upgrade requested by the tenant, or the flood was the result of the tenant's forgetting to turn off the bathtub faucet, the tenant should bear the expense of living elsewhere.

What is the tenant responsible for?

You aren't the only one with responsibilities—the tenant has some too. These include:

- **Keeping the rental unit in a reasonably clean and safe condition.** If the tenant doesn't do things like mop the tile floor in the kitchen every once in awhile, in which case you'd have to replace the caked grout before the next tenant moves in, you can legitimately deduct the costs from the security deposit. Before the end of the tenancy, if you discover that poor housekeeping has resulted in the need for repairs or property replacements, you can either cover the cost from the security deposit (and demand that the deposit be replenished to its original level), or simply bill the tenant for the cost.

- **Disposing of waste cleanly and safely.** Tenants are responsible for the consequences of unsanitary habits. For instance, if mice or ants invade the kitchen because your tenant forgot to wash the dishes before leaving on a two-week vacation, the tenant is responsible for the extermination and cleanup costs.

- **Keeping plumbing fixtures clean.** For example, bathtub caulking that has sprouted mold and mildew will render the tub unusable (or at least disgusting). Because it could have been prevented by proper cleaning, the tenant is responsible. On the other hand, if the bathroom has no fan and the window has been painted shut, the bathroom will be hard to air out, so the resulting mildew might be your responsibility.

- **Using electrical, plumbing, sanitary, heating, ventilating, air-conditioning, and other facilities and systems properly.** Examples of abuse by tenants include overloading electrical outlets and flushing large objects down the toilet. Catherine, who rents out a cottage behind her house, says: "After I had to call Roto Rooter out for the third time in six months, I had them put what they pulled out into a baggie, and told my tenant, 'If you put this stuff down one more time, you're paying the plumbing bill.' It was

Clorox wipes, which say they're flushable, but not with our old Berkeley pipes. And I'd already warned the tenant about flushing anything other than toilet paper."

- **Fixing things the tenant breaks or damages.** If a tenant causes a serious habitability problem on your property—for example, by carelessly breaking the heater—the tenant is responsible. You are responsible for making sure the repair happens, but you can bill the tenant for it. (The tenant can't just choose to forego heat, either.)

- **Reporting problems in the rental.** Many states require tenants to inform the landlord, as soon as practicable, of defective conditions on the premises that the tenant believes to be unknown to the landlord and believes are the landlord's duty to repair. As we'll explain further, below, your best bet is to ask the tenant to notify you of problems immediately, even if the law doesn't require it.

To protect yourself (and to notify your tenants of their responsibilities), make sure your lease or rental agreement spells out these basic tenant obligations. And use common sense in dealing with tenant psychology. For example, many tenants will ignore their maintenance obligations if they have to pay extra to comply. Gordon, a landlord with property in San Jose, California, says, "If the tenants have to pay for the water, they're not going to water the lawn. One way around this is to have an irrigation system on a timer. Another way is to keep the water in your name, and just raise the rent a bit."

> TIP
> **Best thing I ever did: Learn to regularly remind tenants of key maintenance obligations.** As Kathy explains, "I've found that the one thing my tenants are worst at remembering is to replace the filter on the air conditioner. Here in Florida, if you don't change the filter at least once a month, it starts freezing up, gets a drainage problem, and the pipes get moldy. By impressing upon my tenants that they must change the filter every time they pay their electric bill, and reminding them about it when we talk, I at least reduce the amount of money I'm spending repairing the AC."

If you don't meet your obligations: What the tenant can do

If you don't maintain your property in a fit and habitable condition, as required by law, your tenants can take action. Their options might include one or more of the following depending on the applicable laws:

- **Withholding rent.** In some states, if you don't keep the property livable, your tenant might be able to stop paying rent until necessary repairs are made. This is called rent withholding or rent "escrowing," because tenants often have to deposit the withheld rent in an escrow account until the repairs are done, at which point the money will be released to make the rent payment (maybe after some negotiations between you and the tenant on how you'll compensate the tenant for the inconvenience).

- **Repairing and deducting.** In states that allow this, a tenant can simply repair the problem and subtract the cost from the next month's rent. In most states there's a maximum dollar limit or a specific percentage of the month's rent the tenant can spend—for example, $300 or less than one half the monthly rent, whichever is greater. Also, states usually limit the use of this remedy to fixing essential services, such as heat or water. And many states limit how often tenants can pursue this option, such as no more than twice in any 12-month period.

> **CAUTION**
>
> **Don't drive tenants to repair and deduct.** Though it will mean the repair gets done with little effort on your part, a repair that isn't done well could cost you in the long run. Moreover, when tenants use repair and deduct, you have no receipt (with your name on it) to prove the expense for tax purposes.

- **Reporting code violations to housing inspectors.** Tenants can complain to a local building, health, or fire department about problems such as inoperable plumbing, a leaky roof, or bad wiring. If an inspector comes out, you might be ordered to correct the problem—and subjected to a fine or penalty if you don't do so within a certain amount of time (often five to 30 business days).

- **Filing a lawsuit.** Aggrieved tenants always have the option of suing. They can ask the court to order a rent refund for the period that housing conditions were substandard; payment for the costs of repairing property lost or damaged as a result of the problem (for example, furniture ruined by water leaking through the roof); and compensation for personal injuries caused by the problem. Sometimes, depending on your lease and/or local law, tenants can also seek attorneys' fees. In some states, courts can also order you to repair the defects, with rent reduced until you show the court proof that you've remedied the defects.

- **Moving out.** If you fail to make the rental property habitable, the tenant ultimately has the right to move out—either temporarily or permanently. Such drastic measures are justified only in the case of truly serious problems; for example, where essential services aren't being provided, or the place has been partly or totally destroyed. Tenants also may move out if environmental health hazards such as lead paint dust make the place uninhabitable. Your state statute might impose specific procedures tenants must follow before they can move out, such as how and when tenants must provide notice before making their exit. Depending on the applicable laws and the extent of the problem, you might have anywhere from five to 21 days to remedy the situation before tenants can move out.

Tenants can't use the first two options—withholding rent or repairing the problem and deducting it from the rent—just because they feel like it. In states that allow these remedies, at least three conditions must be met:

- **The problem is serious, not just annoying, and imperils the tenant's health or safety.** Not every building code violation or annoying defect in a rental home justifies such extreme action.

- **The tenant told you about and gave you a reasonable opportunity to fix the problem.** In some states, the law will tell you exactly how much time you have to make the repairs (ten days to three weeks is common); in others, you must respond within a reasonable time under the circumstances.

- **The tenant (or a guest) didn't cause the problem.** If they did, then you can't be expected or required to pay for it.

RESOURCE
More information on state rules on repairs and maintenance.
The State Landlord-Tenant Laws area in the Landlords section of Nolo.com includes state-by-state charts of tenant rights to withhold rent or use the repair-and-deduct remedy. Also see the Rental Repairs & Maintenance section for useful articles.

Adopting a Good Maintenance and Repair System

Early attention to repair and maintenance issues will forestall many problems—but not all of them. And unexpected problems are, in most situations, your responsibility. You'll need a system that helps you prevent problems when you can and deal with them quickly when you can't. (At least maintenance and repair costs are tax deductible, as discussed in Chapter 6.)

Creating a maintenance and repair strategy

We suggest creating a systematic approach to maintenance and repairs, such as the one that follows.

When you have a new tenant:

- **Get everything shipshape before move-in.** Do a thorough evaluation and fix any problems. You'll want to repeat this every time there's tenant turnover. You might want to create a checklist, tailored to your property, to make sure you don't miss anything.

- **Clue the tenant in.** Specify the tenant's responsibilities for repair and maintenance in your lease or rental agreement, and discuss them before the tenant signs.
- **Show new tenants how to handle routine maintenance.** Explain the basics, such as how to avoid overloading circuits, proper use of the garbage disposal, how to turn off water to the toilet in the event of an overflow, and the location and use of the fire extinguisher. Identify problems the tenant definitely shouldn't tackle, such as electrical repairs. Include a brief list of all these maintenance dos and don'ts as part of your move-in materials (discussed in Chapter 5).

Throughout the tenancy:

- **Be accessible.** Make sure tenants can reach you to report problems immediately. Have voicemail or other answering service available at all times, and check your messages frequently. Also consider creating a form tenants can use to make repair requests, then give tenants a few copies at move-in with directions on how to get the form back to you.
- **Keep a written log of all complaints (including those made orally).** Include sections for recording your immediate response, follow-up responses, and any subsequent tenant communications. Be sure to enter the date you fixed the problem, and give some brief details of what you did. Try to respond in writing to every tenant repair request (even if you also do so orally).
- **Respond quickly.** Handle repairs (especially urgent ones) as soon as possible, but definitely within the time any applicable law requires. Notify tenants by phone—and follow up in writing—if repairs will take more than 48 hours (excluding weekends). Keep tenants informed of the repair status—for example, if you have problems scheduling a plumber, drop the tenants a quick note to let them know what's going on and that you're doing your best to address the issue. We'll discuss responding to complaints in more detail below.

On a regular basis:

- **Have biannual tenant reviews.** Twice a year, give your tenants a checklist for reporting any potential safety hazards or maintenance needs, such as an entryway rug showing signs of fraying (replace it now, before it gets worse and someone trips). You might want to create a form checklist you can use over and over. Set specific dates on which to hand it out to tenants, and provide a deadline for the tenants to fill it out and return it to you. Respond promptly and in writing to all returned forms, and keep copies in your file.

RESOURCE
Looking for checklists, move-in letters, and more? Go to *Every Landlord's Legal Guide,* by Janet Portman, Ann O'Connell, and Marcia Stewart (Nolo). The book includes detailed information on how to use all the landlord forms and documents you need. Purchasing the book will give you access to downloadable versions of all the forms, which you can customize to your needs.

- **Use written reminders.** Remind tenants of your policies and procedures for keeping the property in good repair in every written communication: Print it at the bottom of all routine notices, rent increases, and other communications. You could even place it in your standard email signature. Tenants will be more likely to tell you about maintenance and repair problems if you remind them that you're truly interested.
- **Conduct an annual safety inspection.** Once a year, make time for a "safety and maintenance inspection," where you check that items such as smoke detectors, heating and plumbing systems, and major appliances are safe and in working order. These inspections are not required by law, but they're a good idea. Be sure not to overdo it—once a year is sufficient.

Your Right to Conduct a Safety Inspection

In many states, you have the right to enter a tenant's home to conduct a safety inspection, but you usually need to notify the tenant first. Some states specify 24 hours' notice, others simply state that you must give "reasonable notice." To be on the safe side, check your state's statutes and, if all that is required is "reasonable notice," allow at least 24 hours.

If a tenant objects to your entry, despite your having given the notice required by law, the tenant's refusal is grounds for eviction. If your state doesn't allow the landlord to enter and inspect against the tenant's will, point out to the tenant that you take your responsibility to maintain the property very seriously. Remind the tenant that you'll be checking for problems that the tenant might not notice, which could develop into bigger problems later. If you still get a refusal, write a confirming letter to the tenant—it might protect you later if the tenant claims there's a safety hazard or damage to the property (especially if the damage could have been prevented had you had the opportunity to inspect).

Responding to tenant complaints

You should respond almost immediately to all complaints about defective conditions. Give the tenant a call, and follow up with an email or other writing. If you can't reach tenants by phone, shoot them an email, and follow up as needed. Explain when repairs can be made or, if you don't know yet, say that you'll be back in touch promptly. Different problems require different levels of action:

- **Personal security and safety problems.** When you're notified about a problem that could result in property damage or personal injury, respond immediately. Arrange to have the problem fixed on an emergency basis, even if getting the work done quickly is more expensive—a rapid response will likely cost less in the long run.

- **Major inconveniences to the tenant.** Respond and attempt to get work done as soon as possible, or within 24 hours if the problem is a major inconvenience to the tenant, such as a plumbing or heating problem. Otherwise, you risk a tenant's using one of the self-help remedies mentioned above, or simply feeling dissatisfied and moving out.

- **Minor problems.** Respond within 48 hours (on business days) if the problem is not too serious. You'll avoid a tenant's major dissatisfaction, and you won't have to worry that your inaction will trigger the tenant's inappropriate but highly annoying use of remedies such as withholding rent or making repairs and deducting their cost from the rent.

If you can't take care of a repair right away, keep tenants informed— let them know your timeline and what actions you're taking. For the sake of speed, do this orally (a voicemail on the tenant's phone should serve), and then follow up in writing. Explain any delays, such as having to wait for a specially ordered part.

As important as these repairs are, you can't just march onto the property to make them until you've taken steps to protect the tenant's rights. You can enter the rental premises only with the tenant's consent, or after having given the amount of notice required by state law, usually 24 hours. Except when there's an emergency or when it's impractical, try to pick a reasonable time of day (such as regular business hours) to make repairs. Respecting the tenant's schedule will keep the peace, and ensure you're acting reasonably under any applicable state or local law.

Can Tenants Alter the Property?

Tenants often want to personalize their homes—paint the living room, install a closet system, or put in a dishwasher, for example. If a tenant you like and would hate to lose makes a request to alter the rental, consider the following to evaluate if it makes sense to allow it:

- **Is the improvement or alteration easily undone?** Repainting is easy to redo, while knocking out a wall to install a wine closet is more permanent.
- **Does the improvement or alteration enhance your property?** For example, resurfaced kitchen cabinets might actually add value.
- **Does the law protect the tenant's right to make the particular improvement or alteration?** For example, in some cases, the law might protect a tenant's rights to install a satellite dish, and you'll need to comply with such laws. See Chapter 5, "Step Aside: Tenants Might Be Allowed to Make These Repairs or Alterations," for more on the subject.

If you and the tenant reach an understanding, put it in writing, carefully describing the project and materials, including whether the improvement or alteration is permanent or portable, the terms of the reimbursement, if any, and how and when you'll pay the tenant, if at all, for labor and materials.

Anything your tenant attaches to a building, fence, deck, or the ground itself (called "fixtures") belongs to you, unless you agree that the tenant can keep it. Either way, it's wise to spell out in your lease or rental agreement who will own the improvement. And make it clear that if the tenant later fails to properly restore the premises, or removes an alteration that was meant to be permanent, you'll deduct the resulting costs from the security deposit or take further legal action if necessary.

Responding to problems at a distance

If your property is in another state and you haven't hired a property manager, you'll face additional challenges when you need to get work done. Laura, who lives in Washington state, describes how she handles repairs for her Nevada and Florida properties: "My tenants know enough not to call me at 3:00 in the morning. Of course, their timing can still be horrible—just before my son's wedding, I got about 50 phone calls concerning the water heater in one of my houses. Still, I've found that I can accomplish a lot by phone. I view dealing with repair issues as a partnership with my tenants. Sometimes I'll have them call the repairperson to make an appointment, which makes more sense given that they're going to have to be the one to let the person in. I tell them to have the repairperson call me after arriving at the house. Then we'll plan the job and I'll usually pay for it over the phone, and ask the repairperson to send me the receipt. This system tends to go smoothly."

It's also smart to line up a list of potential repairpeople while you're in town visiting the property, rather than waiting until an urgent situation arises. We'll discuss how to find good people later in this chapter.

No Thanks! Hiring Someone Else to Do the Work

If you live far from your rental property, don't have time to deal with the hassle of repairs or maintenance, or are simply too busy or not very handy, you might want to hire someone to take care of maintenance and repairs for you. Your primary options are to hire a property manager, a handyperson, or the tenant.

> **TIP**
> **Learning some maintenance and repair skills might be smart.**
> "I do a lot of my own maintenance," says John, who has owned multiple properties since 1975. "It gets me on the property and shows a presence; it shows that I care. Besides, you have to learn to do some repairs yourself, because you can't afford to hire someone for every little thing."

Hiring a property manager

If you hire a property manager, that person's package of services will probably include overseeing maintenance. This can have its advantages, especially since many property management companies have professionals on staff to deal with maintenance problems, and have vetted a host of other specialized professionals like plumbers, electricians, and general contractors.

But watch out for a few potential bumpy spots, too. For example:

- **Make sure the property manager will respond immediately.** Ask for a commitment to a specific turnaround time. You don't want your property damaged, or your tenant injured, because the property manager didn't get around to acting promptly.

- **Confirm that the property manager is available 24 hours a day, 365 days a year.** That will avoid issues like a desperate call from a tenant on Christmas morning, complaining that the heater is broken and the manager is nowhere to be found.

- **Find out whether you'll be charged extra for maintenance calls.** Some property management companies make money by tacking on administrative fees when hiring outside contractors or vendors.

- **Know whether the property manager is authorized to conduct repairs without your prior approval.** Your contract should specify what level of repairs may be done without getting an okay from you first. You want your property manager to be able to act quickly if there's an emergency, especially if you're on vacation or otherwise unavailable. On the other hand, you don't want to give a manager authority to undertake a major or expensive repair or replacement, such as replacing the stove without consulting you first.

Also, keep in mind that the property manager will probably not conduct annual inspections or periodically ask the tenant whether any repairs are needed. This is something you'll either have to do yourself, negotiate with the property management firm to include in your agreement, or pay extra for.

For more information on hiring a property manager, see Chapter 10.

Hiring a handyperson

As a middle-ground option between doing the work yourself and paying for the deluxe services of a property manager, you can hire others. Your best bet is to find a reliable handyperson for basic repairs, and hire a contractor (discussed below) for more specific or skill-intensive tasks.

A good handyperson will have an extensive background in home repair. Many are even trained and licensed contractors. You'll want someone who is available 24 hours, in case of emergencies. Choose someone who's been in business for awhile, as an established professional is more likely to stick around and become familiar with your property.

To find a competent handyperson, ask other rental property owners or real estate professionals for recommendations, as well as friends and colleagues. It's best to find one who carries primary health insurance and liability insurance, which will protect you if the handyperson is injured on the job, causes any property damage, or injures others. A reputable worker will be willing to provide proof of insurance. An insured handyperson will probably charge more than an uninsured one might— but it's worth it for the extra security of knowing you or your insurance company won't end up paying for the consequences of any accidents.

Also, for the sake of both your project and your financial risk, make sure the person you hire has complied with any state rules and licensing requirements. In some states and cities, for example, it's illegal to hire unlicensed contractors for certain kinds of work.

Hiring a contractor

When you, your handyperson, or your property manager don't have the skills needed for the task at hand, you'll probably hire a contractor, such as a plumber or an electrician. Again, you're looking for someone who's available quickly when you're in a jam—especially if you're not in the area.

Ask other rental property owners or real estate professionals for recommendations. Look for someone who is properly licensed and insured. You can often find this information on your state's contractor licensing board website, but get confirmation from the contractor in case anything has changed.

Don't Become an Accidental Employer

You probably don't consider someone you hire someone to fix a leaky faucet, mow the lawn, or retile the bathroom to be your "employee." But the IRS or other federal or state governmental agencies might feel differently if that person becomes a regular worker who takes orders from you—unlikely in a single-family rental, but something to bear in mind if you expand into multiunit properties.

When the government considers you an employer, and not simply someone who hires an independent contractor for a specific job, your obligations to the worker (and the government) change dramatically. For example, you'd need to secure proof of the worker's authorization to work in the United States, to withhold and pay Social Security and Medicare taxes, and maybe also pay workers' compensation insurance and state unemployment taxes.

For IRS purposes, the more control you exercise over a worker's tasks, the more likely the IRS is to consider the person your employee. Workers are more likely independent contractors if they:

- can earn a profit or suffer a loss from the work
- furnish the tools and materials needed to do the work
- are paid by the job, not by the hour
- work for more than one place at a time
- invest in equipment and facilities
- pay their own business and traveling expenses
- hire and pay any assistants, and
- set their own working hours.

For more information, see IRS Publication 15-A, *Employer's Supplemental Tax Guide*, and the articles in the Employment Law section of Nolo.com.

Hiring the tenant

You might want to delegate some of the responsibility of managing the property to your tenant. It's not always a bad idea. After all, the tenant is aware of the problems, and is highly motivated to fix them. On the other hand, because tenants aren't normally interested in the long-term condition of the property, many won't attend to repairs with the same concern that owners bring to the job.

You'll want to make sure the tenant has the necessary expertise to make repairs—which will probably depend on both the task and the tenant. Second, make sure hiring the tenant is cost-effective. While such an arrangement is convenient—you don't have to find a professional to handle certain tasks—it isn't necessarily cheaper. If you credit or pay the tenant hourly, but it takes twice as long (or causes further damage), you won't save money.

Compensating the tenant for repairs

If you decide to allow tenants to make repairs from time to time, you have two options for how to compensate them. You can:

- **Reduce the rent.** You'll want to agree to this practice ahead of time, agree to the payment terms, and lay out your agreement in writing, within the rental agreement.

- **Pay directly for the work.** Paying an on-site tenant to do repair and maintenance is preferable to giving the tenant a reduction in rent for work performed, because if the job isn't done right, you can simply cancel the work arrangement rather than amend the lease or rental agreement. Plus, there will be no question that the tenant is still obligated to pay the full rent as usual. If you choose this route, be sure to write down what you expect your tenant to do, and for how much money.

> **TIP**
> **In a multifamily property, beware of turning a tenant into an employee.** No matter which method of compensation you choose, if your tenant will be performing regular maintenance duties in a multi-family rental situation (such as dealing with minor plumbing repairs and sweeping the lobby and front steps), your tenant will be your employee. As an employer, you'll need to comply with the requirements described in "Don't Become an Accidental Employer," above. (In a single-family situation, it's unlikely that making a tenant responsible for yard upkeep, and including that provision in your lease, would carry the same risk.)

Types of repairs a tenant can't do

Even though it might be cheapest to buy a book at a local hardware store, throw some parts into your cart, and hire the tenant to replace the water heater or repair faulty wiring, it's not a good idea for such major repairs. Here's why:

- **You're risking low-quality work.** Unless your tenant just happens to be a skilled contractor, the repairs might be inadequate, so that you end up having to redo them (or worse).

- **You're legally responsible if the tenant gets injured or injures someone else.** Tenants who don't know what they're doing can easily cause injuries, especially if dealing with sensitive systems like heating or wiring. Hiring the tenant means you'll be responsible for these injuries—even if they occur later (for example, when the newly installed light fixture comes crashing down during a dinner party). Of course, you could always try to recoup your losses by suing that tenant (called "seeking indemnity" in legalese), but your chances of recovery will be slim unless your tenant has significant assets. On the other hand, a maintenance or repair service will normally carry its own insurance (confirm this before you engage its services).

- **The law might not permit you to delegate major repairs to the tenant.** Judges and legislators fear that tenants will rarely be in the position, either practically or financially, to do the repairs necessary to bring a structure up to par—and, no matter what you delegate, it's still your duty to make the place habitable. Even in the few states that allow landlords and tenants of single-family dwellings to agree in writing that the tenant is to perform some of the landlord's statutory duties, landlords remain bound by the implied warranty of habitability and responsible for compliance with health and safety codes.

Avoiding problems

Repair and maintenance arrangements between landlords and tenants often lead to dissatisfaction—the landlord feels that the tenant has neglected certain tasks, or the tenant feels that there's too much work for the money. To keep things flowing smoothly:

- **Put it in writing.** Any repair or maintenance agreement should be written and signed, either as part of the lease or rental agreement or as a separate employment agreement. This will avoid mutual misunderstandings about who's responsible for what.

- **Provide enough detail so that the tenant knows exactly what's expected.** Whether it's repairing a broken window, dealing with a routine plumbing problem, or landscaping, you'll want to specifically describe and limit each task—and make sure the tenant is qualified to do these tasks.

- **Pay fairly.** If you don't, you'll increase the tenant's resentment, while decreasing motivation to get the job done. If you ever have a dispute with the tenant, a judge won't look kindly on an unreasonably low payment for the tenant's hard work, especially if it doesn't add up to minimum wage.

- **Treat the delegation of duties as separate from your other duties as landlord.** Your agreement with your tenant has nothing to do with your other responsibilities. For example, if you and your tenant agree that the tenant will do gardening work in exchange for a reduction in rent, and you're watching the shrubs die or take over the sidewalk, you cannot respond by shutting off the water or otherwise retaliating. The proper recourse is to discuss the problem with the tenant and, if it persists, to cancel the arrangement. ●

Landlord Liability for Injuries, Crimes, and More

As a landlord, you have some legal responsibility for your tenants' safety. In addition to providing a well-maintained place to live, you're legally required to create an environment that protects tenants from various dangers. In this chapter, we'll cover those dangers and how to avoid them, including:

- your responsibility for tenant injuries
- dealing with environmental problems like mold and lead
- protecting tenants from crime, and
- buying insurance to protect yourself.

Fortunately, the likelihood of having problems that will result in serious legal or financial liability is low, especially if you follow the preventative measures we recommend throughout this book. And with a good insurance policy, even if you're confronted with some surprises, you'll be covered.

Ouch, That Smarts: Liability for Tenant Injuries

It's probably no surprise that you must keep your property safe for your tenant and any guests—and it's a responsibility to take seriously. After all, an injured tenant can seek financial recovery for medical bills, lost earnings, pain and other physical suffering, permanent physical disability and disfigurement, and emotional distress. Tenants can also look to you for the costs of property damage that resulted from faulty or unsafe conditions. As Jason, a landlord in Texas, remembers, "The tree in front of our rental house was overgrown and overdue for a trimming, but I put it off. Last winter, a storm broke a major branch, crushing my tenant's car, which was parked in the driveway. My insurance carrier paid for it, because I'd been remiss in not taking care of the tree, but my premiums went up."

Consistently practicing good maintenance serves a double purpose: It will not only help prevent tenants from getting injured (or having their property damaged) in the first place, but will help you defend yourself if a tenant claims you're responsible for an injury or damage.

You're not responsible for everything

It isn't always easy to determine whether you're legally responsible for a tenant's injury. Basically, you might be liable for injuries resulting from:

- **Negligence.** An injured tenant might claim you acted negligently— that is, carelessly, in a way that wasn't reasonable under the circumstances—and thus caused the injury. Courts have found landlords liable for negligence when a tenant fell down a staircase due to a defective handrail, a tenant's child was scalded by water from a water heater with a broken thermostat, and a tenant received electrical burns when attempting to insert a stove's damaged plug into the wall outlet.

- **Violation of a health or safety law.** Many state and local laws require smoke detectors, sprinklers, inside-release security bars on windows, childproof fences around swimming pools, and so on. Some states say that a landlord who doesn't take reasonable steps to follow the laws will be considered negligent, and responsible for any resulting tenant injuries. Additionally, your violation of a health or safety law could indirectly cause an injury and lead to liability. For example, if you let the furnace deteriorate in violation of local law and a tenant is injured trying to repair it, you could be liable, unless the tenant's repair efforts were extremely careless themselves.

- **Failure to make certain repairs.** If your lease or rental agreement prohibits the tenant from making repairs or alterations without your consent, you can get into trouble if you're told about such a problem but don't fix it, and then the tenant gets injured as a result. The legal reason is that you breached the contract (the lease) by not making the repairs. (You could be found negligent, as well.)

- **Failure to keep the premises habitable.** If a problem is so serious that the rental unit becomes unfit for human habitation—and you knew of the problem and had a reasonable amount of time to fix it—you could get into trouble for any resulting tenant injuries. What type of problem makes a house uninhabitable can vary by circumstance, however. For example, a large, jagged broken window would make the premises unfit for habitation in North Dakota in winter, but a torn screen door during summertime in southern California would not.

- **Reckless or intentional acts.** If you harm a tenant on purpose or "recklessly," you might be in hot water. In the legal sense, "recklessness" usually means extreme carelessness regarding an obvious defect or problem (like ignoring a fire hazard for months). Acting recklessly can be expensive, making you potentially liable for "punitive" damages: extra damages, beyond the cost of the injury, to punish you for bad behavior.

Me? I'd Never Hurt a Fly!

If you hit a tenant during an argument, that's an intentional act. But so are emotional or psychological injuries inflicted intentionally, such as:

- **Sexual harassment,** or repeated, disturbing attentions of a sexual nature (or a single outrageous act) that leave a tenant fearful, humiliated, and upset

- **Assault,** even if it's nonphysical—for example, threatening or menacing someone, and

- **Repeated invasions of privacy,** such as by unauthorized entries into the tenant's living space.

- **Other duties imposed by law.** In rare instances, courts or state legislatures have decided that landlords are automatically liable for certain kinds of injuries. This legal principle is called "strict liability," or liability without fault. It's usually imposed only when a hidden defect poses an unreasonably great risk of harm to people who can't detect or avoid the danger. For example, Massachusetts landlords are strictly liable if their tenants are poisoned by lead-based paint.

Liability for injuries to guests and trespassers

If you act negligently and a tenant's guest or even a trespasser (who wasn't invited by you or the tenant onto the property) is injured, will you be responsible? In a few states, you're liable without regard to why the injured person was there in the first place. As a general rule, however, you don't owe the same "duty of care" to a nontenant as you do to your tenant, especially if it's a trespasser. For example, a tenant who gets hurt by falling from an unfenced porch can make a fairly strong argument that you were negligent; but a trespasser, even an innocent one who entered onto the wrong property, and fell off the same porch, might have a harder time recovering from you.

Dog Bites and Other Animal Attacks

Dog bites cost insurance companies close to $700 million in 2018 to settle around 18,000 claims, with the average cost paid out per claim around $39,000. (Source: Insurance Information Institute, III.org.) And it's not just pet owners who are liable for injuries their animals inflict. Landlords might also be financially responsible for injuries caused by their tenants' animals, be they common household pets, such as dogs, or more exotic, wild animals.

Dangerous domestic pets. If a person injured by a vicious animal can prove to an insurance adjuster (or a jury) that the landlord knew (or should have known) that the animal had dangerous tendencies, and failed to take reasonable steps to prevent the injury (such as demanding that the animal leave the property or evicting the tenant), the landlord might be held liable.

Dangerous exotic pets. Keeping wild animals is generally considered an "ultrahazardous activity." So if your tenant keeps a monkey or tiger and you know about it (or should have), a court will assume that you understood the dangers presented, and might hold you responsible if the animal injures someone.

If a tenant is at fault, too

If the tenant is partially to blame for getting injured, your picture isn't so grim. For example, a drunk tenant who, while stumbling around, trips on a loose brick on the front steps might not be able to collect as much, or anything at all, from the landlord.

If a tenant knows of a danger and takes a chance anyway, thus causing or worsening the injury, the law will say that the tenant has "assumed the risk" of injury. In some states, such a tenant might not be entitled to recover anything, regardless of any negligence by the landlord. In other states, a tenant's recovery will be lowered based on how much the tenant appreciated (but ignored) the danger involved.

While a tenant's own carelessness might decrease the hit to your wallet (or your insurance policy), it won't decrease the time you'll spend dealing with the incident. For example, Walt, with a single-family rental in Miami explains, "My tenant, Dorothy, definitely knew that the bedroom casement window had become hard to lift and secure, but she didn't say a word about it. The first I heard was one night when she called from the hospital, after the window had come crashing down on her arm and hurt her wrist, real bad. She sued me. At least the jury got the picture that Dorothy was partly at fault, so she got only a portion of the damages she'd asked for. (My insurance company paid.) Still, I had to spend days going to the lawyers' offices and preparing for and attending the trial."

How to prevent liability problems

Here are ways to protect yourself from lawsuits and hefty insurance settlements and at the same time make your tenants' lives safer and happier:

- **Follow the maintenance plan in the last chapter.** Look for dangerous conditions and fix them promptly; comply with all health, safety, and building codes; conduct regular safety inspections; ask tenants to report problems; and document problems and resolutions.

- **Warn of dangers you can't fix.** With some dangers, like a steep driveway or winding stairs, there simply isn't much you can do to improve the situation. But if you know, or should know, about such dangers or defects, you have a duty to tell the tenant about them. The best way is to mention them in your lease, rental agreement, or move-in letter. If appropriate, post warning signs near the hazard.

- **Look for tenant security issues.** Install and maintain basic security features such as deadbolt locks, smoke detectors, fire extinguishers, window locks, outside lighting, and any other features appropriate for making your property safer.

- **Be vigilant about dangers to children.** If children are drawn onto your property by an irresistibly interesting (to children) but dangerous feature, such as a stack of building materials or an abandoned refrigerator (known in legal jargon as an "attractive nuisance"), you must exercise special care. Because young children can't read, or tend to ignore warnings, you should place physical barriers between children and the attractive feature. And if the danger is of the type that can be cleaned up or removed (like the refrigerator), you should do so.

> **CAUTION**
> **Tenants can't sign away rights to be compensated for injuries.** Landlords used to protect themselves from most tenant lawsuits with an "exculpatory clause"—lease language absolving the landlord in advance of responsibility for tenant injuries, even those caused by the landlord's negligence. There might be unusual situations when a narrowly worded exculpatory clause would be appropriate—for example, if you've delegated appropriate repair and maintenance duties to a tenant (described in Chapter 8)—but in general, they're rarely enforced by courts, so our advice is not to use them.

- **Supervise contractors.** If construction is being done on your property, make sure the person in charge secures the site and removes or locks up dangerous tools or equipment when the site is left unattended. Consider sending your tenant written notice of the intended project, suggesting extra precautions during the construction period.

Liability for Environmental Health Hazards

If your property poses any environmental health hazards to tenants and you know about them, you've got to tell tenants, and most of the time, you must remedy the problem—even if you didn't cause it. This liability is based on many of the same legal theories described above, such as negligence and negligence *per se* (negligence that's automatic when a statute is broken).

Asbestos

Exposure to asbestos is linked to an increased risk of cancer. Homes built before the mid-1970s often contain asbestos insulation around heating systems, in ceilings, and in other areas. Until 1981, asbestos was also widely used in many other building materials, such as vinyl flooring and tiles. Asbestos that breaks down and enters the air—for example, when it's disturbed during maintenance or renovation work—can give rise to significant health problems.

If you learn there's asbestos on your property, you can't pretend not to know about it. It becomes an undisclosed and dangerous defect that you must tell tenants about and take steps to remedy. Some states might also say you've breached the implied warranty of habitability when, despite knowing about the problem, you do nothing, potentially giving the tenant the right to break the lease and move out without notice, pay less rent, withhold the entire rent, or sue to force you to make the place habitable.

Unless the asbestos material has begun to break down and enter the air, however, it's usually best to leave it alone and monitor it. You can do this as part of your regular safety inspection, discussed in Chapter 7, and you can also require your tenant to report any deterioration to you.

If you must disturb asbestos, warn the tenants first, and give them an opportunity to avoid the area. You might even consider temporarily relocating your tenant. The costs of a few days or weeks in alternate housing will pale compared to the expense of a personal injury lawsuit.

OSHA Regulations and Asbestos

The U.S. Occupational Safety and Health Administration (OSHA) requires rental property owners of homes built before 1981 who employ maintenance employees (including outside contractors for repair and maintenance jobs) to notify these people that a property may contain asbestos, and in some cases, test for it. You can avoid the responsibility only by having a licensed inspector test and confirm no asbestos is present in the home.

OSHA regulations also require custodial workers (such as the handyperson who installs smoke detectors in the acoustic tile ceilings) to have gone through specialized training and use particular work procedures. The procedural rules get extra strict after any intentional disturbance of asbestos or asbestos-containing materials.

If you hire a contractor to perform major renovations or repairs that involve asbestos, the contractor must comply with OSHA's education and prevention rules. But if your own employees do the work, the burden falls on you to learn and implement the rules (see our resource suggestions later in this chapter).

If you learn that asbestos material is airborne (or is about to be), seek an expert's advice on remedies. When removal is necessary, hire trained asbestos removal specialists, and check to make sure the debris is legally disposed of in approved hazardous waste disposal sites. Don't allow tenants to make repairs to or otherwise invade any spaces containing asbestos, for example, by drilling holes in the ceiling to hang plants.

RESOURCE
Asbestos resources. For more on asbestos rules, inspections, and control, see OSHA's website at OSHA.gov or call 800-321-OSHA.

Lead

As we all know, exposure to lead-based paint and lead water pipes can lead to serious health problems, particularly in children. Buildings constructed pre-1978 are likely to contain some lead, whether it's in the paint, pipes, or solder used on copper pipes.

You must, under federal law, inform the tenant, even before signing or renewing a lease or rental agreement, of any information you have on lead paint hazards on the property. If you've had your property tested, that includes showing tenants a copy of the report, or a summary written by the inspector. It also includes giving the tenant the lead hazard information booklet *Protect Your Family From Lead in Your Home*, by the Environmental Protection Agency (EPA) and available at www.epa.gov/lead. Agencies in many states have developed their own pamphlets, which you can use instead of the EPA version if the EPA has approved them.

With a few limited exceptions, every lease and rental agreement must include a disclosure page, even if you haven't tested for lead. You can use the one developed by the EPA, "Disclosure of Information on Lead-Based Paint and/or Lead-Based Paint Hazards," available at EPA. gov. The form has a place for tenants to initial, indicating that they've received it. Note the date they received it, and if you and the tenant are also signing the lease or rental agreement on the same day, enter the time you signed it, too. If you're ever challenged, or investigated by a government agency, you'll be able to prove that the tenant received the disclosure form before signing the rental documents.

> ⓘ **CAUTION**
> **You have additional obligations if you renovate the property.**
> When you renovate a building constructed before 1978, EPA regulations require that current tenants receive lead hazard information before any renovation work begins. The type of renovation depends on where the renovation is taking place. If an occupied rental unit is being worked on, you must give the tenant a copy of the EPA pamphlet *The Lead-Safe Certified Guide to Renovate Right*.

Most states also require landlords to carefully maintain any existing lead paint and lead-based building materials, and they mandate who may work on lead paint abatement. You must comply with any applicable statute in your state as well as the federal law.

There's no federal legal requirement that you be proactive and test for lead. But you might want to anyway, for these reasons:

- **Controlling lead is much easier than going through a lawsuit.** Besides, do you really want to live with the knowledge that a child's health has been damaged?

- **Ignorance might not shield you from liability.** At some point, a court will no doubt rule that the danger of lead paint in older housing is so well known that owners of older housing can be presumed to know of the danger.

- **You can't simply refuse to rent to tenants with children.** Though you might feel this protects them, such a refusal qualifies as illegal discrimination in all states.

- **You can't shift responsibility with a clause in your lease or rental agreement.** An exculpatory clause, which attempts to absolve you from any responsibility for lead-based injuries, won't protect you. In fact, it could work against you, as a court could infer from your requiring the clause that you knew of the lead problem.

- **Any refinance or sale will probably bring the problem to light.** Your lender might require lead testing before approving a loan.

- **Your insurance company might start requiring lead testing as a condition of issuing a policy.** Claims arising from lead-based injuries are expensive—expect the insurance company to require testing before issuing a homeowners' policy, or to exclude claims based on lead. Review your coverage with your insurance broker.

> **RESOURCE**
> **Lead hazard resources.** Information on the evaluation and control of lead-based paint and other hazards, disclosure forms, copies of the *Protect Your Family From Lead in Your Home* and *Renovate Right* pamphlets, lists of EPA-certified lead paint professionals, and more can be obtained at 800-424-LEAD or www.epa.gov/lead.

Lead is relatively easy to detect—you can buy home-use kits that contain a simple swab, which turns color when drawn over a lead-based surface. Knowing how much lead is present, and how to best clean it up, however, are subjects for a certified lead abatement specialist. Plan on speaking with one if a lead test, done professionally or with an at-home kit, comes up positive.

Radon

Radon is a naturally occurring radioactive gas associated with lung cancer. It can enter and contaminate a house built on soil and rock containing uranium deposits or through water from private wells drilled in uranium-rich soil. Radon can become lethal when trapped in tightly sealed homes (well insulated or with poor ventilation), when escaping from building materials that have incorporated uranium-filled rocks and soils, or when released from aerated, contaminated household water. Problems occur most frequently in areas where rocky soil is relatively rich in uranium and in climates where occupants keep their windows tightly shut.

You're not legally required to test for radon, but you should do so if levels are known to be high in your area (ask your city planning department or insurance broker). For the best results, hire an EPA-certified inspector. Testing takes at least three days, and sometimes months. Do-it-yourself radon testing kits are also available; make sure the kit says "Meets EPA Requirements."

If testing indicates high radon levels, be sure to warn tenants and correct the problem. Start by giving them the EPA booklet *A Radon Guide for Tenants*. Ventilation measures will effectively disperse the gas in most situations. These measures range from the obvious (open the windows and provide cross-ventilation) to the somewhat complex (sealing cracks in the foundation or sucking radon out of the soil before it enters the foundation). According to the EPA, a typical household radon problem can be solved for a reasonable sum, in line with other basic home repairs.

> **RESOURCE**
>
> **Radon resources.** Contact the EPA Radon Hotline at 800-767-7236, or visit the EPA website (www.epa.gov/radon). The site gives information on finding a qualified radon reduction provider, and includes a map of radon zones by state. You can also download a copy of *A Radon Guide for Tenants* and other publications.

Carbon monoxide

Carbon monoxide (CO) is a colorless, odorless, lethal gas; a byproduct of fuel combustion produced by nonelectric home appliances, such as gas dryers, refrigerators, ranges, water heaters or space heaters, oil furnaces, fireplaces, charcoal grills, and wood stoves. If appliances or fireplaces aren't vented properly, CO can build up within a home and poison the occupants. Unlike radon, whose deadly effects work over time, CO can build up and kill within a matter of hours. And, unlike any of the environmental hazards discussed so far, CO cannot be covered up or managed.

If you have a regular maintenance program, discussed in Chapter 7, you should be able to spot and fix the common malfunctions that cause CO buildup. Here's how to avoid problems:

- Install carbon monoxide detection devices in the home (many states require these already).
- Check chimneys and appliance vents for blockages.
- Prohibit tenants from using indoor, portable gas or charcoal grills.

- Warn tenants never to use a gas range, clothes dryer, or oven for heating the rental unit.
- Prohibit nonelectric space heaters, or specify that they must be inspected annually. Tenants can get recommendations from fuel suppliers.
- Check the pilot lights of gas appliances regularly. They should show a clear blue flame; a yellow or orange flame could indicate a problem.

RESOURCE
Carbon monoxide resources. The EPA website offers useful instructional material, including downloadable educational pamphlets, at www.epa.gov under "Environmental Topics." Local natural gas utility companies often offer consumer information.

Mold

Across the country, tenants have won multimillion dollar cases against landlords for significant health problems—such as rashes, chronic fatigue, nausea, cognitive losses, hemorrhaging, and asthma—allegedly caused by exposure to "toxic molds." But not all mold produces toxins, and most mold is not otherwise harmful—for example, the mold that grows on shower tiles isn't dangerous. The trouble is, it takes an expert to know whether a particular mold is harmful or just unsightly and annoying.

Mold often grows on water-soaked materials, such as wall paneling, paint, fabric, ceiling tiles, newspapers, or cardboard boxes. However, all that's really needed is an organic food source, water, and time. Throw in a little warmth, and the organism will grow quickly, sometimes spreading within 24 hours. Humidity sets up prime growing conditions. Floods, leaking pipes, windows, or roofs can lead to mold growth in any structure.

No federal law sets permissible mold exposure limits or building tolerance standards for residences, and only a few states have taken steps toward establishing permissible mold standards. Some local ordinances identify mold as a legal nuisance or a property condition that the landlord must clean up. Check with your city building, health, or environmental health departments to find out whether your city or state has passed any relevant laws.

Law or no law, your legal duty to provide and maintain habitable premises naturally extends to fixing leaking pipes, windows, and roofs—the causes of most mold. If you're lax, and mold grows as a result, you could be held responsible for a tenant's resulting health problems.

But instead of worrying about unlikely lawsuits, focus on preventing the conditions that lead to mold growth. The following steps are especially important if your rental house is in a humid environment or has a history of mold problems:

- **Check for and fix moisture or mold problems before new tenants move in.** This will help prevent problems before they start.

- **Make sure every tenant understands how to help prevent mold growth.** Use your lease or house rules to educate tenants about sensible housekeeping practices and how to fix problems should they arise. Give tenants specific advice, such as how to ventilate the rental unit, avoid creating areas of standing water, and clean vulnerable areas, such as bathrooms, with cleaning solutions that will discourage mold growth.

- **Encourage tenants to immediately report signs of mold.** This includes reporting conditions that could lead to mold, such as plumbing leaks and weatherproofing problems.

- **Do all necessary repairs and maintenance to clean up or reduce mold.** For example, consider installing exhaust fans in rooms with high humidity (bathrooms, kitchens, and service porches) or provide tenants with dehumidifiers in chronically damp climates or rental units with poor ventilation.

Should You Test for Mold?

Properly testing for mold will cost you. Although over-the-counter kits can be bought for around $30, their results are questionable. A professional's basic investigation for a single-family home will run you $1,000 or more. To further complicate matters, relatively few competent professionals have entered this field, and no state or federal certification programs exist to govern them.

If you have visible signs of mold, you're much better off simply getting rid of it, using the procedures described below. The procedures are the same no matter what kind of mold it is.

Most mold is relatively harmless and easy to deal with. A weak bleach solution (one cup of bleach per gallon of water) will remove mold from nonporous materials. Use gloves and avoid exposing eyes and lungs to airborne mold dust (use a mask). Allow for frequent work breaks with plenty of fresh air.

Clean or remove all infested areas, beginning on a small patch to make sure you don't develop adverse health reactions such as nausea or headaches. (If you do, call in an experienced professional.) Contain the work space with plastic sheeting and enclose debris in plastic bags. Don't try removing mold from fabrics such as towels, linens, drapes, carpets, and clothing—you'll have to dispose of these already ruined items.

If the mold is extensive, consider hiring an experienced mold remediation company with excellent references.

RESOURCE
Mold resources. For information on mold detection, removal, and prevention, visit the EPA website at www.epa.gov/mold.

CAUTION
Check your insurance policy. You might be dismayed to find that it excludes mold damage from coverage (or will on the next renewal). Even if mold is covered, many insurers try to wiggle out by claiming that it falls within the "pollution exclusion." Most policies won't cover you if you commit or allow pollution, the classic example being deliberately dumping solvents onto the property. Talk to your insurance broker if you're concerned about mold coverage.

Bed bugs

Bed bugs are biting, obnoxious pests that nest in mattresses, bed frames, and beyond. In fact, they can infest an entire room or house, spreading via cracks in the walls, heating ducts, and other openings. They're also excellent stowaways, crawling into luggage, clothing, pillows, boxes, and furniture as these are moved from an infested home or hotel to another location. Secondhand furniture is a common source of infestation.

You'll learn that bed bugs have infested your property when the tenant complains of widespread, annoying bites that appear during the night (fortunately, bed bugs don't carry disease-causing germs). To minimize the outbreak, take the following steps immediately:

- **Confirm the infestation.** Make sure you're not dealing with some other pest, such as fleas. Because several kinds of insects resemble bed bugs, you'll need to capture a critter or two and study them. Go online for pictures, and compare your samples. If it looks like a bed bug, call an experienced pest control operator, pronto.

TIP
Bring in the pro. A can of Raid isn't going to do the job, and will end up costing you more in the long run. Depending on the size of the rental, expect to pay a total of anywhere between $300 and $2,500 for the initial service and follow-up treatments. If you find a company that offers to control bed bugs for a lowball amount like $50 per unit, get another bid.

- **Declutter, move the tenant out, exterminate, vacuum—and do it again.** Bed bugs thrive in clutter, so tenants must remove all items from closets, shelves, and drawers and wash all bedding and clothing in hot water. Put washed items in sealed plastic bags, then move the tenant out during treatment. Most of the time, tenants can return the same day. Upon return, the tenant—or you—must thoroughly vacuum. Exterminators might recommend a second and even a third treatment, with exhaustive cleaning and clutter removing in between.

Your insurance will probably not cover the cost of hiring a pest control company for bed bugs (nor for any other vermin or insect infestation). However, insurance might cover you for the tenant's claims for lost or damaged belongings, medical expenses, and related moving and living expenses, as well as your loss of rent. If your tenant has renters' insurance, suggest referring the matter to the insurance company.

No tenant is going to be happy to hear that you've had a past bed bug problem. Nevertheless, if a prospect questions you directly about bed bugs, especially if the issue is clearly of critical importance to the person, you must answer truthfully. Otherwise you risk the tenant's breaking the lease or suing you for damages. Even if you don't disclose, if you had a problem and it reappears, the tenant could still pursue these options, creating quite a headache for you. Also, some states such as Maine, specifically require landlords to disclose a history of bed bugs in the rental.

RESOURCE

Bed bug resources. Useful information on identifying and eradicating bed bugs is available on the EPA website at www.epa. gov/bedbugs and on www.techletter.com (maintained by a pest management consulting firm).

Keeping Tenants Safe: Liability for Crime

Even the safest neighborhoods have occasional incidents of crime, and depending on the circumstances, you could be held at least partially responsible for resulting tenant injuries and losses. For example, if you know about drug dealing on the sidewalk right in front of your rental property, you might have a duty to take steps to deal with it (starting with involving the police). Once again, preventive measures are your best response. Thankfully, the most successful prevention techniques—proper lighting and good locks, for example—are inexpensive. And they'll help you avoid the greater costs produced by actual incidents of crime, including increased insurance premiums and lost income due to rapid turnover.

Here are some suggestions to effectively and reasonably protect your tenants:

- **Meet or exceed basic legal requirements for safety devices.** Buy and maintain deadbolt locks, good lighting, and window locks, especially when they're required by state and local housing codes. (Ask your state or local housing agency or rental property owners' association.)

- **Respond to the environment.** Examine and research the vulnerability of your property and neighborhood. If your tenants will pay more rent if you make the building safer, you'd be foolish not to do it.

- **Tighten up management practices.** For example, strictly control who has a key to the property.

- **Educate your tenants about crime problems and prevention strategies.** Make it clear that they—not you—are primarily responsible for their protection. Explain what they can do to minimize the chances of assault or theft (avoid being alone on the street or in outside parking lots late at night). Also warn tenants of the limitations of the security measures you've put in place.

- **Don't hype your security measures.** You don't want to inadvertently promise a higher level of security than you're prepared to provide. Derek, who rents out a house in Atlanta that he inherited from his mother, learned this lesson the hard way: "I'd described the neighborhood as 'safe and secure,' and basically promised my new tenant that the security service hired by the homeowners' association was on duty 24/7. Guess what: The tenant got mugged at about 7 p.m. while walking his dog. Then I found out that the 'security service' consisted of an off-duty policeman making the rounds now and then. The tenant's lawyers argued that my tenant would never have ventured out if he'd known the true state of security, and I lost the case."

- **Deal with common security problems.** At the top of your list should be fixing burned-out exterior floodlights and broken locks (the top reason landlords are found liable for tenant injuries caused by criminals) and cutting back overgrown shrubbery that provides a convenient lurking spot for criminals. Also ask tenants for their suggestions about safety concerns, and quickly respond. If an important component of your security systems breaks, be prepared to fix it on an emergency basis and provide appropriate alternative security.

- **Purchase adequate liability insurance.** This will protect you from lawsuits related to crime on your rental property.

These steps will not only limit the likelihood of criminal activity on your property, but will also reduce the risk that you'll be found responsible if an assault or robbery does take place.

Protecting Neighbors From Illegal Tenant Activities

It shouldn't be your fault when tenants break the law. Yet, increasingly over the last decade, stricter laws and court decisions have made landlords liable when they fail to sufficiently address tenants' activities, especially ongoing illegal activities, such as drug dealing. Landlords have faced:

- **Nuisance lawsuits.** A legal "nuisance" is a pervasive, continuing, and serious condition—like a pile of garbage or group of drug dealers—that threatens public health, safety, or morals. Every state has a nuisance abatement law, which allows the government, and sometimes the neighbors, to fight back, often by court order and fines against the landlord. In some states, neighbors can sue in small claims court, seeking monetary compensation (each neighbor may sue for the maximum limit) and an order requiring the landlord to evict the troublemakers, install security, and repair the premises.

- **Property seizure.** Federal and state forfeiture proceedings— where the government takes your property because of the illegal activities of one or more tenants—are the most dramatic and devastating consequence of owning crime-ridden rental property. Forfeitures are relatively rare, but can be ordered on the basis of a single incident.

If you suspect that a tenant or potential tenant might be up to something illegal—or that you're being paid rent from ill-gotten gains—check out *Every Landlord's Legal Guide*, by Janet Portman, Marcia Stewart, and Ann O'Connell (Nolo) for advice on dealing with these situations.

TIP

Protect yourself, too. Take precautions for your own personal safety:

- **Promptly deposit rent checks and money orders.** If possible, do not accept cash.
- **When showing your property, bring someone with you.** If you must show the property alone, at least let someone know, and say when you expect to be done.
- **Go high tech.** Especially if the property is in a high-crime area, carry a cellphone and small alarm device (such as beeper-sized box that emits a piercing alarm when its pin is removed).

RESOURCE

More information on liability issues. The Landlord Liability section of Nolo.com includes useful articles on a landlord's liability for tenant injuries, environmental hazards, criminal activity on the rental property, and injuries caused by a tenant's dog.

Insurance Coverage for Property and Liability

After scaring you with everything you can be sued or otherwise held responsible for, here's a reason to breathe a sigh of relief: You can protect yourself from many problems by buying adequate insurance. A well-designed insurance policy can cover your rental property for both physical losses and people's injuries.

Getting adequate liability coverage

Commercial general liability coverage will reimburse for injuries or losses suffered by others as the result of defective conditions on your property or your carelessness, up to the limits of the policy. Equally important, it covers the cost of settling personal injury claims, including lawyers' bills for your defense.

For example, if your tenant gets injured falling down a defective staircase that you knew about, had a chance to fix, but failed to repair, your insurance company would handle any lawsuit or claim brought by the tenant and pay any settlement or award (again, within your policy limits). The same would be true if your tenant's child's playmate, over for the afternoon, drowned in the backyard pool that you'd failed to equip with a legally required antisuction device.

Liability policies usually state a dollar limit per occurrence and an aggregate dollar limit for the policy year. For example, your policy might say that it will pay $300,000 per occurrence for personal injury or a total of $1 million in any one policy year.

Depending on the value of your property and of your personal assets, buying even more coverage (called an "umbrella policy") is an excellent idea, especially if you're in a large metropolitan area where personal injury damage awards are likely to be high. Umbrella policies are not expensive. Don't put your property at risk of being sold to pay a court judgment!

When choosing liability coverage, consider buying a policy that covers not only physical injury claims, but also claims of libel, slander, discrimination, unlawful and retaliatory eviction, and invasion of privacy suffered by tenants and guests.

You can also suggest, and in most states you can require, that your tenant buy liability insurance as part of a renters' policy. Having a renters' policy in place will protect your own insurance. Here's how it works: Suppose the tenant starts a fire on the stove and burns the kitchen. Your own property insurance would cover the damage—but so would the tenant's insurance. If you require that the tenant's policy be "primary," (that is, applied first to any claim), you can insist that the tenant's carrier, not yours, cover the damage. You're always better off when you don't have to go to your carrier with a claim.

Getting adequate property coverage

Your property insurance should cover losses from a whole host of perils, such as damage from fire, storms, burglary, and vandalism. In negotiating coverage, there are five main questions to consider:

- **What features of the rental property are insured?** Be sure your insurance covers all the property you want protected, be it outdoor fixtures, appliances like washing machines, property used to maintain the house (such as gardening equipment and tools), personal property you're leaving in the house (for example, if it will be partially furnished), and personal business property such as computers.

> **TIP**
>
> **Make sure your tenants know that your insurance doesn't cover loss or damage to their personal property.** If a thief steals your tenants' jewelry or a fire damages their clothing and electronics, they're on their own. Your tenants will need to purchase their own renters' insurance to cover personal property losses—it's relatively affordable, at around $160 to $300 per year.

- **What perils will be insured against?** Coverage for damage caused by fire and smoke is common in the most basic policies. Standard policies also cover damage from wind, hail, lightning, explosions, volcanoes, riots and vandalism, theft, water damage (from burst pipes, for example), and similar events.

- **What perils will be excluded from coverage?** Damage from mudslides, windstorms, the weight of snow, police activity, power outages, sewer backups, dry rot, vermin, war, nuclear perils, losses if your house is vacant for 60 days or more, or losses caused by your own—or your tenant's—intentional or criminal actions, poor maintenance, or failure to preserve or protect the property after it's been damaged, are often excluded from standard policies.

Earthquake insurance on the house itself and flood insurance are typically separate. (They're usually expensive and have very high deductibles, but are still worthwhile if your building is highly susceptible to earthquake or flood damage.)

TIP

Check out "loss of rents" insurance. This will reimburse you for the lost rental income if your property is sidelined—for example, due to a fire or another calamity.

- **How much insurance should you buy?** While you don't want to waste money on pricey premiums, you should carry at least enough insurance on the building to rebuild it. There's no need to insure the total value of your real property (land and house), because land doesn't burn. If you're unsure how much it would cost to rebuild, get an appraiser's estimate. Be sure to get a rebuilding quote, not a quote on the sales value of the structure. Your insurance agent should be able to help you with this, and a local contractor might also provide useful advice on the cost of rebuilding your house in the current market.

  Look for insurance that covers "full replacement value" of your property, including legally required upgrades (requirements adopted since your house was constructed). Stay away from policies with "actual cash value coverage" (these pay only for the costs of replacing your house, minus any depreciation or wear and tear since it was built).

- **Is your house old enough that it will need code upgrades during reconstruction?** Building codes normally require that an older building be rebuilt to modern standards and codes, which is often much pricier than simply replacing it as it was. Ask for "ordinance or law coverage." It's almost never included in standard policies, but is worth paying a little extra for.

Converting your existing homeowners' policy

If you're an accidental landlord converting your own house to a rental, you might want to continue with your current insurance company. However, you can't just sit back and expect your homeowners' policy to remain in effect. Contact the insurer and ask that the policy be rewritten to fit your new role as a landlord. (Current industry practice is to actually split rental property insurance into two separate policies, one for property and one for liability.) If you don't change your coverage, your insurer could simply deny any of your later claims. Of course, you don't have to stick with your existing insurer—comparing prices is a fine idea, too.

> **TIP**
> **Buying a new home to live in?** You can save money, according to Mike Mansel, Certified Insurance Counselor, by "looking into using the same insurance company for both your rental property and your new home. That way the insurer can simply extend the liability portion of your homeowners' policy to the rental property—which will be less expensive than buying two separate liability policies. After that, you'll just need to buy a separate policy for the rental that leaves out liability coverage, also with the same company."

During the conversion, your insurer will reassess the level of risk regarding the property's structure. It might say that your property is now at higher risk of damage because of possible vacancies and because tenants tend to be harder on a property than a homeowner. Your rates could go up a bit for this part of the policy. However, your overall rates will probably go down, because you'll no longer need coverage for personal possessions (unless you're leaving a lot behind).

> **CAUTION**
> **Don't let your house sit empty for 60 to 90 days or more.**
> If you have a typical homeowners' policy, this will result in its being canceled. Check your policy to be sure, and talk to your insurance agent if you think this might become an issue.

Carefully compare your new and old policies before signing. You might discover that coverage you assumed would still be included is no longer there, but can be added in.

Working with your agent to get the best coverage

Not all insurance agents are created equal. Get recommendations from other landlords, or from real estate people with several years' experience. A good agent will listen to your needs and help you find a policy that addresses them, and will:

- **Analyze your business operations.** Steer clear of any agent who, without learning the specifics of your property and business, whips out a package policy and claims it will solve all your problems.

- **Make you feel comfortable discussing your needs.** While some policy buyers try to keep their rates down by downplaying areas of unusual risk, this is a bad idea. If you don't disclose all the facts, you might not get the coverage you need, or the insurance company could later try to deny you coverage because you misrepresented the nature of your operation.

- **Explain what's excluded.** Does the policy exclude damage from a leaking sprinkler system? From dog bites? From an earthquake? If so, and these are risks you face, find out whether they can be covered, and at what cost.

- **Represent only highly rated carriers.** Insurance companies are rated according to their financial condition and size. The most recognized rater is the A.M. Best Company, which assigns letter ratings according to financial strength (A++ is the highest) and Roman numeral ratings reflecting a company's financial size (XV is the best). Because 80% of American companies receive an A rating or higher, there's no reason to choose a company rated anything less. As to surplus, you'll be on solid ground requiring an "X." You'll find the *Best's Key Rating Guide* at AMBest.com.

Saving money on insurance

Few landlords can afford to adequately insure themselves against every possible risk. Here are some guidelines to help you keep costs down:

- **Set priorities.** Ask yourself: What types of property losses would threaten the viability of my business? What kinds of liability lawsuits might wipe me out? Tailor your coverage to protect against these potentially disastrous losses. Get enough property and liability coverage to protect yourself from the most common claims, adding coverage for serious risks where it's reasonably priced.

- **Select a high deductible.** The deductible is the amount you must pay out of pocket before insurance coverage kicks in. The cost difference between a policy with a $250 deductible and one with a $500 or $1,000 or even higher deductible is significant— particularly if you add up the premium savings for five or ten years. Consider using the money you save to buy coverage you would have otherwise gone without, such as for loss of rents.

- **Reduce your risk.** Good safety and security measures, such as regular property inspections, special fire prevention measures, adding deadbolt locks, or requiring that tenants buy renters' insurance, might eliminate the need for some types of insurance or lead to lower rates or discounts. Also ask your insurance agent what you can do to get a better rate.

- **Comparison shop.** No two companies charge exactly the same rates. But be wary of an unusually low price, which could be a sign of a shaky company. Or it might be that you're unfairly comparing policies that provide very different types of coverage. Make sure you know what you're buying, and review your coverage and rates periodically.

RESOURCE
For more information on choosing business insurance:
See the Insurance Information Institute's website at www.III.org. ●

Living in Perfect Harmony?
Dealing With Difficult Tenants

Despite your careful screening, you're bound to eventually encounter a less-than-perfect tenant: one who's chronically late with the rent, disturbs the neighbors with loud parties or a constant stream of visitors, or brings in a dog without your permission. Whatever the problem, you'll want to know how to resolve it quickly, with minimum hassle or expense.

In this chapter, we'll help you figure out how to deal with difficult tenants and enforce the terms of your lease or rental agreement. We'll cover:

- common tenant problems and what to do about them
- different methods for resolving disputes, and
- how to evict a tenant, if that becomes necessary.

> **TIP**
> **Lesson learned the hard way: It's not my house anymore.** Amy, who rents out her former home in Austin, Texas, while she attends graduate school out of state, says, "After my first set of tenants left, I discovered that they'd painted all the rooms different colors and that their dogs, which I hadn't known about, had destroyed the backyard and the storm door. That was crushing—I still felt like it was my house."

Common Tenant Problems— And What to Do About Them

Most tenant problems boil down to a few common and recurring themes. Here, we'll cover some of the problems you're likely to encounter, and how you might wish to approach them. Later in the chapter, we'll explain specific negotiating strategies, as well as how to legally get a tenant to leave.

Late rent

While being a day or two late every once in awhile shouldn't be a reason to evict—especially if it's an otherwise reliable tenant—you probably do want to enforce on-time payments. This will help show that you're serious about this business relationship and avoid reinforcing late-payment habits.

The first time rent is late, simply call the tenant and make sure the payment didn't get lost, forgotten, or misplaced. If the tenant apologizes profusely and pays you immediately—especially a tenant with a history of on-time payments—you might have nothing more to worry about. The next time it happens, however, you should probably invoke the late-fee clause in your lease or rental agreement.

> 💡 **TIP**
> **Enforce your right to the late fee.** Your tenant might decide to pay the rent, but not the fee. If you're thinking, "I'll take it out of the security deposit," check your state's laws first—might forbid this practice. Instead, if your lease or rental agreement says that the fee is considered "additional rent," you'll be able to use a "pay or quit" notice to demand the late fee, and you can begin eviction proceedings if the tenant doesn't pay the fee (or move). If your rental document doesn't describe the fee as additional rent, you'll have to sue in small claims court to get it—hardly a worthwhile task to pursue such a small amount.

If the tenant promises to send a check soon but doesn't, fails to respond to your call, or says "Sorry, I can't make the payment," your next step will probably be to send a termination notice (often called a notice to pay or quit). This notice should explain that the tenant must pay rent within a designated time or move out. If the tenant doesn't comply, you can file an eviction lawsuit. (Proper termination notices and evictions are covered later in this chapter.)

Nip Security Deposit Deductions in the Bud

At the end of your tenant's lease, you'll get inside the rental to assess its condition. You can fairly deduct from the security deposit those sums needed to remedy damage beyond normal wear and tear and any cleaning needed to restore the unit to its level of cleanliness at move-in.

But don't wait until then to take a look around. You might want to have a look mid-lease, to make sure minor problems don't develop into big ones, and to educate your tenants as to what to expect when they move out. As Stuart, with property in Davis, California, says, "No matter how clearly we try to explain security deposits in advance, each time the lease is up and I inspect the place, the tenants' mouths drop at the deductions. They always seem to think the security deposit is just for rent, not for cleaning."

If you want to do a mid-lease inspection, follow your state's rules regarding landlord entry, giving the required amount of notice and scheduling the visit for an agreed-upon day and time. When you find a problem—a hole in the wall, stained carpets—decide whether to fix it now or later (maybe it will be just as efficient to clean the carpets in six months, when the tenants leave).

Who pays? As long as the problem is one for which you could legitimately use the security deposit, you can demand that the tenants pay directly, or you may use the deposit. If you use the deposit, be sure to demand, in writing, that the tenants replenish the deposit. Their failure to do so would be grounds for terminating the lease.

Breaking the lease early

A lease obligates you and the tenant for its entire term. But tenants' life circumstances don't always cooperate, and you'll likely encounter at some point a tenant who needs or wants to break the lease and move out early. Sometimes, their leave-taking is recognized by the law as a permissible tenant remedy (for example, when the landlord refuses to repair a problem that makes the rental unfit). But more often, a tenant's desire to leave is prompted by love, a job, school, or the prospect of a better deal somewhere else.

What can you do about it? If you suspect that the tenant is about to split, have a conversation. Together, you might be able to address an underlying issue, such as the tenant's fear that you won't change your no-pets rule to make room for a new puppy. Or maybe the tenant is leaving because you haven't held up your end of a bargain—by failing to repair a leaky roof, for example—in which case, you might negotiate a last chance to do your part. (By the way, if that tenant leaves for such a reason, you won't be able to ask for rent on the balance of the lease.)

But suppose the tenant is departing for purely personal reasons, and you can't work something out. Now, you're faced with a vacancy you weren't prepared for. The tenant is still responsible for the balance of the rent left on the lease, but that's not the end of the story. In most states, you must take reasonably prompt steps to rent the unit again. Once it's rented, your former tenant's liability for the balance ends.

Other violations of the lease or rental agreement

Even rent-paying tenants are frequently known to violate important terms of the lease or rental agreement. Here are some of the most common violations, and what steps to take before terminating the agreement:

- **Moving in a pet.** If your agreement specifically forbids pets, or limits them to a certain type of pet, but your tenant moves one in anyway, you must decide whether you're willing to allow it. You might decide to ignore your rule if the tenant is reliable, the pet appears well-behaved, and you have not promised other tenants in a multifamily building that the property will be pet-free. Sometimes, it's not worth the bother of forcing the tenant to get rid of the animal or move out. However, if you decide to let the pet stay, you should amend your rental agreement to reflect it, and you might want to increase the security deposit or require an additional "pet deposit" (check your state's security deposit laws to find out whether you're allowed to charge additional sums or separate pet deposits). Also remember that certain types of animals—namely nondomestic pets, such as monkeys and certain dog breeds—might heighten your legal liability. Talk to your insurance company to find out, and for more information on liability, see Chapter 8.

> **TIP**
> **Best thing I ever did: Build a fence.** Stuart thought his tenant was bringing only one dog—a small, sweet pit bull. But, he says, "Then a friend joined them, who had other pit bulls—which were not so sweet or friendly. The neighbor, who has some small dogs, started complaining, afraid that the tenants' dogs would eat hers. But the pit bulls hadn't actually done anything wrong, and if I kicked out the tenants I wasn't likely to get replacement ones for a few months. So I went up and built a reinforced chain-link fence. That kept the neighbor satisfied."

- **Moving in other occupants.** A new boyfriend or girlfriend, an out-of-town buddy who's job hunting—any of these people might have the tenant saying, "Sure, stay as long as you like," without remembering your rental terms. But your lease or rental agreement should prohibit tenants from moving in additional occupants without your consent—other than the occasional short-term personal (that is, not Airbnb) guest, or a new spouse or child, whom you probably can't legally refuse. If you suspect that someone has moved in, talk with the tenant. If you're inclined to allow the new occupant to stay, you still need to go through the same formal screening steps you took when selecting your original tenant. If you don't want to accept the newcomer, or your screening turns up red flags, you can demand that the person leave. Depending on your state's law, you might need to give your original tenant a "cure or quit" termination notice, which offers two choices: Either get rid of the unauthorized occupant or move out.

TIP
You can terminate any month-to-month tenancy with proper notice (30 days in most states). You needn't give a reason, as long as your motives aren't discriminatory or retaliatory. Note, however, that tenants in rentals covered by "just-cause" eviction protection laws (rent control), and all tenants in New Hampshire and New Jersey (which have statewide just-cause protections) might be able to resist a termination when the landlord can't provide a justifiable reason.

- **Illegal subleasing.** Instead of moving others in, the tenant might simply move out, either permanently or temporarily, and have a newcomer (a "subtenant") move in without asking your consent. You might find out what's happening when you see a new name on the rent checks. If you're willing to allow the arrangement, you can do so—but should first do careful screening, and create a direct legal relationship with the subtenant. With a permanent subtenant, terminate the original lease and sign a new one (the subtenant now becomes your tenant). With a temporary subtenant, you can write a sublease signed by all three of you, which will expire on the agreed-upon date. If you prefer not to consider the subtenant at all, or you find the subtenant unacceptable, you can refuse your consent and, if the newcomer moves in anyway, begin eviction procedures.

- **Excessive noise.** Some degree of noise is normal, but a tenant's loud parties, blaring music, or early morning carpentry projects can disturb neighbors and others. You'll want to act immediately to put a stop to the problem. First, point out any clauses in your lease or rental agreement prohibiting excessive noise. Even without a written provision, talk to the tenant immediately if you hear a complaint, then follow up with a warning letter if it isn't resolved. Not taking action could lead to legal troubles like code citations or lawsuits brought by those affected by the noise. In fact, if your rental property has other tenants, they have a legally enforceable right to quiet enjoyment of the premises.

RESOURCE
For more information on state and local noise laws, visit the Noise Pollution Clearinghouse's website, at www.nonoise.org/lawlib.htm.

Of course, there are plenty of other lease or rental agreement terms that your tenant could violate. Your state's law will most likely insist that you give the tenant a few days (anywhere from three to ten days is common) to correct, or "cure," a lease or rental agreement violation. You would do this using a cure or quit notice—that is, telling the tenant to fix the problem or leave. However, there are two important "but ifs" that would allow you to use the less generous "unconditional quit" notice:

- **Repeated violations.** In some states, if the tenant has violated the same lease clause two or more times within a certain period of time, the tenant might lose the right to a second chance.

- **A violation that can't be corrected.** Some lease violations have a permanent—and therefore incurable—effect. For instance, if your lease prohibits tenant alterations without your consent, and your tenant nevertheless removes the living room wallpaper, you can hardly demand that the tenant cease violating the lease clause. It's simply too late to save the wallpaper.

Past criminal convictions

Although you're generally free to reject prospective tenants with criminal records, you won't necessarily find out about these convictions until you've already rented the unit. At that point, your first impulse might be to look for a way to get the tenant out of your building, particularly if the conviction is for a recent, violent crime. With a month-to-month tenant, it's easiest to just give the regular, required amount of notice to move out. (But there's an exception if the conviction was for drug use, and the tenant is currently not using illegal drugs. Such a tenant is protected from termination under federal fair housing laws.)

TIP

Your tenant-screening report might not have told you everything. "I ordered a background report on a prospective tenant," said Alex, a landlord in Cleveland. "It came back clean—but luckily I didn't stop there. When talking to a prior landlord, I learned that this guy had been convicted of a drug sale, though he didn't end up serving time. That's probably why the report didn't include the conviction. But with that information, I denied the application."

If your tenant has a lease, and is otherwise law- and rule-abiding, you won't be able to terminate the agreement just because you now know about the criminal record, no matter how unsavory or alarming. But it's a different story if your lease or rental agreement states that false or incomplete material information on the rental application will be grounds for termination. In that case, you can take steps to terminate the tenancy and evict. Surveys show that almost half of landlords have had to evict a tenant at some point.

Violations of a tenant's basic legal responsibilities

Virtually every state allows you to end the tenancy of a tenant who has violated basic responsibilities imposed by law. Violations might include grossly deficient housekeeping practices that cause an unhealthy situation, like allowing garbage to pile up; seriously misusing appliances, like defrosting the freezer with an ice pick; or substantially damaging the property, perhaps by knocking holes in the walls.

The obligations to keep the property liveable and to refrain from damaging it should already be set out in your leases or rental agreements. But even if they're not, tenants are still legally bound to observe them.

If a tenant or guest substantially damages the premises, you'll be within your rights to use an unconditional quit notice. The law does not require you to give tenants accused of serious misbehavior a second chance. Tenants who have earned this type of termination notice generally get only five to ten days (it varies by state) to move out.

Tenant's illegal activity on the premises

In recent years, many states have made it easier for landlords to evict tenants for dealing drugs or other illegal activities. You don't always have to wait until the tenant is convicted of a crime or even arrested—you might be able to evict based on your fact-based suspicion that illegal activity is afoot. But first, check your state's law to learn what level of proof you'll need to support this termination.

Evictions based on criminal activity are often called "expedited evictions," because they take less time than a normal eviction. Expedited evictions are preceded by an unconditional quit notice that tells the tenant to move out (and do it quickly). If the tenant stays, you can go to court and file for eviction. The court hearing on the eviction is typically held within a few days, and, if you win, the physical removal occurs within a very short time.

Resolving Disputes

If you have a problem tenant who won't listen to reason, but eviction doesn't seem like your best option (or perhaps you don't have solid legal grounds for it), there are other means for settling your dispute. Here are some ideas.

Try to negotiate a settlement

Because fighting a court battle costs time and money, you're almost always better off trying to settle disputes out of court before filing a lawsuit. Your goal should be to achieve the best result at the lowest cost. If you decide to sue based on your conviction or principle (whether right or wrong), chances are you'll spend far too much time and money.

Your first step in working toward a compromise with a problem tenant is to arrange a time to meet. Dropping over unannounced to talk is typically not a good idea, because the tenant might feel threatened and react defensively.

Try writing a letter or email in which you offer to meet with the tenant to work something out—it's a good way to let the tenant know you want to settle the matter. Here are some negotiating pointers:

- **Ask to hear the tenant's point of view.** Once the tenant starts talking, listen closely and don't interrupt.

- **Acknowledge hearing key points, even if you disagree with them.** Sometimes it's even a good idea to repeat the tenant's concerns, to demonstrate that you know what they are.

- **Avoid personal attacks.** This only raises the level of hostility and makes settlement more difficult.

- **Be courteous, but not weak.** Let the tenant know you have the resources and evidence to fight and win if you can't reach a settlement.

- **If possible, try to structure the negotiation as a mutual attempt to solve a problem.** For example, if a tenant's guests have been disturbing the neighbors, brainstorm solutions that might allow the tenant to still have guests, while limiting the noise and other impacts on the neighbors.

- **Put yourself in the tenant's shoes.** What would you want to get out of the settlement? Let the tenant have at least a partial sense of victory.

- **When you propose settlement terms, make it clear that you're compromising.** Offers of settlement (clearly labeled as such) can't be introduced against you if you ever end up in court.

- **For a powerful incentive, try money.** To avoid later costs, be willing to pay—perhaps by reducing rent for a short period, lowering the amount owed for damages to the premises, or offering an outright cash settlement for the tenant to leave (with payment made only when the tenant hands you the keys). Many tenants will settle at a surprisingly low figure if they can walk away from the bargaining table a little richer.

- **If you reach an understanding, promptly write it down and have all parties sign it.** You or your lawyer should volunteer to prepare the first draft. If you're paying the tenant some money as part of your agreement, make sure the tenant acknowledges in writing that your payment fully satisfies the claim.

Send a warning notice

Giving the tenant a written notice to cease the disruptive activity can be effective. Even if your oral warning or attempts to negotiate have been unsuccessful, people tend to take written notices a bit more seriously.

Your letter should include:

- details of the problem behavior, including dates and times of the occurrence
- what exactly you want the tenant to do (such as stop having noisy parties, pay for damage to the rental unit, or get rid of a long-term guest)
- the specific lease or rental agreement provision that prohibits this behavior, such as a clause requiring tenants to repair damaged property, or a lease restriction on guests, and
- the consequences for the tenant's failure to comply (such as termination or eviction proceedings).

TIP

Involve the cosigner when you send your warning notice. Jim, who rented to three college students in Boston, insisted that each student's parents cosign the lease. When Jim learned that the students had brought in two unauthorized occupants, he wrote to them, pointing out that their lease forbade unapproved residents; and he cc'd their parents. That did the trick. "Once the parents realized that they could be financially responsible for damage caused by these newcomers, they apparently got on the phone, and the newcomers were gone within a couple of days."

What if the tenant doesn't reform, despite your reminder? If you want to get the tenant out, you certainly have grounds for terminating. However, in a sense, you'll have to start over, by giving the tenant a formal termination notice that meets your state's requirements. (Termination notices are explained further, below.)

Try mediation

If your settlement efforts don't work out, you might wish to try bringing in a neutral third party to mediate. Mediation is often available at little or no cost from a publicly funded program. A mediator has no power to impose a decision, but simply helps both sides work out a mutually acceptable solution.

Mediation can make good sense, especially if any of the following are true:

- You've had otherwise positive experiences with the tenant, who seems worth dealing with in the future.
- The tenant agrees to split the cost (if any) of mediation.
- The tenant wants to avoid eviction and the expense and delay of litigation.
- The tenant is up to date on rent (or has cooperated by putting the rent money into some type of escrow account).

Mediation in landlord-tenant disputes is usually fairly informal. The mediator will ordinarily have everyone sit down and express all their issues—even emotional ones. This often cools people off and results in a quick compromise. If not, however, the mediator might talk to each person separately to try and determine each party's bottom line. Then, shuttling back and forth, the mediator helps everyone structure an acceptable solution. At some point, the group gathers to sign off on the written settlement agreement.

RESOURCE

Need information on local mediation programs? Call your mayor's or city manager's office, and ask for the staff member who handles "landlord-tenant mediation matters" or "housing disputes." That person should refer you to the public office or business or community group that attempts to resolve these disputes informally, and at little or no cost. Most local courts also provide referrals to community mediation services. For lists of professional mediators and extensive information on mediation, see Mediate.com.

Represent yourself in small claims court

If your attempts at settling a dispute fail, you might end up having to sue. Fortunately, if the dispute is over a relatively small amount of money (less than $10,000 in most states), you can cost-efficiently represent yourself in small claims court. A few states call small claims courts by other names (such as landlord-tenant court), but the purpose is the same: to provide a speedy, inexpensive resolution of disputes. In a few states, eviction suits can also be filed in small claims court.

Small claims court procedures are relatively simple and don't normally require a lawyer's help. You pay a small fee, file your lawsuit with the court clerk, have the papers served on your opponent, show up on the appointed day, tell the judge your story, and present any witnesses and other evidence. The evidence you bring with you is usually the most important part of your case—for example, photographs or a video of a damaged house and the convincing testimony of someone who helped you fix it are usually all you need to prevail and recover money over and above the tenant's deposit.

Don't immediately head for small claims court just because it's relatively easy and you're sure you have a good case. If you suspect you won't be able to collect the money owed—from your tenant's paycheck, bank account, or other financial resource—small claims court will be a waste of time. A judgment you can't collect is worthless.

Avoiding Retaliation Charges

Tenants have a number of legal rights, such as the right to complain to governmental authorities about health or safety problems or the right to be free from illegal discrimination. To ensure that these rights protect tenants, most states forbid landlords from retaliating against tenants who assert them.

A tenant who is trying to avoid eviction or legal liability might claim your legitimate actions are retaliatory. To counter such claims:

- Create a paper trail documenting important facts of your relationship. For example, set up clear, easy-to-follow procedures for tenants to ask for repairs, and respond promptly.

- Demonstrate that you have a good reason to end the tenancy. In other words, be prepared to prove that your reasons were valid and not retaliatory.

- Have legitimate business reasons for any rent increase or other change in the conditions of the tenancy, and make the changes reasonable. Although you might not legally need a reason to increase the rent (unless you live in a rent-controlled area), if you have no plausible business reason for your actions—such as evidence that local rents have risen—you'll have a harder time countering a tenant's claim that the increase was illegal.

- Consider the timing of your actions: If a tenant files a complaint with a government agency just before you were going to raise the rent or give the month- to-month tenant a termination notice anyway, wait. In some states, if a landlord's negative act occurs within a certain time from the date of a tenant's complaint, the landlord will have a harder time countering the claim of retaliation. Wait until that time period is up.

RESOURCE
For more information on small claims court, see the Small Claims Court & Lawsuits section of Nolo.com, which includes a chart of small claims court limits and rules for all 50 states, plus useful articles on preparing your case and testifying in court.

When All Else Fails: Terminations and Evictions

Unfortunately, even the most sincere and professional attempts at resolving disputes fail, and you need to get rid of a troublesome tenant. A key step in winning an eviction lawsuit (sometimes called an unlawful detainer, or UD, lawsuit) is properly terminating the tenancy before you go to court. If you don't strictly adhere to all applicable termination procedures, you can't proceed with your lawsuit, let alone get a judgment for possession of your property or for unpaid rent. In order to properly terminate, you must give your tenant adequate written notice, in the manner and form specified by your state or local laws. If, after receiving the termination notice, the tenant doesn't move (or cure the issue), you can file a lawsuit to evict.

The hard reality of evictions is that they can result in people not having a roof over their heads. For this reason, state and local termination and eviction laws are usually very demanding of landlords. Each state, and many localities, have their own procedures for drafting and delivering ("serving") termination notices. Different types of notices are often required for different situations. You must follow the rules and procedures exactly. Otherwise, you'll run into delays in evicting the tenant—and might even lose your lawsuit—no matter how prolific your tenant's violations.

Even when you have extremely solid reasons for evicting, you should prepare for the tenant to mount a defense—and possibly win. For one thing, the way that you've conducted business with the tenant might affect the outcome. For example, if the tenant can make even a slightly halfway believable argument about your actions being inappropriately motivated by a desire to retaliate, the argument might shift attention away from the tenant's own wrongdoing and sour your chances of victory.

Eviction itself—that is, physically removing tenants and their possessions from your property—can't be done until you've gone to court, won the eviction suit, and received an order of removal from the court. And even then, you can't just move the tenant's stuff out onto the sidewalk and say goodbye. In most states, you must hire the sheriff, marshal, or other designated law enforcement personnel to perform those tasks.

Sending termination notices

Terminating a month-to-month tenancy is, in theory, easy: Simply give the proper amount of notice (30 days in most states). You don't usually need to give a reason (unless your property is covered by rent control). For a tenancy governed by a lease, you'll have to wait until it expires on its own at the end of the lease term. You ordinarily aren't required to renew a lease.

But if your tenant has done something wrong, you might not want to wait the 30 days or until the lease expires. State laws allow you to terminate by serving the tenant with one of three different types of notices. Although terminology varies somewhat from state to state, the substance of these notices is remarkably the same. Most states set standards for the content and look of a termination notice, requiring certain language and specifying the size and appearance of type:

- **Pay rent or quit notices.** These notices are typically used when the tenant hasn't paid the rent. They give the tenant a few days to pay or move out ("quit").

- **Cure or quit notices.** Use these to terminate when a tenant violates a term or condition of the lease or rental agreement, such as a no-pets clause or the promise to refrain from making excessive noise. Typically, the tenant has a set amount of time in which to correct, or "cure," the violation; a tenant who fails to do so must move or face an eviction lawsuit.

- **Unconditional quit notices.** This is the harshest type of termination notice. It orders the tenant to vacate the premises with no chance to pay the rent or correct the lease or rental agreement violation. In most states, unconditional quit notices are allowed only when the tenant has repeatedly violated a lease or rental agreement clause, has been chronically late with the rent, has seriously damaged the premises, or has engaged in illegal activity.

Many states have all three types of notices on the books. But in some states, unconditional quit notices are the only notice statutes on the books. This means that you are free to give your tenants a number of days to pay up, fix the problem, or cease the violation, but you don't have to—you can demand that they leave without giving them a second chance.

Terminating for late rent payments

Not surprisingly, the top reason landlords terminate a tenancy is nonpayment of rent. In most states, this is grounds for immediately sending a termination notice, giving the tenant a few days—usually three to five—to pay up. The exact number of days varies from state to state. In some states, you don't even need to give the tenant a chance to pay up, but can go straight to using an unconditional quit notice.

> **CAUTION**
> **Make sure you know your state rules as to the earliest date you can serve a termination notice.** Some states won't let you send a termination notice of any kind until the rent is a certain number of days late. These states essentially give tenants a statutory "grace period," plus the time specified in the pay rent or quit notice (if applicable), in which to come up with the rent. (In most states, you also have the option of providing for a grace period in your lease or rental agreement.)

If the tenant is late with the rent and you deliver a termination notice—whether or not it gives the tenant a few days to pay the rent—expect a phone call, an email, or a visit from your tenant, hoping to work something out. If you accept rent for the entire rental term, you have canceled the termination notice for that period. In most states, it's as if the tenant had paid on time in the first place.

After all this, what if the tenant is late again with the rent? Check your state's law. In several states, you don't have to give such tenants a second chance—or at least not a third chance, within a certain time period.

If you accept even a partial amount of rent owed—whether for past months or even just the current month—you will, in most states, cancel the effect of a termination notice. But you can still go ahead with your attempts to get the tenant out—just pocket your tenant's payment with one hand and hand over a new termination notice with the other, demanding that the tenant pay the new balance or leave.

CAUTION

If your tenant is in the military or the activated reserves, special rules apply. Federal law (the War and National Defense Servicemembers Civil Relief Act) requires a court to stay (postpone) an eviction for up to three months unless the judge decides that military service does not materially affect the tenant's ability to pay the rent. The law applies only to evictions for nonpayment of rent, not for other reasons, such as keeping pets in violation of the lease. Nor does it apply if you've terminated a rental agreement with a 30-day notice.

How eviction lawsuits work

When the deadline in the termination notice passes, your tenant is supposed to pack up and leave. Unfortunately, that doesn't always happen. Once the deadline to move out has passed, you cannot just call the police and have them escort the person out. Instead, you must file and win an eviction lawsuit. The resulting court order will give you the right to call a sheriff or marshal and arrange to physically evict a tenant who refuses to leave. The whole process can take weeks—or months—depending on whether the tenant contests the eviction in court.

Eviction lawsuits are filed in a formal trial court (called "municipal," "county," or "justice") or (in some states) small claims court. A few states and larger cities have separate landlord-tenant courts specifically set up to handle evictions. In some areas, landlords can choose the court in which to file suit; others confine eviction lawsuits to only one court. Call the clerk of your local small claims court to find out whether it handles evictions.

If small claims is an option, it's usually best for an eviction, because of its speed and simple procedures. And, if you want to (or if the court doesn't allow attorneys), you can limit your expense by going to court without a lawyer. Your main job will be to gather evidence to persuade the court to believe your side of the story. But, if lawyers are allowed in small claims court in your state, you might want to use one. As described just below, eviction lawsuits are rather tricky, so it might be more effective to hire a pro. (By the way, you can always consult with an attorney; what some states don't allow is for litigants to actually bring lawyers to small claims court to present cases.)

If small claims court isn't an option, you'll have even more reason to hire a lawyer. Regular court is far more complex, with more rules about what kind of evidence can be submitted, and more procedural steps to get to a resolution.

RESOURCE
Nolo's Lawyer Directory can help you find an attorney who's right for you. Nolo's profiles provide in-depth information about each attorney's experience, qualifications, and personal approach to practicing law. See www.nolo.com/lawyers for details.

To get an eviction lawsuit going (in any court), you'll usually have to follow these steps:

- **File a complaint.** This legal document lists the facts that you think justify the eviction. It also asks the court to order the tenant to leave the property and pay any back rent, any damages directly caused by having unlawfully remained on the property, court costs, and possibly attorneys' fees. Your complaint doesn't need to be long or complex—in fact, in many states, landlords use a preprinted complaint form, prepared by the court. Check the court's website to see if you can download the forms you need, or contact the court's clerk to obtain copies.

- **Serve the tenant.** When you file a complaint, the clerk will assign a date on which the case will be heard by the court. That date is entered on the "summons," a piece of paper that tells the tenant about the lawsuit, and informs the tenant about answering your charges in writing and appearing in court within a specified number of days. The summons states that failure to follow the directions in the summons or to answer the complaint might result in the tenant losing the lawsuit. You must then arrange for the tenant to be given the complaint and the summons. In legal jargon, this is called "service of process." State laws are quite detailed as to the proper way to deliver, or "serve," court papers. Most critically, neither you (including anyone who has an ownership interest in your business) nor your employees (if you have any) can serve these papers. The method of delivery is specified as well: Normally, the preferred way is "personal" service, which means that a law enforcement officer or professional process server personally hands the tenant the papers. Failure to properly serve the tenant is one of the most common errors landlords make, and can result in court dismissal of your lawsuit before trial. Even a seemingly minor mistake—such as forgetting to check a box on a legal form, checking one you shouldn't, or filling in contradictory information—will increase the chances of your tenant's successfully contesting the lawsuit.

- **The tenant answers.** The tenant must typically file a document called an "answer" on or before the date printed on the summons. (If the tenant doesn't, and then doesn't show up in court, the court will usually issue a default judgment in your favor, meaning you win the lawsuit automatically.) Like your complaint, the answer need not be a complex document, and might be a preprinted form. In the answer, the tenant can dispute the truth of the statements in your complaint. Alternatively, the tenant might try to put forth a good legal reason (such as discrimination or retaliation) to excuse what would otherwise be grounds for eviction. This is called an affirmative defense.

Tips on Dealing With a Tenant During an Eviction

To keep things businesslike:

- Avoid all unnecessary personal contact with the tenant during the eviction process unless it occurs in a structured setting, such as a mediation.
- Keep your written communications to the point and as neutral as you can.
- Until the day the sheriff or marshal shows up to evict, the tenant's home is legally his or her castle. Don't treat the tenant like someone who doesn't have a right to be on the property until this point.

Once you're done with these preliminaries, your lawsuit will proceed. Many eviction cases never end up in trial—for example, because the tenant moves out or negotiates a settlement with the landlord. But each case that does go to trial will have its own unpredictable twists and turns, which can greatly affect trial preparation and tactics. For this reason, you'll probably need to hire a lawyer, if you haven't done so already.

How Tenants Can Stop or Postpone an Eviction

In rare instances, tenants might be able to get a judge to stop an eviction that's already been ordered by convincing the court of two things:

- Eviction would cause a severe hardship for the tenant or the tenant's family.
- The tenant is willing and able to pay any back rent owed (and your lawsuit costs and expenses) and future rent, as well.

It's very unusual for a judge to stop an eviction—after all, if the tenant's sympathetic predicament (and sufficient monetary reserves) weren't persuasive enough to win the case in the first place, these arguments probably won't be given new weight after the trial. The tenant might instead ask for a postponement of the eviction. Typically, courts postpone evictions only in the following situations:

- **While an appeal is pending.** A tenant who files an appeal can ask the trial judge to postpone ("stay") the eviction until a higher court decides the case.
- **When the tenant demonstrates a specific need.** For example, a tenant might be able to persuade a judge that special, personal circumstances (such as a recent job loss) warrant allowing the tenant a little more time to find a new home.
- **When the weather makes evictions difficult.** In most states, judges are not required to postpone an eviction on frigid days, but there's nothing to stop a tenant from asking.

> CAUTION
> **Complete your lawsuit, even if you think you've won already.**
> Never walk away from a lawsuit without formally ending it, even if the
> tenant moves out or pays what's owed without going to court. Doing
> so preserves your reputation as someone who uses the courts with
> respect. If you're simply a no-show, expect a chilly reception the next
> time you appear in court. In addition, if you don't appear for trial but
> the tenant does, the tenant might win, and the court might order you
> to allow the tenant to move back in and pay the tenant's court costs
> and attorneys' fees.

Eviction lawsuits are typically decided on the spot or very soon after
the judge has heard the witnesses and reviewed any relevant laws. If
you win, you get an order from the judge (a "judgment") declaring that
you're entitled to possession of the property. You might get a money
judgment for back rent, court costs, and attorneys' fees, too.

You'll need to take the order to the local law enforcement official,
along with the appropriate fee, which the tenant will be expected to pay
back as part of your costs. The sheriff or marshal will give the tenant a
notice saying that the official will be back, sometimes within just a few
days, to physically remove the tenant if necessary.

Unfortunately, having a judgment for the payment of money isn't
the same as having the money itself. Your tenant might be unable (or
unwilling) to pay you, despite the fact that you have a formal court
order. Unless the tenant voluntarily pays up, you will have to collect the
debt—for example, by using the tenant's security deposit or hiring a
collection agency.

If you lose the eviction case, your tenant can stay, and you'll likely end
up paying for your tenant's court costs and fees. You might also be hit
with money damages if the judge decides you acted illegally, as in the
case of discrimination or retaliation.

How not to evict: Illegal "self-help"

As any experienced landlord will attest, there are occasional tenants who do things so outrageous that the landlord is tempted to bypass normal legal protections and take direct and immediate action to protect the property. For example, one landlord with whom we spoke said, "Out of desperation, I asked two tough-looking, armed friends of mine to come over and tell the tenant it was long past time to go."

Don't do anything like this. Shortcuts such as threats, intimidation, utility shutoffs, or attempts to physically remove a tenant are illegal and dangerous. Today, virtually every state forbids these "self-help" evictions. If you resort to them, you will likely find yourself on the other end of a lawsuit.

Even if your state hasn't legislated against self-help evictions, throwing your tenant out on your own is dangerous, and could land you in more legal entanglements than if you had filed an eviction suit in the first place. The potential for nastiness and violence is great; the last thing you want is a patrol car at the curb while you and your tenant wrestle on the lawn. And you can almost count on a lawsuit over the "disappearance" of your tenant's valuable possessions, which the tenant will claim were lost or taken when you removed them. Using a neutral law enforcement officer to enforce a judge's eviction order prevents these problems.

RESOURCE

Finding your state's laws and resources on terminations, evictions, mediation, and lawsuits. The Evicting a Tenant or Ending a Lease area of the Landlords section of Nolo.com includes many state-by-state articles and charts on topics covered in this chapter, including state rules on termination for nonpayment of rent or violation of a lease term, tenants' rights to break a lease, illegal eviction procedures, notice requirements to terminate a month-to-month tenancy, and security deposit disputes in small claims court. The Small Claims Court & Lawsuits section of the Nolo site includes useful articles on mediation, filing a lawsuit, and working with a lawyer. You can also find a list of landlord-tenant lawyers in your state in Nolo's online Lawyer Directory. ●

Don't Want to Do It Alone?
Hiring a Property Manager

Being a landlord can, at times, turn into a busy job. In the words of Sarah, a San Francisco landlord who rents out half her duplex, "You don't get something for nothing." If your time is already stretched super-thin, you might consider getting help. Fortunately, lots of people make it their business to work as a stand-in rental property owner—they're property managers, and if you find the right one, your rental business will get a lot simpler.

A property manager normally focuses on renting and maintaining property, by handling tasks from finding and screening tenants to maintaining the property to getting it cleaned after a tenant moves out. Of course, there's a catch: Property managers normally charge setup and monthly fees for their services, plus extra for additional tasks you want handled such as terminations or evictions.

In this chapter, we'll help you decide whether paying to hire a property manager is right for you, by explaining:

- what a property manager does
- when hiring a property manager makes the most financial sense
- how to find and choose a property manager, and
- what to include in your signed agreement with a property manager.

What a Professional Property Manager Does

Depending on what's in your contract with the property manager (covered in "Put It in Writing: Drafting an Agreement with Your Property Manager," below), these are some tasks you'll be able to offload, for a set fee or as extras:

- **Setting the rental price.** Although the final figure will be up to you, a good property manager should research the going rate for local rentals like yours. Setting a realistic rental price will help keep vacancies low and your income stable.
- **Advertising the property.** A good property manager will know how to best advertise your rental, online and off.

- **Preparing the property.** When you're between tenants, the property manager will clean the place up and arrange for any necessary maintenance work like painting, replacing fixtures, and more. Instead of you trying to cram these tasks into the odd break in your schedule, the property manager will bring in professionals to handle them. That means faster results and shorter vacancy periods.

- **Screening tenants.** Your property manager might take phone calls from applicants, show them the property, have them fill out applications, interview them, run credit or criminal background checks, and verify employment and rental history. The property manager uses this information to find the best tenant (though you can have a say in the final selection).

- **Moving tenants in.** Once you find an appropriate tenant, the property manager will negotiate the lease or rental agreement, coordinate the tenant's move and provide keys, give the tenant a move-in checklist, and handle any other move-in responsibilities.

- **Collecting rent.** The property manager will collect monthly rent and, depending on the terms of your contract with the manager, deal with problems when a tenant doesn't pay. In most cases, managers will be motivated to collect the rent because their pay is a percentage of it—if there's no income, they don't get a penny.

- **Handling tenant problems.** Late rent isn't the only tenant problem that could crop up (as discussed in Chapter 9). Your property manager will work on resolving all manner of problems and deal with tenant complaints or concerns (though most will not handle an eviction for you). As Rosario, a landlord in El Paso, Texas, says, "I've found that tenants feel more comfortable approaching the property manager than me about issues with the property— maybe they think I'll take it personally if they complain. Anyway, it all works out, because that way they don't wait until the small problems turn into big ones."

- **Keeping the property in good condition.** This means taking care of all repairs and maintenance (described in Chapter 8), as well as regular, general upkeep like mowing and pruning the yard. Usually, a property manager has someone on staff or on call—such as a handyperson—to handle immediate problems, and a list of seasoned professionals to call for more serious issues.

> **CAUTION**
> **Your maintenance and repair costs could go up.** The fees you pay to a property manager probably mean any maintenance problems will be identified quickly—and you'll end up paying someone for even simple tasks (like fixing a broken door lock or tightening a loose hinge), which you might otherwise have been able to handle on your own. When a property manager hires someone to fix a problem, you'll separately pay the worker, on top of your usual fee to the manager; or perhaps an extra fee to the manager, if you agreed to this arrangement within your original contract.

- **Performing inspections.** A property manager can handle the regular inspections that every property requires, to make sure there's no major damage or problem that needs repair.
- **Managing finances.** Your property manager should also perform certain financial tasks, including collecting, holding, and returning deposits; tracking income and expenses; and sending you regular (monthly or quarterly) reports on these items.
- **Complying with laws and regulations.** A good property management company will know applicable federal, state, and local laws and regulations, like those governing security deposits, rent control, and evictions. This will save your having to study and figure out how to comply with these laws—although you (the property owner) will still retain the ultimate liability for compliance.

> ⊘ **CAUTION**
> **Lesson learned the hard way: Don't expect regular monitoring from the property manager.** As Darla, who rented out her former home in Seattle, explains: "Because I lived several hours away, I relied on the property managers for regular maintenance. Mostly, I was happy with them, but they didn't catch the fact that my tenants were keeping dogs—and that the dogs were ruining the carpets. Worse yet, before I sold the place and asked the tenants to move, they sprayed the carpets with some oily substance—perhaps to mask the dog odors—which cost me $400 to remove and clean. If I'd lived locally, I could have driven by occasionally, and probably would have spotted the dogs."

Should You Hire a Property Manager?

If you're not sure whether you're ready to pay someone a relatively large amount of cash to manage your property, consider two things: whether you're in a good position to manage the property yourself, and whether property management makes financial sense.

Are you ready to take care of the property yourself?

Having just read about the process of managing a property, you know the basics of what's involved—selecting and managing tenants, keeping the property in good repair, making sure your tenants don't cause trouble in the neighborhood, and handling tenants' departures and the return of their deposits, for example.

Even if you think you're able to handle the serious tasks, there are situations in which hiring a property manager makes good sense. Here are some of them:

- **You live far away.** Maybe you're renting out a vacation home in a remote part of the state, or maybe it's an investment property across the country. If you can't be right there to handle management tasks, you'll waste a lot of time trying to do so remotely—and your property will probably suffer without someone there to see how the tenants are treating it, handle emergencies, and so forth.

- **You don't want to study the ins and outs.** If you're not interested in learning about and complying with federal, state, and local laws, understanding how to find and screen tenants, or figuring out at least the basics of home repair and maintenance, hiring a property manager is a good idea.

- **You don't have time to spare.** Maybe your full-time career is more lucrative than your time spent managing a property could ever be, or maybe you've got your hands full caring for children or an elderly parent. If your life is already jam-packed, adding the stress of managing a rental property might simply be too much to deal with, and you'll be content to receive a smaller but mostly stress-free profit.

- **You own multiple properties.** If you own a multiunit property or several different properties, the amount of time you'll spend being a landlord will go up—but so will the income you'll get from the rent, so hiring a property manager might become more affordable. Even if you aren't at that sweet spot yet, if you plan to be, it's worth keeping in the back of your mind.

TIP

You can hire a property manager for a short period of time. That's what Laura, a landlord with properties in Washington, Nevada, and Florida, did in preparing for a month-long trip to Europe. It allowed her some stress-free travel. On the other hand, she discovered that, "I'd rather work with tenants myself, especially when it comes to choosing new tenants. I think I'm more concerned than the property manager about finding someone who's easy to deal with. I ended up with an angry tenant (chosen by the company) who tried to get out of paying for damage."

Comparing Pros and Cons

Use this checklist to help you decide whether the benefits of hiring a property manager outweigh the costs. The more boxes you check in each category, the more you should lean toward that choice.

On the plus side of hiring a manager (check every box that describes you):

☐ I have very little free time to take care of maintenance, tenant communications, and other tasks.

☐ I don't relish the idea of interacting with tenants personally.

☐ I live far from the property.

☐ I can earn enough from rents to comfortably pay the property manager's fees, leaving me free to spend my time elsewhere.

On the minus side of hiring a manager (check every box that describes you):

☐ I have enough free time to spend managing the property, or it's so close to my current house that the time requirements will be reduced.

☐ I'm handy myself, or know a lot of good repairpeople, so there wouldn't be much point in delegating those tasks.

☐ I enjoy the idea of earning money by taking an active role as a landlord.

☐ The fees for high-quality local property managers would all but obliterate my profits.

How much does property management cost?

Typically, you'll pay an initial setup fee (between $100 and $300) and then between 6% and 12% of the rental income to the manager; or else a flat rate in the range of $100 per month for a single-family home. Single-family homes are almost always on the higher end of the percentage scale, because it's more costly to deal with them, per unit, than multifamily properties. To get an idea of what property managers in your area cost, call a few and ask.

> ⚠ **CAUTION**
> **High-maintenance properties mean higher management fees.**
> If your property isn't in good shape, expect to pay more—not only in repairs, but in the property manager's fee. A manager will rightfully assume that it's going to take more time and effort to manage your property than it would to handle a similar property in good condition.

Of course, an advantage to paying a percentage-based fee out of your monthly rental income is that the property manager will be highly motivated to keep the place occupied. Still, you might also need to factor in various add-on costs, such as:

- **Extra fees to find a new tenant.** Some property managers charge an extra fee to advertise, screen, and move a new tenant in, such as one half the first month's rent. While your initial reaction might be, "Whoa, I'm not paying for that!" take a closer look at the numbers: The manager might negotiate by setting your monthly fee comparatively lower. And if the manager helps you find a stable tenant who stays several years, wouldn't it be better to pay 8% per month plus the occasional leasing fee rather than 10% a month without a leasing fee? (Then again, if you don't see an adjustment in the manager's prices to account for this fee, this argument loses its luster.)

- **Administrative fees for repairs and maintenance.** You'll need the property manager to hire outsiders—plumbers, electricians, and other repairpeople. What you don't need or want is for your manager to tack on a fee for doing this, so negotiate that ahead of time. Find out also whether you'll have to pay extra fees if the company buys supplies on your behalf, like paint or carpeting.

TIP
If your homeowners' association maintains the property, don't pay your property manager to do it. If you live in a condominium or another common interest development, your homeowners' association might take care of communal areas, such as garden areas and shared hallways. Make sure your property manager knows what the association is responsible for: You don't want the manager to handle and charge you for repairs you weren't responsible for in the first place. Instead, the property management company should notify the association when it receives a tenant complaint concerning a common area. You might be able to negotiate a lower than usual fee with your property manager because there's less to manage.

- **Minimum monthly fees for unoccupied property.** Some property managers set a baseline monthly fee that they'll get paid even if the property isn't occupied—or if it's occupied by a deadbeat tenant who doesn't pay the rent. This decreases the manager's impetus to find you a tenant, not to mention to choose a good, reliable one who'll pay on time.

- **Full fees regardless of whether the tenant pays the rent.** Allowing the management company to collect its fee even if the tenant hasn't paid on time is a bad idea. You want the property manager to be as motivated as you are to collect the rent, which means you'll want them to have a financial stake in the tenant's timely payment.

- **Late fees going to the property manager.** Some property managers specify that they get to keep any late fees the tenant pays. Again, this isn't ideal, because it reduces their motivation to make sure the rent is collected on time. You'll also want to be certain late fees don't exceed legal maximums—if they do, look for another property manager.

Will the costs undo your profits?

A 6%–12% fee can seem steep if you're squeezing out only a small profit to begin with. To decide whether it makes financial sense, add it to the expense portion of your Monthly Property Expense Estimate, in Chapter 1, and then rerun the numbers to show your expected profits.

Also adjust the other expenses on your worksheet, where appropriate —a slight bump upward in your repair and maintenance costs, but (unless the property manager charges you extra), removal of the costs to market your property. Take a close look at what's included in any prospective property manager's fees, and make additional expense adjustments—for example, if lawn care is part of the package, remove your expected weekly payment to the mowing service.

> **TIP**
> **The property manager's fee is tax deductible.** We discussed various tax deductions in Chapter 6—and this is one of them.

Even if the fees for property management will wipe out all or much of your rental income, you don't have to rule it out entirely. You might find a property manager who will provide limited services for a lower fee—for example, agree that you'll find your own tenants, while the manager collects the rent and coordinates repairs. The expense could be worth it if it frees you of whichever parts of your responsibilities are hardest to juggle or to handle at a distance.

As you study your adjusted numbers, keep in mind that a property is usually least profitable in its early rental years. If you wait a couple years more—either paying for property management and losing money, or managing the property yourself until you turn a profit—you might be in a better financial position. At that time, paying for a management company might fit more comfortably within your budget, especially if you can increase rents.

How to Find the Best Property Manager

Anyone can manage a property for you—but that doesn't mean you should let them. Instead, you're looking for a professional manager who knows the business. Many professional property managers are licensed real estate brokers or work for them (as some states require). But it's better if the company is dedicated to property management, not buying and selling real estate. The skills required are very different, and you want someone who is focused on management, not doing it as a side business in the hopes that you, the landlord, will decide to sell the property and use the broker as your selling agent.

Several trade organizations offer education and training leading to designations such as "Certified Property Manager." (These designations are not, however, legal licenses.) What's probably the best program is offered by the Institute of Real Estate Management (IREM), which offers three designations: Certified Property Manager (CPM), Accredited Residential Manager (ARM), and Accredited Commercial Manager (ACoM). To find out more about what these designations mean, visit IREM.org.

Getting recommendations

You might already know of reputable property managers in your area, but if not, you'll need to start looking for one. Here are some likely search methods:

- **Ask friends and family.** Talk to people who are familiar with the rental property market in the area you're looking to hire. Neighbors can be another good resource, especially if you're in an area with a lot of rentals, such as a condo complex.

- **Talk to colleagues and your local apartment association.** Other owners of properties similar to yours are probably your best bet— your needs won't have much in common with those of a landlord for a 50-unit building, for example. However, you might find out whether those large owners belong to an apartment owners' association, and ask whether the association has a "small owners" group.

- **Search professional directories online.** Try IREM at IREM.org or the National Association of Residential Property Managers (NARPM) at NARPM.org.

Follow up on leads by checking the managers' own websites, paying particular attention to whether a firm specializes in any particular area of residential property management, or whether it's located in close enough proximity to handle your property.

Meeting and choosing among potential managers

Once you've narrowed down your list of potential hires, call three or four and arrange to meet and discuss working together. Be prepared to ask targeted questions, such as:

- **Do you hold any licenses?** Find out whether the agent is a licensed real estate agent (required in some states), and whether he or she has earned any special certifications, like the Certified Property Manager designation through IREM.

- **How long have you been in the property management business?** You're looking for someone with several years' experience.

- **Who will handle my property?** Make sure you meet with the person who will actually be responsible for managing your property (if it's one person). Then find out that particular person's experience level, and make sure you get along—remember, you could be working together quite a bit. Finally, make sure you know who's going to help you out if that person isn't available.

- **How many (and what types of) properties do you manage?** You're looking for someone who's not too busy to comfortably deal with you. If you're working with an individual manager, find out not only how many clients the company has, but how many properties that individual is responsible for. Someone in charge of several multifamily complexes will have little time or incentive to spend on your lowly single-family home (larger contracts are more lucrative). Also find out what type of properties the company deals with—be sure they have experience with properties similar to yours.

- **What are the fees?** You want to know all fees—your initial setup, monthly fees, and any add-ons, for things like finding a new tenant, cleaning a property after a tenant moves out, or delivering a termination notice. Also ask whether you'll be charged, and how much, if the place is vacant.

- **How will you advertise the property?** Be sure your property manager uses effective advertising methods, especially ones you might not have access to (anyone can put a posting on Craigslist).

- **How do you screen tenants?** Take a look at the written application form (and ensure it doesn't violate any laws on its face, such as those prohibiting discrimination) and find out what background checks the company will conduct and how. Make sure the company is as focused on finding a reliable tenant as you are—despite the fact that the company might be all too happy to receive extra payments for late fees or tenant turnover.

- **How do you handle repairs and maintenance?** Make sure someone will be available to handle any problems, 24 hours a day, seven days a week. Refer to Chapter 8 for a full list of repair and maintenance issues to discuss with your property manager.

- **Do you have a standard property management agreement?** Most management companies do, and as we'll explain below, they're written to benefit the company, not you. Make sure the standard agreement can be altered if necessary. Most companies will resist changes, but it's not impossible to find one that will make reasonable adjustments.

- **Do you have a standard lease?** Most property management companies do, and you want to take a look before signing on. As with a property management agreement, a lease agreement will be written to benefit the company first, not you or the tenant. Make sure the lease is fair and legal. In particular, check that the late fees don't exceed the maximum allowed in your state.

- **How will you send financial information?** Your property manager should provide you a regular report that details income and expenses. You'll want to know how often you can expect to receive the report and what format it will be in. Ask for a sample.

- **What kind of insurance do you carry?** It's important that the company carry comprehensive general liability insurance, workers' compensation insurance (to pay for any injuries sustained by employees), automobile insurance, and errors and omissions insurance (in less legal terms, malpractice insurance). Ask to see proof (a "certificate of insurance," on an "ACORD" standard form).

- **Do you have a fidelity bond?** Property managers handle a lot of money—and it isn't unheard of for a less-than-honest employee to skim some off the top. A fidelity bond (in the $1,000,000 range) will protect you if someone makes off with some of your rent money.

- **Do you have references?** Get names and call two or three, and make sure they own properties similar to yours. Find out whether they're satisfied with the service they've received, how long they've been working together, and specifics like how long it takes the property manager to respond to inquiries, requests, or complaints—both the owner's and the tenant's.

Once your questions have been answered satisfactorily, drive by the properties owned by the references of any manager you're considering hiring, and any other properties you know the manager handles. Take a close look at how well they're maintained. If you have a chance, talk to the tenants—they're likely to give you an unbiased answer on what it's like to deal with the management company. Once you've made your decision, get ready for the next step: signing a property management agreement.

Put It in Writing: Drafting an Agreement With Your Property Manager

For convenience' sake, your property manager's company doubtless has a standard agreement that it will ask you to sign. Every agreement will include some basic provisions, which you'll want to review carefully. Make sure the agreement:

- **Identifies the parties.** This should be fairly straightforward—you and any co-owners should be named, as should the property management company. However, if it's important to you to work with a specific employee, you might ask for that to be spelled out in the agreement.

- **Specifies the property.** Make sure the property is sufficiently identified, particularly if it's in a multiunit building or complex.

- **Details the fees you'll pay.** You want the fees clearly spelled out—the regular fee ("10% of the monthly collected rent") as well as any add-on fees, or minimum monthly fees paid even if the property is vacant. Watch out for language that makes the monthly fee a percentage of "rent due," "scheduled rent," or "rental value," any of which would mean you owe money regardless of whether the property manager was successful in getting the tenant to pay. How often you'll have to pay the fees is also important to see spelled out—often, they're deducted from the rent payment, with the rest of the payment forwarded to you (be sure the agreement specifies how quickly the company must forward the rent to you, minus its fee). Also be sure you know where and how your rent money is held before it's divvied up— ideally, in an individual trust account.

- **Explains the manager's responsibilities.** Look back to the list of responsibilities at the beginning of this chapter. Are they all covered in the agreement? If not, you'll have a hard time getting the manager to take care of them.

- **Explains your responsibilities.** Your list of responsibilities should be short—making timely reimbursements to the management company for repair expenditures is probably the most important one. But if you've agreed to hire a property manager for limited services only, it will be important to clearly list what you'll still be responsible for handling.

- **Includes the contract's duration.** You don't want a management agreement with an end date in the far future—it decreases the manager's motivation to make sure you're a satisfied customer. On the other hand, you shouldn't expect the contract to be significantly shorter than the tenant's lease period—it wouldn't be fair to the property manager to bring a tenant in, only to have you take over managing the property. No matter how long you agree to continue the management relationship, make sure it's spelled out in the agreement, as well as how much notice will be needed if you or the management company want to end the relationship early (for example, 30 days' written notice). Avoid an agreement that allows you to terminate only for specified reasons.

- **Addresses how much the manager can spend without your authorization.** You'll probably create a reserve account into which you'll deposit money that the manager can use for necessary expenses like repairs. Make sure your agreement specifies how much the manager can spend without prior approval—as well as where and how the money will be held.

- **Doesn't disclaim responsibility.** In many contracts, you'll find a provision in which the property management company attempts to hold itself harmless if its own errors and those of its employees cause you harm or injury. You might also see a related clause, called an indemnity clause, in which you promise to reimburse the company for any losses it suffers as a result of its negligence. Obviously, these are onerous clauses and you should get rid of them if you can. If you can't, you can take some solace if both you and the company have adequate insurance—with insurance properly in place, these clauses will seldom come into play.

- **Is signed.** Both you and a representative of the property management company should sign and date the agreement.

> ⚠ **CAUTION**
>
> **What happens if there's a dispute between you and the property manager?** Your agreement should specify whether you must resolve any legal disputes through specific avenues, like mediation or arbitration.

If you find that any of the provisions of an agreement are unacceptable, you'll have to decide whether to challenge them or sign anyway. A property management company should agree to alter an agreement, if your request is reasonable. If not, you might want to consider going elsewhere. ●

Ready to Quit? Exiting the Rental Property Business

No matter how much you enjoy being a landlord or how profitable it is, at some point, you might be ready to give it up. Maybe you're ready to spend time on other projects, or spend money on other investments. Or perhaps you're simply ready to enjoy the benefits of selling the property—the appreciation that's accumulated, thanks, in part, to your conscientious maintenance.

In this chapter, we'll discuss the decision to stop being a landlord. We'll cover:

- identifying your objectives and developing an exit plan to meet them
- deciding when it's the right time to get out
- exploring different ways to exit the business, and
- preparing the property for sale.

What's the Driving Force? Exit Plan Objectives

People have lots of different goals when they decide it's time to stop being a landlord. You might share one or more of the most common ones:

- **Realizing profit.** Over the years, you might have watched the value of your property rise. While that looks good on paper, it won't pay your son's college tuition or buy you the sailboat you've always wanted. Perhaps it's time to cash in on that gain.

- **Avoiding taxes.** The downside to ongoing property appreciation is that the taxes you'll owe on profits when you sell are also going up. Many exiting landlords hope to avoid, or at least limit, this tax liability—and, if they previously lived in the property, to preserve their eligibility for the capital gains tax exclusion.

- **Reducing workload.** For some, dealing with a rental property simply gets to be too much bother, or interferes too much with their day job.

- **Passing money to heirs.** Lots of landlords want to make sure they have adequate assets to pass on. A landlord might exit the business due to a worry that leaving property to their heirs could be more complicated and stressful for the heirs than leaving money.

- **Keeping a property that you want to use yourself.** Some landlords might be done with the business—but not the property. For example, you might have inherited and rented a cottage that you're now ready to retire in.

As you read through this chapter, keep your own objectives in mind, and see which of the options here best meets them.

What Are Your Options? Exploring Opportunities

There are many ways you can stop being a landlord. It could be as simple as putting the house on the market, or as complex as executing a tax-deferred exchange to buy another investment property. We'll explain the details of these and other strategies, below. Chapter 12 explores a "soft" exit strategy: rent-to-own arrangements with tenants. Chapter 13 discusses yet another variation—moving into the house yourself and renting out a room.

Sell the property

The most straightforward way to get out of the rental property business is to sell the property. You might have experience with selling a personal residence—and know that it gives you an immediate (and often large) amount of cash to spend any way you please.

But selling your rental has some disadvantages, too. First of all, it involves high transaction costs. If you hire a real estate agent, you'll pay a commission (usually 5%–6% of the total sales price). That doesn't include the cost of getting the property ready for sale, or any of the other transaction costs that are commonly paid by the seller (which vary by geographic area). Altogether, you could spend up to 10% of the sale price just on these costs.

How to Estimate Your Capital Gains Tax

Worried about how much you're going to pay in capital gains taxes? Do some rough calculations first. Your capital gains tax liability is based on your purchase price, but you're allowed to increase that amount (called the "basis") to account for certain expenses, thereby decreasing your taxable gain. Include these adjustments when you calculate your tax liability.

Step 1: Start with your purchase price. Then add your closing costs, such as title fees, escrow fees, and recording fees. Add only the costs you paid, and don't count any amounts in escrow for future payment, like taxes or insurance premiums. (If you're not sure whether an expense qualifies, look at IRS Publication 551, *Basis of Assets*, available at IRS.gov.)

Step 2: Did you make any improvements to the property? If they have a useful life of more than one year, you can add those costs to the basis. There are a few other expenses that can adjust your basis, but they don't apply to most people. These include things like zoning fees and legal fees—for example, for defending a challenge to title. See Publication 551, above, if you think one of these exceptions might apply to you.

Step 3: Estimate how much you think you can sell your home for, based on an honest assessment of its fair market value.

Step 4: Reduce the sale price by the cost of your sale expenses, such as broker fees, title fees, and escrow fees.

Step 5: Subtract the Step 2 figure—the adjusted purchase price—from the Step 4 figure—the adjusted sales price. This is the amount you can be taxed on as a capital gain, not counting any depreciation you must recapture (at a higher tax rate).

But the transaction costs might not be your only expenses—capital gains taxes could also take a bite. For example, if you bought an investment home four years ago for $200,000 and you sell it now for $300,000, you'll potentially owe capital gains tax on approximately $100,000, though probably a bit less after adjusting the basis, which we'll explain further below. (There's no exclusion for houses that weren't the owner's primary residence for two out of five years before the sale.) Assuming a long-term federal capital gains tax rate of 15% (it's either 0%, 15%, or 20%, depending on one's income level, but most investors pay 15%), that's $15,000 to the federal government alone. States also collect capital gains taxes.

$\bigcirc$ **CAUTION**
Short-term capital gains are taxed at ordinary income tax rates. If you've owned your property for a year or less and are selling it at a gain, you'll be taxed at your ordinary income tax rate—which can go up to 37%! Taxpayers in the higher brackets might be better off waiting to sell until they've held the property for more than one year.

In addition to taxes on your gain, you'll have to pay taxes on the "recapture" of depreciation you took over the years. As explained in Chapter 6, the IRS requires you to take annual deductions to account for the decreased value of your rental building (but not the land it sits on) caused by normal wear and tear.

The IRS arbitrarily set the "lifespan" of residential property at 27.5 years. That means that over 27.5 years, you're allowed to deduct the purchase price of the property (minus the land) in equal amounts. So if you bought a property with a house on it worth $100,000, each year you probably deducted around $2,750.

This works great while you're a landlord and are taking the deduction, but when you're ready to sell, you must pay tax on any profits that essentially paid you back for the depreciation deductions you took.

Avoid taxes with a 1031 exchange

If you are horrified at the tax bill that might accompany a home sale, you might be interested in the "1031," "like-kind," or "Starker" exchange. In a 1031 exchange, you can defer paying taxes on the sale of a business or investment property when you reinvest your gain in other business or investment property.

Despite the name, you don't literally swap one property for another—you can sell your property to any buyer and find a property you want to purchase from any seller. But to qualify as an exchange, you must meet certain requirements. Most importantly, you have 45 days from the sale of the first property to find and identify potential properties to purchase. Within 180 days of the sale, you must actually purchase one or more of those properties. During that time, the sale proceeds can never be in your hands, or the transaction won't be considered an exchange. Instead, all the cash from the sale must be held in an escrow account. (You'll usually hire a third party, called a qualified intermediary, to hold the cash for you, and your transaction costs will be a little bit higher as a result.)

> ### The number of Americans being audited is falling
>
> According to a 2020 report by USA TODAY, your odds of being audited are half what they were five years before. Oddly enough, it's the rich and the poor who get audited most frequently—those with incomes below $25,000 or above $500,000.

Although this arrangement allows you to defer capital gains taxes from the sale, you'll have to pay tax eventually, when you sell the property bought in the exchange. (The exception would be if you do another exchange, in which case your taxes will be deferred again.) However, to fully defer your taxes, the new property you buy has to be worth the same as or more than the old property you are selling. You can also defer the taxes on the recapture of depreciation you've taken on your current property, discussed above.

Exchanging property provides other advantages, too. For example:

- **You can leverage your investment into a higher value property.** If the value of the property you currently own increases significantly, you might want to trade up to a more expensive property (or properties) that yields higher rents. For example, if the rental house you bought for $100,000 is now worth $500,000, you may use your gain to purchase an eight-unit building that costs $900,000. Because you aren't paying taxes, you have more cash available for such a leveraged investment.

- **If you're tired of the day-to-day management of being a landlord, you can buy a lower-maintenance property or buy into an exchange company.** For example, you can exchange an active rental property for undeveloped land you think will appreciate soon. Or you can purchase a fractional share in an investment property (known as a tenancy in common). In the most sophisticated arrangements, you own a part of a large commercial property, with a professional company managing it and distributing rent payments to you, with very little other responsibility. Be aware, however, that exchange companies charge fees, and you'll pay capital gains on the dividends as they're paid each year. Additionally, the buy-in price is high—often several hundred thousand dollars.

- **You can buy multiple properties.** While there are some rules about the number and types of properties you can buy, you can exchange a single property for several different investment properties.

- **You can continue to depreciate property.** If you have depreciated your current property to or near the maximum amount allowed, a 1031 exchange gives you the opportunity to start fresh with a new property. However, the adjusted basis of the current property transfers to the replacement property. That means you can take depreciation deductions only on the new property reduced by the depreciation you've already taken on the old one.

If you're considering a 1031 exchange, see your tax or legal adviser to help you navigate these highly technical requirements. Also, if you pass away during the exchange period, your heirs could face adverse tax consequences.

Offer seller financing to home buyers

If you're ready to sell your property but aren't interested in reinvesting in another business or investment property, you have another option to help soften the tax blow: an installment sale, sometimes called "seller financing." With an installment sale, you act as a lender as well as a seller, letting the buyer pay you over time. You might be the primary mortgage holder or a secondary mortgage holder.

Buyers are attracted to installment sales because they avoid the expense or hassle of dealing with a traditional lender, and because installment sales offer flexibility.

For example, a buyer who is self-employed—and can't show regular income despite a profitable business—might have a hard time getting a traditional loan. Or maybe the buyer needs a lower monthly payment than the bank will offer, and you're able to offer more creative financing.

But installment sales aren't just good for buyers—you might benefit, too. First of all, you'll earn interest on the money lent to the buyer, receiving a stable, steady return on your investment. Additionally, you can spread out payment of your capital gains taxes, which need to be paid only in the year you receive the actual gain. And your gain will be partly the loan principal, so in the early years, when most of each payment is usually interest, your capital gains tax bill will inevitably be low. (You will still be taxed on the interest income, at ordinary income tax rates.) This frees more money for other investments or uses.

Of course, there are drawbacks to installment sales. Perhaps the biggest risk is the possibility that the buyer won't make the payments. As a secured lender (one who has filed a mortgage or deed of trust), you'd have the right to seek payment through a foreclosure, but that's an expensive and time-consuming process. And if you were the second mortgage holder, you'd be paid only after the first mortgage holder is paid.

The other major drawback is the risk that the buyer will pay the loan off early. If this happens, you'd have all the remaining taxable gain due in that year, which could wreak havoc on a well-planned tax strategy. Although you might be able to limit this possibility by including prepayment penalties on the loan, many states limit the amount of any prepayment penalty.

> **TIP**
> **You can combine a 1031 exchange with an installment sale.** This topic is beyond the scope of this book, but if you're interested, speak with a financial or tax adviser.

Move into the property yourself

Perhaps you've been holding onto your property so that you can someday retire or move into it. This approach offers certain tax benefits.

If you convert a property you have owned for at least two years to your main home and live there for two out of the five years before its sale, you don't have to pay tax on the portion of your gain that's attributable to your personal use. The maximum exclusion under this provision is $250,000, or $500,000 if you're married and filing jointly. If you own and live in a multiunit property, you can use the exclusion on a fractional basis, excluding gain on the portion of the property that was your principal residence.

For example, if you buy a house and rent it out for four years, then live in it for an additional six years, you can exclude 60% of your gain, and will face potential taxes on only 40%. But this won't help you avoid taxes on your recaptured depreciation deductions.

For more information, see IRS Publication 523, *Selling Your Home*, available at IRS.gov.

> **CAUTION**
> **Did you acquire your property in a 1031 exchange?** If so, you must live in it for five years, not two, before you can take the primary residence exclusion.

Bring in a co-owner

If you're tired of being the sole owner and caretaker of your property, you could ask someone to buy in. Legally speaking, you'd turn the ownership into a tenancy in common—a form of joint ownership that allows you and co-owners to hold property in unequal shares. Neither of you needs the other's permission to sell your interest, and you can decide how to divide up, use, and care for the property.

You might be able to find a buyer who's interested in this arrangement, and is willing to manage the property. If you also act as the mortgage holder, you'll have monthly income at the same time. See a legal or tax adviser for details.

Donate the property to a charitable remainder trust

Though donating your property to a charity might seem like a money-losing proposition, it can have significant tax advantages. You can name yourself and your spouse as beneficiaries of the trust, creating an income stream for the rest of your life, then donate the remainder (the property) to a charity of your choice.

You can also take a significant tax deduction, based on the projected value of the benefit the charity will receive (after your death) and the type of charity you donate the property to. For more information on this and other estate planning strategies, see *Plan Your Estate*, by Denis Clifford (Nolo).

What Rights Does the Tenant Have If You Sell?

If you have tenants living on your property at the time you decide to put it on the market, you'll need to understand their rights (and yours) during the selling process and beyond. (If the property is vacant, you can skip this section.) Dealing with current tenants can be a challenge (and a possible hindrance to a sale), which is why many owners wait until the property is vacant before selling.

Tenants with leases will continue to have the right to live on the property until the lease ends, despite the change in ownership. In other words, the new owner will step into your shoes, and must honor the lease just as you did. This doesn't mean, however, that you or a prospective owner can't approach tenants and ask to buy them out of their leases. Tenants have no obligation to negotiate with you or the buyer, but many will, seeing an opportunity to make some money.

What Does a Buy-Out Cost?

When deciding how much rent to charge, you looked at the state of the market—was it hot or cold, and what were the rents for properties like yours? You'll use the same approach, and add in some individual factors, if you decide to try to end a current tenancy early by buying out your lease-holding tenants.

First, understand that the tenants will have to find another place to live. What rent will they have to pay to find a comparable unit? If they are long-term, good tenants, whom you've wisely kept around by making modest rent increases over the years, if the market is hot (and rents for comparable rentals are high), and there are few comparable rentals available, your tenants will be facing a steep uptick in rent per month. Expect to pay at least the difference between their current rent and the expected new rent, times the number of months left on the lease. On the other hand, if the market is soft and the cost of a similar rental is close to their current rent, your offer could be much lower.

Next, determine whether you'll include help on moving costs. You might be inclined to skip this—after all, you wouldn't be helping them move at the end of the lease. But here is where you need to think creatively and keep your goal—a vacant property—in mind. Suppose you're asking them to leave six months early. Your tenants will be losing interest on the moving money when they spend it six months early. Offer at least to cover this sum. Throw in a bit more to compensate them for the inconvenience this sudden move entails—and keep in mind that disruptions that involve kids' schooling, commuting, and loss of a familiar neighborhood are hard to quantify but mighty important to the people involved.

Before concluding that existing tenants will enjoy continued residence under a lease that exists at the time of the sale, check the lease itself. A few, especially those custom-drafted by attorneys familiar with the property and the current owner/landlord, include a clause providing for early termination in the event that the property is sold before the lease termination date. Such a clause might say, for example, that the lease will terminate 60 days after escrow once a sale has closed. In a lawsuit, courts tend to uphold these clauses, especially if they provide tenants with a reasonable notice period.

Tenants who rent on a month-to-month basis present you and the new owner much more flexibility. As you know, you can terminate month-to-month tenants with proper notice, 30 days in most states. While you may not terminate for an illegal (retaliatory or discriminatory) reason, ending a tenancy in order to prepare and show the property (which you would do), or to live in it once it's purchased (which the new owner would do) is legal in every state. Some long-term monthly tenants are entitled to slightly more notice in some states, but the general rule is the same—you can end their tenancies with relative ease.

If You Decide to Sell: Getting Ready

If you decide to sell the property, even in a 1031 exchange or an installment sale, you'll have to deal with putting your house on the market and finding a buyer. A little advance planning will help you maximize your return.

Is now a good time to sell?

Many factors affect whether it's a good time to sell your rental property. Unless you have no choice in the matter—for example, you need the cash, or a life change has made managing a property impossible—it's worth considering whether now is the best time to put your place on the market. Consider these factors:

- **Your local real estate market.** Real estate markets fluctuate—and they're often intensely local. What's happening can vary by city, neighborhood, block, or even street, so make sure you understand what's being sold nearby and at what price. If you know the market is cold—that there are more houses on the market than there are buyers—you can't expect to command the same price for your property as you would if the market were hot (if there were more buyers than available houses). In a cold market, consider whether you'd rather wait to see if prices increase. (But keep in mind—if the property isn't producing income, this could end up costing you more in the long run, as you continue to pay for taxes, maintenance, insurance, and to make regular monthly mortgage payments.)

- **The condition of the property.** Over the years, you've worked to conscientiously maintain the property. But you can't necessarily say the same for your tenants. And if you have long-term tenants, you might not have made a lot of improvements or accounted for regular wear and tear, either. You might need to wait until you can invest some cash up front before putting the property on the market.

- **Whether the property is currently occupied.** Whether you want to offer an occupied property when you sell might depend on who you expect your buyer to be—an individual looking for a home, or an investor looking for an income-producing property. Either way, it's usually easiest to show the property when it's empty, so if you are between tenants, this might be a good time to make a sale. (On the other hand, some buyers will be happy to find a property with a stable, income-producing tenant— particularly if they themselves are first-time landlords.)

- **The effect that selling will have on your tax liability.** As discussed above, when you sell can significantly impact your tax liability. Make sure you understand the consequences—for example, if you sell at a gain after owning a property less than a year, any gain will be a short-term capital gain, taxed at your current income tax rate. If that's higher than the current applicable long-term capital gains rate, you might want to hold off.

Real Estate Agent Interview Questions

☐ Do you work full-time as a real estate agent? (Best answer: Yes.)

☐ How long have you been in the real estate business? (The longer the better, but at least three years.)

☐ Do you have additional certifications beyond your general real estate license? If so, what are they? (More certifications show a commitment by the agent to professional development.)

☐ In what percentage of your real estate transactions in the past year have you represented the seller? (Should be at least half.)

☐ What was the price range of homes you sold in the last year? What was the average price? (Should be about your price range.)

☐ Do you specialize in certain types of property? (Should be the type of property you're selling, like a single-family house or condo.)

☐ Do you specialize in a certain geographic area? (Should be the geographic area where you're looking to sell.)

☐ Do you partner with other agents or use assistants? (If so, find out whom you'll be working with, what their real estate experience is, and what they'll be doing.)

☐ How will I reach you? Are there days or times you're unavailable, or do you have vacations planned? (Make sure you can reach the agent when you need to. If you plan to sell soon, make sure the agent will be readily available.)

☐ Can you provide at least three names of recent clients who sold their properties with you, who will serve as references? (Only acceptable answer is "Yes," and ideally at least one of these references will be a landlord who sold an investment property.)

Hire an agent or sell it yourself?

The vast majority of property owners enlist real estate agents to help them sell. Real estate agents serve many functions: They help set a realistic price for the property, prepare it for sale, advertise it, show it to prospective buyers, negotiate and close the sale, and handle paperwork to make sure the whole process goes smoothly.

Of course, these services come at a cost—typically 5% to 6% of the sale price, paid by you at closing, with your agent sharing the commission with the buyer's agent.

Some sellers choose to sell the property themselves. They reason that they can handle a lot of the basic tasks an agent takes care of, and that the biggest challenge—marketing the property—should be no problem, because many buyers look at properties on the Internet.

Having saved the cost of the commission, they can easily afford to hire an attorney or title officer to help with the closing. Other expenses may include the cost of online listing services, like ForSaleByOwner.com or FSBO.com, which help increase exposure and traffic to the property.

But selling a property yourself can be harder than it looks. First, you've got to do enough research to set your starting price just right— too high, and you might drive away potential buyers, who are unlikely to return after your house goes stale (sits unsold) on the market. Also expect to spend large amounts of time on tasks like coordinating prospective buyer showings, evaluating offers and deciding whether to accept or counteroffer, and making sure all the formalities that lead to a closing— title insurance, removing contingencies, and more—are properly handled.

If you decide to work with an agent, you'll want to choose the best (especially because you won't pay a premium to do so—the local market usually dictates the total commission, regardless of the experience of the agent). You're looking for someone who is experienced, trustworthy, and professional. Ideally, this means someone who's been operating in the area where you're selling for at least three years, has handled many transactions involving rental properties, returns calls and inquiries, and promptly schedules appointments with interested buyers. If you're doing a 1031 exchange or an installment sale, find an agent experienced in handling these transactions.

Ask other rental property owners in the area for recommendations, and interview at least three potential agents. See above for some questions you can ask.

Will the buyer be an investor or a home buyer?

You'll want to evaluate what type of buyer will likely buy your rental. Namely, will investors be interested, or will your property attract buyers who intend to live there? These two types of buyers have very different objectives. A home buyer looking for a place to live will walk in and say, "Can I imagine myself spending years here, cooking in this kitchen, walking in this neighborhood?" On the other hand, a shrewd investor will want to know, "Will I make money renting this property out?" A hybrid situation might arise, for example, if you're selling a duplex in which the buyer could live in one part and rent out the other.

Of course, you won't always know who the buyer will be, and you'll want to be prepared for all possibilities. But there are clues that can help you make an educated guess. For example, if your property has been the only rental on the block in a desirable neighborhood for the last several years, it's highly likely it will attract buyers who intend to live there themselves. Alternatively, if you're selling a condo in a development in which more than half the units are rented, investors will probably be interested.

If there's any possibility you'll sell to an investor, part of your sales preparation should involve showing that the property is capable of delivering a healthy return. Your real estate agent, if you work with one, will likely help you prepare a brochure, "pro forma," or similar document that shows prospective buyers the property's potential profitability. This document will include much of the same information you might have had access to when you bought, including the number of units (in your case, probably only one or two) and how much each one rents for each year. This figure—the income—is reduced by the vacancy rate and normal operating expenses.

Your agent will probably encourage you to present these numbers in the best possible light. In fact, the numbers will likely be based on the property's potential, even if you're not realizing that full potential (but make it clear that the numbers are potential, to avoid a charge later that you misled the buyer). For example, even though you've rented your house for $1,000 per month to the same reliable tenant for the last six years, the new owner might actually be able to ask $1,200 per month if it's clear that the market for a property like yours has gone up. Or, perhaps you spent $15,000 replacing the roof last year, which made your expenses unusually high—call this out as an unusual and long-lasting improvement, and note that you don't anticipate significant spending in the next year.

> CAUTION
> **It might be time to cut expenses.** Because investors may ask how much you actually spent on maintenance and improvements in the previous year, try to keep these numbers reasonable in the months before you sell. Don't defer needed maintenance—it will cost you more in the long run—but consider holding off on unnecessary improvements.

The savviest investors will want to know what you've actually spent, and will base their own profitability calculations on these numbers. If you get a lower offer as a result, be prepared to justify a higher asking price. For example, you could tell a prospective purchaser, "Because I live far away and didn't have a lot of time to deal with this property, I rented it to a reliable tenant at a below-market rate, even after rents went up in the area. But in this great neighborhood, with low vacancy rates, you could easily find a tenant willing to pay $200 more per month."

If you think the likely buyer will live in the house, you'll have a whole different set of tasks to complete. Most important will be making the property physically attractive, as discussed below, under "Preparing the property for sale."

Of course, it's difficult to make a house sparkle if a tenant is still living there. You can't control the tenant's taste in furniture or level of cleanliness. To forestall resistance from the tenant, consider:

- **Negotiating a move out.** As explained above, if the tenant is on a lease, you might be able to work out an early termination. For example, you could offer to pay moving expenses, pay the tenant a small fee, or reduce the rent for a short period in exchange for moving out more quickly.

- **Paying for a cleaning service.** If you don't want or can't get your tenant to move out, you could instead hire someone to clean the place—maybe once for a thorough cleaning, then regularly to maintain it in good condition. Don't expect the tenant to pay for this. It will be worth the cost, if it presents your property in the best possible light.

- **Offering to pay for the spruce-ups.** If your tenant has a lot of stuff cluttering the place up, offer to pay for a storage facility, or provide onsite storage if available. You might also want to buy inexpensive items—a new door mat, shower curtain, and so forth—to enhance the appearance of the place.

CAUTION
Be sure to follow state law when showing an occupied property. Most states regulate the reasons you may enter rented property, and how to give notice to your tenants. Check your state's entry laws (find yours in the Landlords section of Nolo.com) and be sure to give adequate notice. Uncooperative or hostile tenants can ruin a showing or an open house, so it pays to get your tenants on your side by, for instance, reducing the rent for the time the property is on the market.

Preparing the property for sale

Whether you're moving a tenant out or dealing with a vacant property, you'll want to make things look their best in preparation for sale. You're looking to appeal to the broadest spectrum of buyers so that you can sell quickly at a competitive price. Our advice in Chapter 3 on sprucing up a rental property applies also to preparing a house for sale.

But before you start sprucing up, determine if you have some deferred maintenance to deal with—repairing dry rot or fixing leaking windows, for example. As much as you tried to stay on top of such problems, some things might have escaped the tenant's and your notice (or been caused by the tenant).

> **Does staging really work?**
>
> It just might—around half of Realtors surveyed by the National Association of Realtors (NAR) said they believe staging usually has an effect on the buyer's view of the home.

Leaving minor maintenance matters for the next owner to deal with is usually a mistake. For one thing, in most states, you'll have to disclose problems that you know about, and you'll be in a weaker bargaining position as you and the buyer argue over each necessary change. Ultimately, your house value will go down.

For another, signs of deferred maintenance are a big red flag for potential buyers, as they could indicate that the property has other, less obvious problems. If potential buyers plan to rent the property out, they might be concerned that your poor maintenance means the current tenants are unhappy or unlikely to stay. Still, if something major like the roof is old but still functional, it might be best to simply reduce your price accordingly, or offer a "credit" to the buyer to make the change. This will save you the effort of either taking care of it yourself or negotiating it in the purchase agreement. If a buyer says, "I'm knocking $15,000 off the offer price to replace the roof," you can confidently reply, "Actually, the asking price was set based on comparable properties, but discounted for the cost of a new roof."

Beyond the basics discussed above, consider "staging" your property. This basically means using design, décor, and lighting to highlight the property's most attractive features, while minimizing its less-than-perfect aspects. In certain parts of the United States, hiring professionals to manage this process is standard. Almost every stager will tell you that it's ideal to move out all occupants and furniture, so that they can move all-new furniture and accessories in.

RESOURCE

For more information on all aspects of selling a home, see *Selling Your House: Nolo's Essential Guide,* by Ilona Bray (Nolo). ●

A Slower Exit:
Rent-to-Own Arrangements

Another exit strategy involves selling your investment property to the current tenants. Of course, when you're ready to sell, you can always let them know that the property is going to be on the market and encourage them to put in a bid. But if you know in advance when you want to sell—say, in one to three or even five years from now—you might be able to set up the tenant-buyer scenario at the beginning of the tenancy. Such an arrangement offers both significant advantages and major risks.

The terms "rent to own" and "rent to buy" are shorthand ways of describing what's legally known as an option contract (to buy the house). Here's how it works: In a contract that's ideally separate from the lease but dependent on the tenant's faithful adherence to the lease terms, the landlord gives the tenant the option to buy the property within a specified period or at a specified date, for a certain price (or sets out a manner of arriving at a price; more on that below).

The landlord doesn't give the option away; tenants typically pay for it, normally in an up-front fee to the tune of several thousand dollars. You can also add to your agreement that all or a portion of the tenant's rent payments—most likely a premium added to the fair market rent—up until the time of sale will go toward paying down the principal amount owed on the sale.

Rent-to-own setups are attractive to tenants who are going through short-term hard times and cannot presently buy a home. Perhaps they've been laid off or lost their own home to foreclosure so that they must rent for a while. Or, a medical situation could have temporarily interrupted work and income. These tenants might well be able to buy a home in the near future, as their financial and employment pictures improve, their credit scores go up, and they become eligible for a loan. For continuity's sake (nearness to jobs, school, friends and family), they might be looking for a rental that they can imagine would be a good permanent home for them someday soon.

Advantages and Disadvantages of Rent to Own

Renting to tenants who hope to someday buy their rented home can be a real boon to an owner planning on selling. Because the accompanying leases are at least two years long, you'll avoid the uncertainty and expense of tenant turnover. If the tenant exercises the option and buys the property, you will skip the cost of a regular sale—no fix-up and staging fees and, most significantly, no brokers' commissions. You'll also be blissfully clear of the hassle and stress involved in selling real estate.

Tenants who hope to someday own their rented home will likely be conscientious when it comes to taking care of the property. You can even formally turn over some maintenance responsibilities to them. And because your option contract should specify that they must be "in good standing" at the time they exercise the option or even throughout the entire life of the lease, they'll be motivated to pay the rent on time and not cause problems.

Option contracts do, however, have their downsides. Granting an option ties the hands of the landlord in significant ways. Before the option is exercised, you cannot sell to another person or entity (unless that buyer knowingly agrees to buy a property that can be bought out from under him or her by the tenant in the near future … a very unlikely prospect). Nor can you readily use the property as collateral for a loan. For example, it could be difficult to get a second mortgage to finance a child's college education—the bank will hesitate because if it has to foreclose and becomes the owner, it will want to sell the home—but the property will be encumbered by the option, which will make it practically unsaleable.

Depending on the laws of your state, you might also have to make disclosures concerning the property and its condition when you and the tenant sign an option contract. These disclosures are no different than the ones that sellers make when involved in a regular house sale, concerning such things as proximity to flood plains and fault lines, the physical condition of the property (mentioning everything from cracked foundations to leaky hot tubs to peeling linoleum), and so on.

Finally, understand that once the tenant properly exercises the option, that contract becomes an irrevocable sales contract. It should be clear on all essential issues, and, to avoid hassles and the possible disintegration of the sale, you should make the terms of the sale clear right now, in the option contract. If you omit issues like when and in what manner the tenant can exercise the option, the terms of payment, time and place of closing, nature of title to be given, and any adjustments to be made at closing, you risk later disagreements about these issues—serious disagreements that might scuttle the deal.

In short, offering a rent-to-own option is not as simple as inserting a lease clause saying, "During the lease term, Tenant will have the option to buy the premises for $XXX." Properly done, it's a sales contract, and will take some work (and professional assistance, from a broker and a real estate lawyer, too). Do not insert an option clause in your lease and think it will work. It won't.

The Option Price

Because you're narrowing your use of the property, as explained above, it's fair to charge the tenant for the option. Ideally, you'll get this fee up front, though some rent-to-own arrangements allow tenants to pay a portion of the option in the form of extra rent each month. Calculating the fee based on 1% of the agreed-upon sale price is common (and we've heard of fees as high as 5%), but don't simply leap at such a figure without doing further analysis.

The amount you should realistically charge depends on the value you place on foregoing the rights just explained, and on how much you can reasonably expect a tenant to pay. Add to this sum the value to the tenants to have a house "set aside" for them, as long as they perform as expected (and assuming they can qualify for a loan). If the house is attractive and likely to draw many buyers, that additional value should be set appropriately high, but if the house isn't really anything special (maybe there are plenty like it on the market), the set-aside portion of the option will be less.

Will the option fee be refunded to a tenant who doesn't exercise the option? Most rent-to-buy agreements say no. However, allowing this fee to go toward the tenant's down payment is a common feature of these contracts (although this means that the landlord is effectively not charging for the privilege of giving the tenant the right to buy the house).

> **CAUTION**
>
> **This isn't play money.** A savvy tenant will require you to hold any amounts meant to go toward the down payment in an escrow account, to be released when the sale occurs. Your tenant might also negotiate a term in your option agreement stating that regular rent payments will go straight toward your home mortgage, real estate taxes, and homeowners' insurance, to avoid the possibility that you'll go into foreclosure on the home while the tenant is working toward exercising the option.

Sale Price of the House

When you give a tenant an option to buy, you'll need to either name the house sale price in your option contract or decide on an objective way in which that price can be determined later. Naming the price now has the advantage of certainty, but it means that you risk misreading the market. You might specify a sale price that turns out to be less than actual market value at the time of sale, leaving you frustrated that you can't put the house on the open market. Of course, it's also possible that you'll misjudge the other way and end up with a set price that is unrealistically high, given the market value at the time the option is exercised.

Because both owner and tenant might be leery of the risks just explained, they often choose a different approach. You can avoid the risk of misjudgment by deferring the price, but you must set up a fail-safe method for arriving at it. For example, your contract might say, "Market value as determined by licensed brokers, one each chosen by landlord and tenant; and if the brokers cannot agree, the price to be determined by a third who will be chosen by the two brokers." That's far better than simply saying, "fair market value at the time the option is exercised," or "price to be negotiated at the time," or even "fair market value based on at least two appraisals." All of these leave wide open the possibility that you and the tenant won't be able to agree on a price or a way to mediate your dispute. In such a situation, you will not be able to go to court and get a judge to settle the house price for you. The option will fall apart.

Although providing a clear method for arriving at the fair market value removes the possibility that the deal will fall apart over price disagreements, it has a significant downside: The tenants will have to exercise the option before knowing the price they will be expected to pay. The tenants can, of course, do some homework and arrive at a figure that probably should be the ultimate price, but there's no guarantee that this estimate will match the price chosen by the neutral experts. Tenants can end up overextended and feeling cheated in these situations, making for a difficult or impossible sale. If some of the tenants' up-front fee or rent payments were meant to go toward the down payment on the sale, and the sale falls through, your contract might well say that you don't have to return those amounts—but you'll have doubly angry tenants (or soon to be ex-tenants). The tenants might even start looking for possible grounds upon which to sue you.

By When the Tenant Must Exercise the Option

You'll want to provide a specific window of time, or a deadline, by which the tenants must tell you they are exercising the option. You could specify that the option be exercised several months in advance of the end of the underlying lease—this gives you time to begin planning for a sale or a successor tenant. Or, you could set a deadline (like the ending date of the lease), and allow exercise at any time before that, regardless of the amount of time left on the underlying lease (exercise of the option will terminate the lease).

If there's a chance that you will extend the lease, be aware that the option to buy might or might not be extended with it. It all depends on the way judges in your state view the matter, and on what your extension and the original option contract have to say. From the landlord's point of view, it's best to leave nothing to interpretation, and to provide for termination of the option contract when the original lease term ends; then, if you wish, you can specifically extend the option to buy into the renewed lease term (and possibly negotiate better terms, too).

Similarly, it's not clear what might happen to the tenant's option if you allow the tenant to stay on, as a holdover tenant (particularly if the option's exercise period is not specified as a specific date, but rather as the end of the lease term). On the one hand, you might think that because a holdover tenant becomes a month-to-month tenant under the same conditions and terms as existed in the expired lease, the option to buy would extend to the holdover period, too. But some courts view purchase options differently, and won't carry them over to a holdover tenant. The lesson for smart landlords is to keep on top of their leases and never allow a tenant to remain as a holdover in the first place.

Seller Financing and the Tenant's Rent-Paying History

Many lease option sales involve seller financing of the sale—in other words, the tenant will make regular (most likely monthly) mortgage payments to the landlord-turned-seller instead of to a bank or another institutional lender. From a practical point of view, eliminating an institutional lender can save everyone time and save the buyer a considerable amount of money. If the tenant has conscientiously made rent payments, perhaps there's no reason why installment payments shouldn't come straight to you.

If seller financing is something you'd consider, you'll want to decide whether the tenant must have been "squeaky clean" in order to take advantage of the option—that is, whether any prior lease defaults will bar the exercise (current lease violations should give you grounds to refuse to honor the option, as explained below). For instance, you might not want a tenant who has a history of paying rent late to be able to exercise the option, because that tenant will probably have a hard time paying you back on the loan, too. (Be reasonable, though—minor and/or one-time lease violations won't justify yanking the tenant's option right.) You might also want to insist on certain financial criteria, such as a minimum credit score.

Involve the Mortgage Lender

When tenants expect to use a mortgage lender, it makes sense for them to consult one now, even though it could be years before they take out the loan. The lender might be able to tell them how long it will take, given their current credit situation and expected earnings, to qualify for a loan. Pay attention to that interval—two to five years is typical—and consider allowing the option right and lease to last that long. If you set a shorter period, the tenant might want to exercise the option but be unable to secure a loan.

How Will the Tenant Notify You?

The manner in which you will accept the tenant's decision to exercise the option should be spelled out in advance. While oral notification is enforceable when there's a written option contract, for obvious reasons written notification is preferable. What's more, personal delivery is the best method (certified mail is a good second choice). It's essential to give your tenant a clear template to use when notifying you, like the example below.

Exercise of Option

The undersigned, _____[tenant's name]_____ , Tenant

of the premises located at _____[property address]_____ ,

hereby exercises the purchase option included or referenced in

the___[option contract]___ , dated _[date contract was signed]_ ,

between _____[landlord's name]_____ as Landlord, and

_____[tenant's name]_____ , as Tenant, affecting the

property therein leased and known as

_____[property address]_____ .

_____[tenant's name]_____ ___[date]___

Restrictions on the Landlord

Tenants who pay for a valuable option will expect that, should they exercise the option, they will not end up with property that has been encumbered in the meantime with burdens, such as mortgages, mechanics' liens, and so on. (But encumbrances existing at the time the option contract is entered into may come with the property if the option is exercised.) Unless the option contract specifically forbids adding new encumbrances, there's nothing to stop the landlord from adding them (or allowing them to be added). One practical step taken by tenants is to provide for the recording of the purchase option, so that it appears on the property's chain of title. Seeing an option contract could scare off would-be mortgagees. But, it won't stop the filing of a mechanics' lien.

Tenant Improvements and Rent

Many tenants will want the ability to begin improving "their" home, with the value of the improvements credited against the selling price. If you agree, be sure to consider what will happen if the tenant decides not to buy the home—will you reimburse the tenant for what was spent?

Similarly, tenants might ask you to apply a portion of the rent toward a down payment. As with improvements, you'll need to address what will happen if the tenant does not exercise the option, or if the sale does not go through.

What Happens If You Need to Evict or the Tenant Breaks the Lease?

Your option contract should be very clear that the option will terminate automatically upon termination of the underlying lease. If you need to terminate the lease (if the tenant fails to pay the rent, causes damage, or otherwise gives you solid legal grounds for ending the tenancy), this will extinguish the option. Similarly, a tenant who breaks the lease, even with justification, will lose the option to buy.

To drive this point home, the option contract should specify that the tenant may exercise the option only if in "good standing" with respect to the lease. A tenant who has been terminated or evicted, or one who has left, is obviously not in good standing. Be sure you do not become obligated to return any option fees already paid.

"Right of Refusal" and "Right of Offer"

Instead of entering into a full-blown option contract, some landlords formally agree to give their tenants preferential treatment when and if the property goes on the market. In these situations, the landlord avoids some of the tricky issues mentioned above, but such agreements still have certain drawbacks.

Right of refusal

A "right of refusal" allows the tenant to match or improve on any deal the landlord hammers out with a third-party buyer. After having secured a buyer, the landlord must give the tenant an opportunity to buy the property on the same or better terms. These arrangements are nothing but a headache for a seller, because it means that any potential buyer runs the risk of having the tenant trump the deal. Knowing this, buyers won't bother going through the effort of negotiating with these sellers, and seasoned brokers (on both sides) avoid these situations like the plague.

Right of offer

A "right of offer" is much milder. The landlord promises to give the tenant the first opportunity to buy the home at the price named by the landlord. If the tenant declines, the home goes on the market. The landlord must not artificially inflate the offering price in order to get rid of the tenant, but must name a commercially reasonable price. As many sellers find out, however, sometimes you don't really know what the house will go for. Selling at your named price might deprive you of a lucrative bidding war (which the tenant could always join, too).

Landlords do not give away rights of refusal or offer—like options, these rights come at a price.

Get Legal Advice

Think long and hard about whether your interests would be served by giving tenants an option to buy, or even rights of first refusal or offer. If you decide to go ahead, consult an attorney who specializes in real estate law and a tax specialist before signing any contract. Remember, you're dealing with a very expensive investment. And once a tenant exercises an option to buy, it's the same as an irrevocable sales contract. Structuring the option contract (or offer rights) and the attendant sales contract in ways that do not protect your interests could be financially disastrous. ●

13

Renting Out a Room in Your Home

The exit strategies in Chapters 11 and 12 have discussed various strategies for getting rid of your rental property. But you might have another option if you can envisage yourself living in the property while renting out a room.

Most landlords don't share their own homes with lodgers, making it their business practice to keep their homes and their rental properties separate. In recent years, though, an increasing number of homeowners have chosen to offer one or more rooms for rent. Often, this decision is prompted by financial necessity (they need the income in order to pay the mortgage). Others simply want the company of another person in the home—whether it's for socializing or to provide extra security—and the rent money is a bonus.

"Tenants" and "Lodgers": What's the Difference?

A lodger is someone who has a bedroom (and perhaps a bathroom, too) in somebody's home, and enjoys the use of common areas such as the kitchen and living room. Legally, the lodger has "non-exclusive use" of these shared facilities.

Tenants, on the other hand, rent space that is theirs exclusively. The landlord can't offer the space to anyone else, nor can the landlord access the premises absent tenant permission or a legally recognized reason (most states specify permissible reasons for landlords to enter tenants' rented homes).

The legal difference between lodgers and tenants becomes important in at least two ways. As explained below, homeowners who rent to no more than one lodger might avoid some dictates of the federal antidiscrimination laws. And if you need to evict a lodger, the rules are a bit different, too (see below).

While all landlords want someone who will pay their rent on time, keep their property in good condition, and not cause any legal or practical problems, there are additional things to consider when you plan to share space with a lodger. The lodger must not only have all the good tenant traits discussed in Chapter 4, but must be someone with whom you feel comfortable and secure. This chapter highlights some of the special considerations involved with renting a room in your home—and will help make sure you choose the right kind of lodger to have around. Keep in mind that the focus here is more traditional rental situations, with long-term lodgers, not short-term renters who come through Airbnb or a similar site. See "Is Airbnb or VRBO for You?" in Chapter 1 for more on this subject.

Is Renting a Room to a Lodger for You?

Here are some questions to consider before you start looking for a lodger:

- **Is it legal?** Zoning might be an issue: If your neighborhood is zoned for single-family residences only, operating a "rooming house," even if you have only one roomer, might violate that law. Or, if you own a condo or townhouse in a planned unit development, the homeowners' association rules (CC&Rs) might restrict you from bringing in a lodger.

- **Do you have the space?** A good-sized bedroom (ideally, furnished with a comfortable bed, along with adequate storage and lighting) and separate bath are ideal. You might have to spend some money to fix up your run-down den before you rent it out.

- **How much rent you can collect?** Before you start dreaming of all the money a lodger will bring in, do some homework. Start by checking out comparable rates on Craigslist and local college housing offices. Then subtract the additional costs of having a lodger (such as higher utility and household supplies bills).

- **How do tax deductions fit into your bottom line?** Figuring out the amount of money you'll net from bringing in a lodger involves calculating the tax benefits of renting out a room. Many of the tax deductions available to landlords who rent out entire properties (discussed in Chapter 6) apply to lodger rentals, but you must divide certain expenses between the room you rent out and the part of the house you live in. For example, if you install new wall-to-wall carpet in the entire downstairs of your house, you can deduct only the expenses for the room you are renting out.

Lodgers and Discrimination

The federal laws that prohibit housing discrimination (discussed in Chapter 4) do not apply to owner-occupied properties of four units or less. Nor do they apply to homeowners who rent out a room in their own home—with one important exception. While you may screen applicants in a way that would otherwise expose you to a charge of discrimination, you may not advertise or make statements in a way that indicates a preference (or avoidance) based on a protected group.

In other words, it is legal for you to decide not to rent to a prospective lodger after meeting this person and learning that he or she is of a certain race, religion, and so on; but if you post an advertisement that reflects your wishes, and if you communicate your preferences to the actual applicant, you're breaking the law. Rather tellingly, this rule is known as "discrimination at the door."

Discrimination at the door does, however, have one exception under federal law. If you have no more than one lodger, you are allowed to advertise for a lodger of a specific gender—but that's all. For instance, it's okay to seek "Female lodger wanted," but not okay to say, "Christian lodger wanted."

Various U.S. states have also weighed in on the lodger question, and might have tighter restrictions.

When it comes to expenses for your entire home (such as replacing the roof or installing a security system), you'll need to divide these expenses between the room you rent and the rest of the house—for example, by dividing the expenses based on the number of rooms in your home or the square footage of your house. *Every Landlord's Tax Deduction Guide*, by Stephen Fishman (Nolo), discusses special tax issues involved with renting out a room in your home. Questions to ask yourself include:

- **What is your motivation for bringing in a lodger?** It's one thing to look for a lodger who will be pleasant to have around; it's quite another to expect this person to perform any kind of work or even commit to being at home for specified hours. If you need a caregiver for your elderly parent or child care for your kids, a rent-paying lodger is not the way to go. Instead, consider a caregiver or a nanny.

- **Is there a market for the room—and for the type of lodger you want?** College towns usually have no shortage of people looking for less-costly alternatives to renting an entire unit. Then again, if you're a 60-year-old woman, you might not be interested in sharing your house with an 18-year-old. Or perhaps you'll discover that there's a market for your room, but only for seven or eight months of the year.

- **Who is your ideal lodger (and would such a person want to rent a room in your home)?** Sharing your home can be intense (especially if you've never lived with roommates or a large family). You'll want to think long and hard about the kind of person you want to live with, perhaps:

  - Someone who will take care of your dogs when you're on one of your regular business trips or someone who will be gone most weekends?

  - A private, quiet person who pretty much keeps to him- or herself, or an outgoing social type who is happy to share meals and watch TV with you?

- Someone who eats all meals out or someone who takes over your kitchen three times a day and loves to hold dinner parties?

- Someone who shares the same values and interests? If you're a vegan or light sleeper, you might not want to live with someone who's grilling steaks every weekend or whose favorite form of exercise is midnight aerobics routines.

• **Do you have children living at home?** If so, you will want to be especially conscientious about choosing a lodger, particularly if the person will be home alone with your children.

• **Are you willing to do the work required to keep the place in good shape?** You might need to make some initial repairs before renting out a room—and be prepared to continue maintenance you might otherwise defer during the lodger's stay. A torn carpet or leaky faucet might not bother you, but they might annoy a lodger.

• **Do you need additional insurance?** Check with your agent to see whether bringing in a lodger will affect your homeowners' insurance (additional costs might at least be tax deductible).

Sharing Your Home With More Than One Lodger

If your house is especially large, you might want to bring in more than one lodger. If so, you'll need to consider how everyone in the house gets along (not just you and the lodger). And as noted above, renting to a lodger might violate zoning rules if you live in a single-family-only zone. While it's not too likely that your neighbors will object to one roomer, they might feel differently when multiple people begin parking in their favorite spots, and increasing the noise and activity level of a previously quiet neighborhood.

- **Do you have the personality for this?** If you've been living alone for quite some time, or really value your privacy, or realize you'll have to give up turning the music loud and spreading a craft project all over the living room, renting out a room might simply not be for you. If certain personality types drive you crazy, you'll want to be sure to weed these people out during the interview process.

Checking References and Credit

Landlords who rent apartments or houses have learned to be diligent when checking out prospective tenants (many have learned the hard way). The only way they can evaluate the likelihood that an applicant will be a good tenant (pay the rent, take reasonable care of the property, not cause problems with other tenants, neighbors, or the landlord) is to question the applicant's former landlords and check the applicant's credit report.

You can—and should—take some of the same steps when choosing a lodger. Ask for references from former landlords, neighbors, or employers. A college transcript of a student applicant will tell you loads—good grades and an absence of "incompletes" indicates some degree of reliability and follow-through.

You won't be able to order a credit report from a credit reporting agency, however, unless you go through the tedious step of establishing your qualifications for handling credit reports (in recent years, Congress has required those who handle these documents to prove to the credit reporting agencies that they have a safe and secure physical setup in their office). Instead, ask applicants to bring a current copy of their report (people can obtain free reports from AnnualCreditReport.com. If you want to be extra sure that the report has not been doctored, ask the applicant to sit down with you at your computer and order a report on the spot, which you can examine immediately.

Basic Steps to Renting Out a Room

Once you've determined that bringing in a lodger makes sense, follow the same basic steps discussed earlier in this book for renting out a room in your home:

- Fix up the room for rent and make other necessary changes in your home.

- Identify your key terms and policies by drafting a rental agreement (a month-to-month contract that can be terminated on short notice). Be sure to cover issues such as kitchen etiquette, quiet times, guests, home business restrictions, shared chores, and so on. California owners can use Nolo's "Renting Out a Room in Your California Home Kit," available for download at Nolo.com.

- Decide the places to advertise for or spread the word about the type of lodgers you want: word-of-mouth, a college housing office, and/or Craigslist are a few possibilities.

- Interview prospects, and give likely candidates a rental application and full disclosure on how the household needs to be run. Be candid and clear here—if you are a neatnik, now's the time to say so. If you don't, you face a future full of silent (or not-so-silent) resentment.

- We'll say it again: Talk more with your prospective lodger about practical issues like pets, noise, drinking, TV preferences, music tastes—everything about your living situation that's important to you.

- Sign a rental agreement.

- Get the lodger moved in. ●

Index

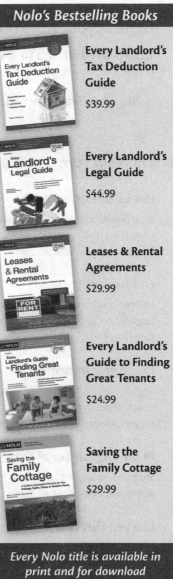